Sri Lanka

DREAM TRIP

SARA CHARE

CONTENTS

THIS IS
SRI LANKA

For many, the island of Sri Lanka conjures up images of tea plantations, white-sand beaches backed by coconut palms, and imposing statues of reclining Buddhas. The pearl-shaped isle does offer all these things but as with everywhere, the real Sri Lanka is much richer than the picture-postcard ideals. Travel beyond the tourist trail, eat outside your hotel and meet some of the locals.

Ringed by beautiful beaches, there is the opportunity to spend time on the coast lounging on the sand, exploring under the water with a snorkel, or tackling some of the waves from atop a surfboard. For wildlife enthusiasts Sri Lanka has some excellent birdwatching opportunities, as well as the chance to see elephants and leopards in the national parks, and to embark on whale- and dolphin-watching trips in Mirissa or on the Kalpitiya Peninsula. The Cultural Triangle is home to Kandy's Temple of the Tooth, the ancient kingdoms of Anuradhapura and Polonnaruwa, Sigiriya Rock, and the breathtaking murals of Dambulla's cave temples, and these sights should not be missed. The Hill Country offers some respite from the heat of the lowlands and whether walking near Ella, watching the sun rise from Adam's Peak or tea tasting at one of the plantations, you may find it hard to tear yourself away. Those who decide to travel north to the Jaffna Peninsula will find it a very different place from the Buddhist south. Palmyrah trees, freshly painted Hindu temples, red chillies drying in the sun and the remnants of war will greet you here. Jaffna is not yet the place to come for a relaxing holiday but the peninsula's beautiful islands will captivate those who make the journey.

The long civil war ended in 2009 and the damage wrought by that and the savage 2001 tsunami are gradually being erased, but Sri Lanka still has a long way to go. As people look to the future and enjoy the fruits of a growth tourist industry, there remain the problems of infrastructure and wildlife welfare. There is also the issue of freedom of the press, and a government that has not yet satisfactorily answered allegations of war crimes. This is a country that is still adjusting to peace and prosperity and if you can, try and ensure you travel sensitively and sustainably.

Sigiriya Rock

FIRST STEPS
PUTTING IT ALL TOGETHER

Choosing which route to take, will depend on your interests, the time of year you travel and how you will be getting around.

One of the great things about Sri Lanka is its size. It's fairly easy to visit most of the tourist sights during your holiday, particularly if you have your own transport. Choosing which route to take, however, will depend on your interests, the time of year you travel and how you will be getting around.

Sri Lanka is affected by two monsoon seasons, which sweep over the country at different times of the year. This won't affect your travel plans too much, but it will dictate which coast you want to spend time on. The southwest monsoon hits between June and October and the northeast between October and January. Weather is not, however, an exact science so the monsoon may start earlier and end later in any given year. The most popular time to visit the island is during the months of December and January, when prices rise accordingly. Another thing to consider when planning your trip is if you would like to be present for any festivals, for example the Kandy Esala Perahera in August, or if you would like to climb Adam's Peak during the pilgrimage months of December to May.

As most people arrive by plane into Bandaranaike International Airport it is best to organize an itinerary that starts from Colombo or Negombo, where you will most likely spend your first and last nights in the country (there is a new international airport near Hambantota, but at the time of writing only Sri Lankan Airlines domestic flights and those linking it with the Maldives were operating). The suggested three itineraries take this into account and cover most of

Sri Lanka's tourist highlights, but note that the timescales do assume a mode of independent transport. Most visitors to the island hire a car and drive for some or all of their trip and this provides more flexibility. That being said, it is possible and easy to make your way around the island by train and bus, hiring three-wheelers where necessary, but journey times will be significantly longer. If you are short on time but have sufficient funds, there are also a number of domestic flights between the main areas of tourist interest.

Trips could be scaled down to a minimum of one week or combined to build a trip of a month or more. Three weeks is a good amount of time to spend on the island to see the major sights and still have time to relax in the Hill Country or on the beach. Those with more time though will be able to hunt out more inaccessible or lesser-visited sights. Do not feel constrained by these itineraries but see them more as a starting point, from where you can add places or activities you particularly want to experience, or combine routes to come up with your dream trip.

Three weeks is a good amount of time to spend on the island to see the major sights and still have time to relax in the Hill Country or on the beach.

→ DOING IT ALL

Negombo → Kalpitiya Peninsula → Anuradhapura → Mihintale → Habarana → Sigiriya → Polonnaruwa → Dambulla → Kandy → Nuwara Eliya → Ella → Uda Walawe National Park → Tissamaharama → Kataragama → Tangalla → Mirissa → Galle → Mount Lavinia → Colombo.

1 Keeping cool whilst elephant riding **2** Get up in time for sunrise to make the most of the morning cool **3** Oruva fishing boat near Negombo

Best time to visit To take advantage of the calm seas on the west coast and spot dolphins at Kalpitiya, visit between November and April, but May to September is best for kitesurfing.

The dry season of June to October is the time to visit Minneriya National Park to see "the Gathering" of the elephants, with perhaps the best sightings being from July to September. Kaudulla is part of the same elephant corridor and its sightings peak slightly later.

As for Kandy, many people choose to visit for the Esala Perahera festival in August. If doing so, ensure your accommodation is booked well in advance.

Many visitors to Sri Lanka start their trip in **Negombo** (page 35), a beach resort near the international airport and just north of Colombo. Spend a couple of nights here, either lounging by a hotel pool or exploring further afield by bike. Travel north to the relaxing **Kalpitiya Peninsula** (page 40), where in season you can try your hand at windsurfing or go on dolphin-watching trips.

After three nights or so head inland to the Cultural Triangle and learn more about the history of Sri Lanka. Your first stop is **Anuradhapura** (page 44), site of the island's most sacred ancient city and home to the Sri Maha Bodhi tree. The area is large and is best explored by bicycle or you can hire a three-wheeler to take you around. Most visitors only spend a day here, followed by a morning at **Mihintale** (page 51) where it's said Buddhism was introduced to the island in the third century BC. It's best to arrive at Mihintale early in the morning, as there is little shade once you reach the upper terrace.

1

Arrange an early start one morning and climb Sigiriya before the crowds arrive.

Habarana (page 58) is the next stop and though the town itself is not that interesting there are some nice hotels here, and if you have your own transport it's a good spot to base yourself when exploring the Cultural Triangle. Aim to stay for about three nights, and from here you can arrange a safari to one of the nearby national parks such as **Minneriya** (page 58) or **Kaudulla** (page 57). Arrange an early start one morning and climb **Sigiriya** (page 67) before the crowds arrive, be sure to visit the museum at the base of the rock. In the

1 Lighthouse at Dondra Head   2 Thuparamaya Dagoba, Anuradhapura   3 Bonnet macaque   4 The lion platform at Sigiriya

afternoon, visit the less touristy and atmospheric Ritigala forest monastery (page 60). If you can, allocate a day to cycling around the ancient city of Polonnaruwa and don't miss seeing the reclining Buddha of Gal Vihara.

Stop in at the richly painted Dambulla cave temples (page 71) on the way south to Kandy and, if you're not "templed out", at the roadside temple of Aluwihare (page 75) where shrines have been carved out of large boulders. Once in Kandy (page 81), ensure you attend a *puja* at the Temple of the Tooth and spend some time in the beautiful Peradeniya Botanical Gardens. From the city you can organize trips out to the Pinnawela Elephant Orphanage (page 115) or the Tea Museum, embark on the three-temple loop, or just enjoy spending time in Kandy's museums. For those who want to stretch their legs, the Knuckles Range can be visited without a guide or you can arrange an overnight trekking adventure. Once back on the coast take a couple of days to see the sights in Colombo (page 97), such as the National Museum, the fort area and the bustling streets of the Pettah. Colombo also offers the best choice of cuisine on the island and is an excellent place to pick up souvenirs to take home.

1 Siva Subramaniya Kovil, Slave Island, Colombo 2 Elephants in the river, Pinnawela 3 Looking down from Swami Rock, Trincomalee

→ GOING FURTHER

From **Anuradhapura**, head east to **Trinco-malee** (page 77) and the beaches of **Nilaveli** and **Uppuveli** (page 78-79), or north to spend a few days on the **Jaffna Peninsula** (page 55).

3

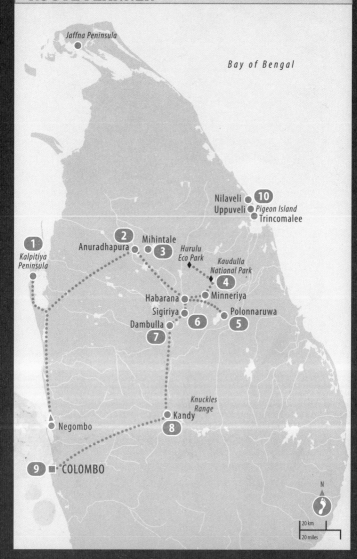

1 Inside one of Dambulla's cave temples

→ **WISH LIST**

1 Dolphin-watching on Kalpitiya Peninsula. **2** Anuradhapura, Sri Lanka's first capital. **3** Mihintale, where Mahinda converted King Tissa to Buddhism. **4** Spotting large herds of elephants in Minneriya or Kaudulla National Park in the dry season. **5** Gazing into the serene face of the Buddha at Polonnaruwa. **6** Admiring the view from atop Sigiriya Rock. **7** The beauty of the Dambulla cave's painted walls and ceilings. **8** Catching sight of the tooth casket in Kandy. **9** Learning more about Sri Lanka at Colombo's National Museum. **10** Relaxing on the white-sand beaches of Uppuveli or Nilaveli.

Elephants taking part in the Esala Perahera, Kandy

DREAM TRIP 2 COLOMBO → KANDY → NUWARA ELIYA → ELLA → COLOMBO

Best time to visit The southwest monsoon hits between May and October, bringing heavy showers to Colombo and rough seas to the coastal resorts. Many people visit during this time, however, to take in the ten-day Esala Perahera festival in Kandy in August.

The Hill Country is also affected by the southwest monsoon, so visit early in the year between February and April. April, during the Sinhalese Tamil New Year, is the busiest time in Nuwara Eliya when prices rise and a carnival atmosphere prevails.

The pilgrimage season of December to May is the best time to climb Adam's Peak. Those interested in tackling the white water at Kitulgala will find April to November the best months for rafting.

After an overnight stay in Colombo (page 97) make your way to Kandy (page 81). Make sure you attend an early evening or morning *puja* at the Temple of the Tooth, and whilst in the temple complex don't miss a visit to the Raja Tusker Museum. If the hubbub of Kandy is getting too much, the peace and quiet of the British Garrison Cemetery may be just what you need, or if you want to travel further out then wander the avenues of the Peradeniya Botanical Gardens (page 91). To see all Kandy and the surrounding area have to offer, consider a three-night stop.

A train journey through the Hill Country is highly recommended and some people choose to travel by rail between Colombo and Kandy, or alternatively from Kandy to Nuwara Eliya (page 118). Note that the nearest station to Nuwara Eliya is Nanu Oya, where you can

1 The tooth shrine in the Temple of the Tooth, Kandy **2** Aluthgama **3** View from World's End, Horton Plain's National Park

either arrange to meet your driver or hotels and guesthouses can often pick you up from here with advance warning. Unless you're a golf enthusiast, there won't be much in Nuwara Eliya to hold your interest for long. A former British Hill Station you can admire the colonial architecture, enjoy the cooler climate and perhaps take a walk through the surrounding countryside. The Labookellie Tea Estate (page 117) is nearby and you can tour the factory before trying the tea and tucking into a piece of chocolate cake. The real reason to stay for a couple of nights, however, is to enable you to get up at the crack of dawn to visit Horton Plains (page 124) and admire the view from World's End before the mist settles in for the day.

Get up at the crack of dawn to visit Horton Plains and admire the view from World's End before the mist settles in for the day.

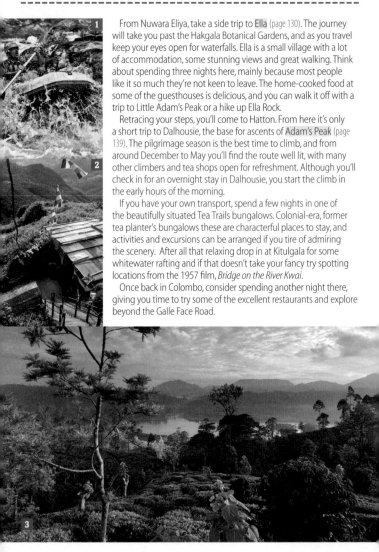

From Nuwara Eliya, take a side trip to Ella (page 130). The journey will take you past the Hakgala Botanical Gardens, and as you travel keep your eyes open for waterfalls. Ella is a small village with a lot of accommodation, some stunning views and great walking. Think about spending three nights here, mainly because most people like it so much they're not keen to leave. The home-cooked food at some of the guesthouses is delicious, and you can walk it off with a trip to Little Adam's Peak or a hike up Ella Rock.

Retracing your steps, you'll come to Hatton. From here it's only a short trip to Dalhousie, the base for ascents of Adam's Peak (page 139). The pilgrimage season is the best time to climb, and from around December to May you'll find the route well lit, with many other climbers and tea shops open for refreshment. Although you'll check in for an overnight stay in Dalhousie, you start the climb in the early hours of the morning.

If you have your own transport, spend a few nights in one of the beautifully situated Tea Trails bungalows. Colonial-era, former tea planter's bungalows these are characterful places to stay, and activities and excursions can be arranged if you tire of admiring the scenery. After all that relaxing drop in at Kitulgala for some whitewater rafting and if that doesn't take your fancy try spotting locations from the 1957 film, *Bridge on the River Kwai*.

Once back in Colombo, consider spending another night there, giving you time to try some of the excellent restaurants and explore beyond the Galle Face Road.

1 Whitewater rafting, Kitulgala **2** The trail to Adam's Peak **3** A tea plantation near Hatton **4** Kitesurfing is popular on the south and west coasts

→ GOING FURTHER

If you have your own transport, it takes just over a couple of hours to reach the famous surf spot of **Arugam Bay** (page 134).

4

1 Scenic train journey near Nuwara Eliya 2 Sri Lanka is one of the world's largest producers of tea 3 The giant fig tree in Peradeniya Botanical Gardens

2

→ WISH LIST

1 Being present for a *puja* at the Temple of the Tooth. **2** Kandy's Peradeniya Botanical Gardens are a great place to people watch. **3** Taking it slow with a scenic train journey. **4** Visiting a tea factory and learning more about your morning cuppa. **5** Trying to spot the south coast from World's End. **6** Tucking into delicious home-cooked food in a guesthouse in Ella. **7** Hill Country walking. **8** Watching the sun rise from the summit of Adam's Peak. **9** Tea Trails bungalows, a trip back in time. **10** Eating rice and curry.

Tea terraces in the Central Highlands

DREAM TRIP 3 COLOMBO →
TISSAMAHARAMA → GALLE → MOUNT LAVINIA

Best time to visit Uda Walawe can be visited year round but if you are particularly interested in migratory birds be there between November and March, and visit Bundala National Park from October to April. As for Yala, November to April is the best time, although it can be wet November to January. The park is sometimes closed for a period between September and October, so check before visiting.

The best time to visit the south and southwest coast is between November and early April (also surfing season), avoiding the monsoon. Divers should head to Bentota, Hikkaduwa and Unawatuna from November to May, and Weligama from December to April. If you fancy whale watching in Mirissa, trips run from December to April.

A two-week trip should give you a taste of the south coast beaches and also enable you to see some of Sri Lanka's famous wildlife. Spend two days in Colombo (page 97), taking in the sights and visiting the famous Odel department store.

From Colombo, make your way to Ratnapura (page 148), known for its precious stones and home to Maha Saman Devale, which is worth visiting if you have the time. Press on to Uda Walawe National Park (page 153) and aim to see one of the feeding sessions at the Elephant Transit Home west of the entrance gate. These elephants are rescued orphans that will be released back into the park when they're old enough. The main attraction of this national park is the number of resident elephants, but a safari here also offers some good birdwatching. The following day, continue on to Tissamaharama (page 156), where three nights will be enough time for one or more trips into Yala West (Ruhuna) National Park (page 157) to look for leopards, and if you're interested in birdwatching arrange a visit to Bundala National Park (page 160). Consider a side trip to

1 The chance of seeing leopard draws many visitors to Yala National Park **2** Relax on one of Tangalla's many beaches **3** Sunset from the rock temple at Mulkirigala

Kataragama (page 159), one of the most important pilgrimage sites on the island.

Follow the coast west towards Tangalla (page 163), where the white-sand beaches will encourage you to stop for a couple of nights. If lounging in the sun is not for you, nearby Mulgirigala (page 164) is a monastic site where the key to translating the *Mahavansa* into English and Sinhala was discovered. Some visitors make their way to from Tangalla to Rekawa Beach (page 165) of an evening to watch for turtles.

Follow the coast west towards Tangalla, where the white sand beaches will encourage you to stop for a couple of nights.

There are a number of coastal settlements that may take your fancy, but **Mirissa** (page 168) is a popular spot best known for its whale-watching trips from December to April. Even if passing through when the whales are not about, it's a nice enough place to relax for a couple of days.

Passing through **Weligama** (page 168) and a number of good surf spots such as **Midigama** (page 169) you could stop at **Koggala** (page 169) to visit the Martin Wickramasinghe Folk Museum. Further west, you may wish to base yourself at the busy resort strip of **Unawatuna** (page 170), where there is a vibrant nightlife, as well as a number of watersports on offer, but if that doesn't take your fancy there are some very pleasant hotels in the surrounding area or within the confines of nearby Galle Fort (page 173). The sights of Galle Fort can

1 Palm trees close to Mirissa Beach **2** Stilt fishing near Koggala **3** The Mount Lavinia Hotel

When travelling through Ratnapura, think about taking a side trip to **Sinharaja Forest Reserve** (page 151), the last significant stretch of rainforest on the island and home to a remarkable array of birdlife.

be seen in one day but if you stay for two or more nights you will be able to soak up the atmosphere of this World Heritage Site. Take a walking tour of the fort, explore the Maritime Archaeology Museum and watch the sun set over the ramparts.

It is possible to jump on the highway from Galle and head straight back to Colombo, or alternatively you could wind your way up the coast, passing through the busy resorts of Hikkaduwa (page 179) and Bentota (page 183). Think about taking a side trip to Brief Garden (page 184), which was created by Geoffrey Bawa's brother Bevis. Instead of finishing your trip in Colombo, spend a night in the beach suburb of Mount Lavinia and enjoy a sundowner overlooking the ocean from the Mount Lavinia Hotel terrace.

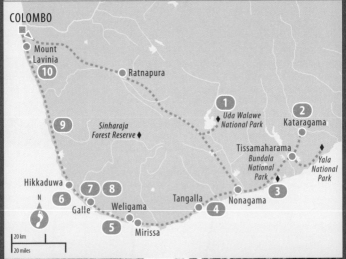

1 The British coat of arms on the Old Gate leading into Galle Fort **2** The islands beaches are just one of many reasons to visit **3** The painted stork is frequently seen in Sri Lanka, keep an eye out for it in the national parks **4** Boys playing cricket on Hikkaduwa Beach

→ WISH LIST

1 Photographing elephants in Uda Walawe National Park. **2** Kataragama, the most important pilgrimage site on the island. **3** Birdwatching in Bundala National Park. **4** Pretending to be a castaway in Marakolliya, north of Tangalla. **5** Surfing on the south coast at Midigama, Weligama or Hikkaduwa. **6** Kicking back at a beachside resort on the west coast. **7** Wandering the streets of Galle Fort. **8** Watching impromptu games of roadside or beach cricket. **9** Brief Garden, an enchanting place **10** Sipping a sundowner in Mount Lavinia.

Flamingoes, once seen in Bundala are now more commonly spotted in the north of the island

The 12-m standing Buddha at Aukana

DREAM TRIP 1
Negombo➔Anuradhapura➔Kandy➔Colombo
14 days

Negombo 2 nights, page 35
Bus or taxi from Colombo (1 hr) or
the international airport (20 mins),
3-wheeler from bus station in
Negombo Town to the beach

Kalpitiya Peninsula 3 nights, page 40
Car and driver (2½ hrs), or bus to Puttalam
(2 hrs) and then 3-wheeler to your
destination on Kalpitiya Peninsula

Anuradhapura 2 nights, page 43
Car and driver (1½ hrs) or bus from
Puttalam (2 hrs)

Habarana 3 nights, page 58
Car and driver (1½ hrs) or bus (2 hrs)

Kandy 2 nights, page 81
Car and driver (1½ hrs) or bus (2¾ hrs)

Colombo 2 nights, page 97
Car and driver (3 hrs), bus (3 hrs)
or train (2½ hrs)

GOING FURTHER

Jaffna Peninsula page 55
Car and driver from Anuradhapura (3½ hrs),
or bus (5 hrs). If travelling from Colombo
you can fly to Jaffna (1 hr).

Trincomalee page 77
Car and driver from Habarana (1½ hrs), or
bus (2 hrs). Note that buses from Habarana
to Trincomalee can be very busy and if you
have big bags it's best to catch the bus from
its starting point in Anuradhapura.

DREAM TRIP 1
Negombo→Anuradhapura→Kandy→Colombo

This route offers visitors the chance to experience Sri Lanka's beaches, enjoy a safari in a national park and explore the Cultural Triangle. The journey begins in Negombo, a beach resort close to the international airport, and then takes in the increasingly popular Kalpitiya Peninsula. Travelling inland, you come to the first capital of the island, Anuradhapura. Over a thousand years of history is represented here; this was one of the greatest cities of its time and is a reminder of the golden age of Sinhalese culture. Using Habarana as a base, you can take a number of day trips to some of the best-known sights on the island, and go looking for elephants in Minneriya or Kaudulla national parks or Hurulu Eco Park. This area is home to Sigiriya and its famous frescoes, the cave temples of Dambulla, the forest monastery of Ritigala, and Polonnaruwa, the island's medieval capital.

Next, head south to Kandy and its Temple of the Tooth. Witnessing a *puja* here and trying to catch sight of the tooth relic is top of many people's lists when they come to Sri Lanka. There is, however, much more to see including a number of museums, the Peradeniya Botanical Gardens and sights in the surrounding area such as the Knuckles Range. Be warned that Kandy can be very busy and the touts tiring. Finish the trip in Colombo, and get a taste of the island's big city. A couple of days will be enough to see the main tourist sights and experience the best restaurant scene on the island.

It is possible to extend this trip by travelling north or east from Anuradhapura or Habarana. The Jaffna Peninsula is still recovering from the long civil war and although a beautiful part of the island, there is as yet little tourist infrastructure. April to October is the best time to enjoy the east coast beaches of Uppuveli and Nilaveli, north of Trincomalee.

NEGOMBO

Owing to its proximity to what is, at the time of writing, Sri Lanka's only international airport, Negombo is the principal resort north of Colombo. It has a wide range of accommodation, and is a convenient place to start or end a holiday, although the beach can be dirty – if you are looking for an unspoilt strip of white sand head to the south of Sri Lanka where the beaches are far superior. Negombo town, although a little scruffy, does have a picturesque lagoon and a few interesting reminders of the Portuguese and Dutch periods.

ARRIVING IN NEGOMBO

Getting there Negombo town is easily accessible from the airport (6 km away) by taxi, three-wheeler or bus. It takes about 20 minutes. Hotels can often arrange a transfer on request. From Colombo, take the No 240 bus (every 15-20 minutes) from Saunders Place bus stand in the Pettah which takes about an hour. The train from Colombo's Fort Station also takes about an hour.

Moving on If you have your own transport (for example, a car and driver) then exploring the **Kalpitiya Peninsula** (see page 40) will be a lot simpler and quicker. That said, it is still possible to take a bus from Negombo to Puttalam and organize a three-wheeler from there to take you to your hotel/guesthouse. It may also be possible to catch a bus from Puttalam up the peninsula. There are trains that make the journey from Negombo to Puttalam but at the time of writing they are very slow, stopping at a number of stations en route.

Getting around The main tourist area is 2-4 km north of the town itself. You can walk most of the way along the beach (which gets progressively more inviting), or take a three-wheeler, or the Kochchikade bus (No 905) from the bus station. Frequent buses run along the main beach road from the bus and railway stations in Negombo Town. Bicycles can be hired to explore area. Three-wheelers offer Negombo town tours.

Best time to visit Swimming and watersports are only safe from November to April, outside the southwestern monsoon period. Easter is celebrated with Passion plays, particularly on Easter Saturday on Duwa island. In July the **Fishermen's Festival** at St Mary's Church is a major regional celebration.

PLACES IN NEGOMBO

The Portuguese originally built a **fort** on the headland guarding the lagoon in about 1600. Since the area was rich in spices, particularly the much prized cinnamon, it changed hands several times before the Portuguese were finally ousted by the Dutch in 1644. In attempting to make Negombo an important centre, the Dutch built a much stronger structure but this was largely destroyed by the British who pulled much of it down to build a jail. Today, only the gatehouse to the east (dated 1678), with its rather crooked clocktower, survives. The place is still used as a prison and the District Court is tucked away in a corner of the grounds.

A more enduring monument to the Dutch is the **canal system**. Originally explored in the 15th century, they were improved and expanded by the Dutch who recognised their advantage in transporting spices – cinnamon, cloves, pepper, cardamoms – and precious

ON THE ROAD
Catholicism and canals

The coastal road runs through the region most affected by Portuguese colonialism. Their imprint is clearly visible in the high proportion of Roman Catholics, and the number of Catholic churches in the numerous villages through which the road passes. Nearly a quarter of the population immediately inland from Negombo is Christian, increasing in the north to almost 40%. The common nature of names like Fernando and Perera gives a clue as to the extent of their success.

Dutch influence is also evident in the now unused canal which was built between Colombo and Negombo. Once it was busy with the flat-bottomed 'padda' boats which travelled the 120 km between Colombo and Puttalam. As the Rev James Cordimer wrote in 1807 "the top of the canal (near Colombo) is constantly crowded with large flat-bottomed boats, which come down from Negombo with dried fish and roes, shrimps, firewood, and other articles. These boats are covered with thatched roofs in the form of huts". The Dutch built canals extensively not just around Colombo but also around Galle in the south, but they were relatively minor works compared to the 1000 km of irrigation canals already dug by the Sinhalese by the 12th century. The boats on these canals were often pulled by two men in harness. These days the canal banks are largely the preserve of people strolling along the waterway. You can hire bikes at several points, including Negombo, and ride along a section of the banks.

gems from the interior and along the coast to the port of Negombo for loading on to ships sailing for distant shores. Today you can see this if you follow St Joseph Road into Custom House Road and around the headland. It skirts the lagoon where mainly fishing boats are moored (witness to its thriving fishing industry). The junction of the canal is just past the bridge crossing the lagoon. Unfortunately at its mouth it is dirty and not that appealing.

St Mary's Church dominates the town. It is one of many churches that bears witness to the extent of Portuguese conversions to Roman Catholicism, especially among the fishermen in Negombo District. Work began in 1874 and was only completed in 1922. There are a number of alabaster statues of saints and of the Easter story as well as a colourfully painted ceiling.

There are three Hindu temples on Sea Street. The largest, **Sri Muthu Mari Amman**, has a colourful *gopuram* in the inner courtyard.

The area is very rich in marine life and although there is much evidence of a motorized fleet in the harbour, you can still see fishermen using catamarans and ancient outrigger canoes to bring up their catch onto the beach every day. The outrigger canoes, known as *oruva* here, are not made from hollowed-out tree trunks but rather the planks are sewn together and caulked to produce a fairly wide canoe with an exceptionally flat bottom. They are often beached in front of the hotels and you can usually see the fleet early in the morning returning to harbour, each canoe under a three-piece sail. Their catch includes seer, skipjack, herring, mullet, pomfret, amberjack, and sometimes sharks. Prawns and lobster are caught in the lagoon. There are a number of fish markets – one is near the bridge on Duwa Island across the lagoon and there is another beyond the fort.

The nearest **reef** is 3 km off the beach hotel area with corals within 10-20 m, though the quality of this inner reef is poor. There are much better reefs further out, teeming with marine life including barracuda (even rare giant barracuda), blue-ringed angels and unusual starfish. Make sure you go with a registered (eg PADI) dive school.

Muthurajawela marsh, in the lagoon, is an esturine wetland that harbours the saltwater crocodile, which can grow up to 9 m in length, as well as many species of birds such as the pied kingfisher. More information and boat tours (with wildlife guide) can be obtained from the **Visitor Centre** ① *T074-830150, Tue-Sun 0700-1800*. Tours are also arranged by hotels and guesthouses in Negombo, and tour operators.

NEGOMBO LISTINGS

WHERE TO STAY

$$$$ Beach (Jetwing), Porutota Rd, T227 3500, www.jetwinghotels.com. 75 rooms with balcony, and 3 suites with rain shower and jacuzzi. Pool (open to non-residents when occupancy is low), sports facilities, gym.

$$$$ Blue (Jetwing), Porutota Rd, T229 9003, www.jetwinghotels.com. 103 large rooms, 6 suites and 3 family rooms, not all with good views. Typical resort hotel, with all amenities and excellent service, good pool, entertainment, and watersports such as kitesurfing organized.

$$-$ Icebear Guesthouse, 103-2 Lewis Pl, T223 3862, www.icebearhotel.com (English). Attractively furnished rooms in bungalows and 'villas', in a well-kept Swiss-owned guesthouse. There's a pleasant garden with a wonderful secluded feel, personal attention, good home cooking (book in advance for evening meals), free Wi-Fi and bicycles.

$ Star Beach, 83/3 Lewis Pl, T222 2606. Clean rooms, downstairs are cheap but gloomy, upstairs most have a balcony, private or shared, and some rooms have a sea view. The restaurant looks out onto the beach. Friendly.

RESTAURANTS

There are a number of places to eat in the Negombo Beach area, from upmarket hotels to smaller restaurants and bars serving a range of Sri Lankan and international dishes. It's often best just to wander along the strip and see where's busy.

$$$ Lords, 80B Portutota Rd, T077-723 4721, www.lordsrestaurant.net. Chic eatery with catfish in small pools in the courtyard. Expensive but tasty food, beautifully presented. British meals such as shepherd's pie if you're feeling homesick but also Asian fusion. If you can't afford a meal, just go for one of the fresh juices. Extensive mocktail menu for non-drinkers. Art gallery.

$$$-$$ Edwin's, 204 Lewis Pl, T223 9164. Excellent Sri Lankan meals such as devilled prawns. Generous portions, attentive host, try the rice and curry.

$$ Bijou, Portutota Rd. Swiss-owned and moderately expensive (although much cheaper than the tourist hotels), excellent for seafood and noodles.

$$ Icebear Century Café, 25 Main St, T223 8097. Owned by the same people as the **Icebear Guesthouse** (see Where to stay), this café offers coffee, tea, cake and sandwiches in an airy space in Negombo Town.

$$-$ Dolce Vita, 27 Poruthota Rd, T077-743 6318, www.freewebs.com/dolcevitasrilanka. Coffee shop selling cake and more filling meals. A good place to watch the kitesurfers.

NORTH TO KALPITIYA PENINSULA

North of Negombo, you cross from the West to Northwest Province, traditionally known as Wayamba Province. It is an area of fishing hamlets and seemingly endless groves of coconut palms, while inland is a rich agricultural patchwork of paddy fields and plantations. The 'carpeting' of the coastal road to Puttalam in 2002 made this the quickest route from Colombo to Anuradhapura, and many pass through without stopping. However, there are some worthwhile attractions along the way: secluded beaches, ancient Hindu temples, a 'forgotten' peninsula and Sri Lanka's largest national park, Willpattu.

→ BEACHES NORTH OF NEGOMBO

There are two main beach areas which lack the bustle (and hassle) of Negombo but are still within easy reach of the airport. **Waikkal**, 12 km north of Negombo, is attractively sited on a meandering river but is quite remote so you are dependent on private transport to get anywhere. It is, however, the site of some impressive eco-resorts, which organize a wide array of nature-based activities.

Some 11 km further north is **Marawila**, which has a large Roman Catholic church, curious Italianate houses and a reputation for producing good-quality batiks. There are a growing number of resort-style hotels here, though the area has never really taken off on the scale of resorts further south. The beach is good in places but sometimes gives way to breakwaters constructed of large rocks.

→ ALONG THE WEST COAST TO PUTTALAM

Beyond Marawila, after crossing the estuary, the road passes between the lagoon and the railway through **Madampe**, which is known for its Coconut Research Institute and **Taniwella Devale**, a colourful harvest festival held in August in which the whole farming community participates.

Chilaw, 75 km north of Colombo, is a small town with a large fish market and a big Roman Catholic church. Its shady claim to fame is as a smuggling centre though there is little in town to warrant a stop. However, 2 km east is **Munneswaram**, which is worth a detour, especially on Fridays, the busiest day for this Hindu temple complex of three shrines. The 1500-year-old inner sanctum of the main Siva temple has Tamil inscriptions and is an important pilgrimage centre. In August there is a month-long festival, which includes firewalking.

A left turn at Battulu Oya leads to the prawn-fishing Tamil village of **Udappuwa** on the Kalpitiya Peninsula, 26 km north of Chilaw. As at Munneswaram, there is a festival with firewalking in July/August at its seaside three-temple shrine complex. Experiments in 1935-1936 showed that the coals were heated to about 500°C.

Marshes and lagoons lie between the road and the sea for much of the route north, which crosses a series of minor rivers and a few major ones such as the Battulu Oya. The largely Muslim and Catholic town of **Puttalam**, 131 km north of Colombo, is a centre for prawn farming, dried fish and coconut plantations. It used to be famous for its ancient pearl fishery but is now better known for its donkeys, and is thus a target of many Sinhalese jokes. The A12 continues northeast through to Anuradhapura.

Though easily accessible by causeway from the main road, Kalpitiya Peninsula has a quite distinctive, almost otherworldly landscape, and there are some important monuments to its history. Kalpitiya's position at the head of Puttalam's lagoon made it an important port for Arab traders from the seventh century and the peninsula remains predominantly Muslim to this day. Later, the Portuguese and the Dutch recognized its strategic use and the Dutch built a fort here in order to strangle King Rajasingha's trade with India. Today it is famous for its dried fish and prawn farming. Its sandy soil has also made its farmers some of Sri Lanka's richest. Despite its proximity to the sea, the land overlies an abundant supply of fresh, rather than brackish, water. Simple wells have been constructed for irrigation and crops including tobacco, shallots, chilli, and even potatoes, grow abundantly.

In recent years Kalpitiya Peninsula has also been recognized as an excellent place to see dolphins, and even whales between December and mid-April. Tours are run from a number of the hotels. Twitchers will also enjoy the abundance of birdlife here.

ARRIVING IN KALPITIYA PENINSULA

Getting there Arrange a car and driver from Colombo or Negombo (2½ hours), or take a bus to Puttalam (two hours) and then change to a local bus or arrange a three-wheeler to take you to your destination on Kalpitiya Peninsula.

Moving on Travel back down to Puttalam and from there either catch a bus or, if you have your own transport, follow the A12 to **Anuradhapura** (see page 43).

TALAWILA

Talawila has an important shrine at **St Anne's Church** ① *remove shoes before you enter; photography is not allowed*. There are two accounts of its history. In one, a shipwrecked Portuguese sailor brought the image of St Anne to shore, placed it under a banyan tree and vowed to build a church here if his business prospered. In the other, a vision of St Anne appeared and left gold coins for the construction of a chapel. The present-day church, set in extensive tree-lined grounds, was built in 1843 and has fine satinwood pillars. There is a wide beach behind the church. The town celebrates two major festivals, in March and June, which feature huge processions, healing and a rural fair. These draw up to 50,000 people, with some pilgrims arriving by boat.

KALPITIYA

The bustling, predominantly Muslim village of Kalpitiya, marks the end of the road. The small **Dutch fort** ① *prior approval from the navy must be sought before visiting, this can be arranged through your accommodation on the peninsula*, built in 1676 on the site of a Portuguese stockade and Jesuit chapel, is one of the best preserved in Sri Lanka. It has a VOC gate (1760), an original wooden door, and inside the remains of the barracks, commander's house, chapel and prison. In the modern base, you may be shown a number of rusting Indian trawlers, impounded for fishing in Sri Lankan waters. Two tunnels lead from the fort to St Peter's Kirk and a school, though these were blocked up during the war. Photography is prohibited and you may need to leave ID before entering. A naval officer will accompany you around the ramparts.

In contrast, the impressively gabled **St Peter's Kirk** nearby has lost many of its original features although inside a heavy stone font remains. There are some well-preserved 17th- and 18th-century Dutch gravestones inside. The church's columns and semi-circular porch date from a 19th-century renovation. Outside, there is a small, weathered cemetery.

→WILPATTU NATIONAL PARK

ⓘ *The park office, information centre and entrance are at Hunuwilagama, 7 km from the Wilpattu Junction turn-off at Maragahawewa on the A12. RS 1700.*

In March 2010, a clamour of excitement greeted the reopening of Wilpattu National Park, Sri Lanka's largest, oldest and – before the war – most popular wildlife sanctuary. The 131,693 ha park had been an important historical and archaeological site, as well as home to some of Sri Lanka's most visible populations of large mammals.

The park was closed in 1985, immediately after an attack on its wardens and officers by a group of LTTE cadres. It was reopened in 2003 before being closed again in 2006 when six Sri Lankan tourists and their guide were killed by a landmine. There has been some controversy over the past year, as roads are being laid in the park causing damage to the ecology and distress to the animals. Visitors may see construction vehicles rumbling around.

Wilpattu has a unique topographical landscape of gently undulating terrain dominated by *villus*, natural sand-rimmed water basins, which fill up with rain and to which animals come to drink. These used to be the best places to see leopards. Certain sections have a distinctive rich, red, loamy soil and there are also areas of dense forest. The western part of the park is reminiscent of Yala (see page 157), while out to sea Dutch and Portugal bays may still support populations of dugong. A further protected area, the Wilpattu Sanctuary, lies to the north within Northern Province.

These days few animals are visible, many were poached and the others will need time to get used to the sound of the jeeps. A small population of leopard remains but is hard to see, while elephants are more likely to be glimpsed in the farming areas to the south. The bird population of resident and migratory waterfowl and scrub and forest species is said to be fairly healthy, as is the reptile population.

NORTH TO KALPITIYA PENINSULA LISTINGS

WHERE TO STAY

$$$ The Mudhouse, Pahaladuwelweva, Anamaduwa, T77-301 6191, www.themud house.lk. For those who want to get back to nature, look no further. Huts made from natural, local materials, scattered around jungle and some even in the trees. No electric lights, lanterns and candles in the evenings, and outdoor showers (no hot water). Prices are all-inclusive, a lot of the fruit and veg comes from **The Mudhouse's** organic garden, Due to its remote location a member of staff can meet visitors in the nearest town, pick-ups can be arranged from anywhere in Sri Lanka, or your driver can ring for detailed directions.

$$$-$$ Palagama Beach, 12 Palmyra Rd, Alankuda, T077-350 7088, www.palagama beach.com. 4 cabanas (the 3 not on the beach have hot water) modelled on fishing shacks. There is a more luxurious villa option, or a house with kitchen and living area. Restaurant, infinity pool, dolphin-watching trips, watersports and trips to Wilpattu.

$$$-$ Bar Beef Resort, Alankuda, T077-772 5200, www.barreefresort.com. 6 large cabanas, 2 family villas, and a house where meals can be prepared by the chef. Saltwater pool, trips arranged, restaurant.

WHAT TO DO

Kitesurfing

Kalpitiya Peninsula is popular with windsurfers and some resorts hire out gear. **Kitesurfing Lanka**, www.kitesurfinglanka. com. IKO-certified windsurfing instructors.

Safaris

Leopard Safaris, 45 Ambagahawatta, Colombo Rd, Katunayake, T077-731 4004, www.leopardsafaris.com, based near Colombo. Offers excellent tented safaris in Wilpattu National Park.

ANURADHAPURA AND MIHINTALE

Anuradhapura is Sri Lanka's most sacred city and one of the points of the Cultural Triangle (Polonnaruwa and Kandy are the others). Along with Mihintale, it represents the first real home of Buddhism in Sri Lanka, and thus contains some of the island's most sacred Buddhist sites. It is here that the Sri Maha Bodhi tree is said to have been planted from a cutting from the original Bo under which the Buddha received Enlightenment, to this day drawing thousands of pilgrims from around the world. Today, Anuradhapura's ruins and monuments are widely scattered which makes a thorough tour exhausting and time-consuming, but for those with more than a passing interest in the island's past it more than repays the effort. Nearby Mihintale, where King Tissa received the Emperor Asoka's son Mahinda and converted to Buddhism, makes an excellent day-trip away from the bustle and noise, and can even be used as an alternative base.

→ ARRIVING IN ANURADHAPURA AND MIHINTALE

GETTING THERE

From Puttalam, buses run east along the A12 and take a couple of hours to reach Anuradhapura. A car or driver will be slightly quicker. By train, Anuradhapura lies on the Northern line, and all trains between Colombo and Vavuniya stop here. Mihintale, 11 km east of Anuradhapura, is a short bus, three-wheeler or cycle ride from the city.

MOVING ON

Drive southeast from Anuradhapura to **Habarana** (one hour, see page 58), or catch one of the buses heading towards Polonnaruwa, which should stop in Habarana (two hours). There are buses to **Trincomalee** (3½ to four hours, see page 77) and also a train with a change at Maho Junction. To **Jaffna** (see page 55), catch a bus to Vavuniya (one hour) and change, or see if there are any travelling direct.

GETTING AROUND

Take a three-wheeler from the train or bus station to your accommodation. The New Town is about 2 km southeast of the central sites. If you want a full-day tour, consider hiring a car or three-wheeler since the ruins, especially to the north, are very spread out and can be exhausting under a hot sun. Many people use a bicycle (available from guesthouses) to get around but you should be prepared to park it and walk when told to. Bear in mind also that unless you follow a prescribed route (and even if you do) it is easy to get lost, as there are many confusing tracks and signposting can be poor. Unlike Polonnaruwa, the monuments are not clustered into convenient groups so planning an itinerary can be difficult. The order of sites below follows a 'figure-of-eight' pattern, starting in the central area, then heading 3 km north and then east to Kuttan-Pokuna, before returning south to the Jetavanarama *dagoba*, and looping across to explore the museums and lakeside monuments south of the central area.

BEST TIME TO VISIT

There are several festivals during the year. In April **Snana Puja** is celebrated at Sri Maha Bodhi. In June, at the full moon in **Poson**, the introduction of Buddhism to Sri Lanka is celebrated with huge processions when many pilgrims visit the area. In July/August, during **Daramiti Perahera**, locals bring firewood in a procession to the Bodhi tree, commemorating a time when bonfires were lit to keep away wild animals.

TOURIST INFORMATION
ⓘ *T222 4546, Mon-Fri 0900-1700, Sat 0900-1300.*

Anuradhapura tourist information office is on Sri Maha Bodhi Mawatha, the best approach road to the ancient city. Here you can pick up a local map and planning advice. There are four ticket offices: one at the Tourist Information Counter, another at the Archaeological Museum, a third at the Jetavanarama Museum, and finally one towards the Dalada Maligawa. A single ticket for the main site costs US$25 (half-price for children). It is worth getting a guide, Rs 500-800 for three to four hours. There are lots of drink stalls around; the ones near the *dagobas* tend to be expensive. The souvenir sellers can be very persistent and unpleasant, so be firm. At Mihintale there is a Rs 500 charge for visiting the sacred centre.

→ ANURADHAPURA

BACKGROUND
From origins as a settlement in the sixth century BC, Anuradhapura was made Sri Lanka's first capital in 377 BC by King Pandukhabhaya (437-367 BC) who started the great irrigation works on which it depended, and named it after the constellation Anuradha. The first era of religious building followed the conversion of King Devanampiya Tissa (ruled 250-10 BC). In his 40-year reign these included the Thuparama Dagoba, Issurumuniyagala, and the Maha Vihara with the Sri Maha Bodhi and the Brazen Palace. A branch of the Bodhi tree (see below) under which the Buddha was believed to have gained his Enlightenment was brought from Bodhgaya in India and successfully transplanted. It is one of the holiest Buddhist sites in the world.

Anuradhapura remained a capital city until the ninth century AD, when it reached its peak of power and vigour. At this time it may have stretched 25 km. Successive waves of invasion from South India however finally took their toll. After the 13th century it almost entirely disappeared, the irrigation works on which it had depended falling into total disuse, and its political functions were taken over first by Polonnaruwa, and then by capitals to the south. 'Rediscovered' by Ralph Backhaus, archaeological research, excavation and restoration was started in 1872, and has continued ever since. In 1988, it was designated a World Heritage Site. The New Town was started in the 1950s, and is now the most important Sinhalese city of the north. It houses the headquarters of the Sri Lanka Archaeological Survey.

APPROACH
Anuradhapura rivals Milton Keynes for its roundabouts. If you are staying in the New Town, the best approach to the ancient city is to cycle northwest across Main Street and the railway line, to Jayanthi Mawatha where you turn right, past the two rest houses, up to **Lion Pillar**. Here you turn left on to Sri Maha Bodhi Mawatha, continue up to the barrier, beyond which the road leads to the **Sri Maha Bodhi**. You are not allowed to cycle past this point, and you will be asked to park your bike in the car park. Don't do this, as you will leave yourself with a long walk back from the central area to pick up your bike, though there are sometimes buses. Instead, continue past the car park for almost 1 km, heading

up Nandana Mawatha (or path) towards the huge white **Ruvanwelisiya Dagoba**. Here you can park your bike (for free) close to the central area. There is a wide pedestrian walkway which leads from the *dagoba* to the Sri Maha Bodhi.

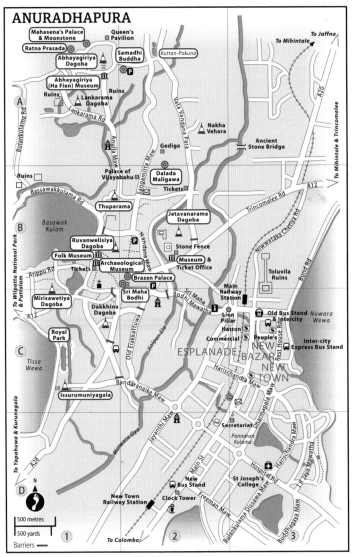

ANURADHAPURA

ON THE ROAD

Five of the best sites not to miss in Anuradhapura

Sri Maha Bodhi – one of the holiest trees in the world.
Ruvanwelisiya Dagoba – impressive *dagoba* with elephant wall.
Samadhi Buddha – serene statue beloved by Jawarhalal Nehru.
Jetavananarama Dagoba – simply enormous!
Issurumuniyagala – bats, reclining Buddha and 'the lovers'.

RUVANWELISIYA DAGOBA

Begun by King Dutthagamenu (Dutugemunu) to house relics, this is one of the most impressive of all Sri Lanka's *dagobas*. Built with remarkable opulence, the king, who was said to have great luck, found a rich vein of silver from Ridigama to cover the expenses. Monks from as far away as Alexandria were recorded as being present at the enshrinement of the relics in 140 BC. The king however fell ill before the *dagoba*'s completion, so he asked his brother Saddhatissa to complete the work for him. Saddhatissa covered the dome with bamboo reeds and painted them with lacquer and imitation gold so that the king could witness the 'completion' of his *magnum opus* on his deathbed. Today, the dome is 80 m in diameter at its base and 53 m high. Apart from its sheer size, you will notice first the frieze on the outer wall of hundreds of life-size (and life-like) elephants, most of which are modern replacements. The *dagoba* is surrounded by the remains of sculptural pieces. You can see the columns, often no more than 500 cm in height, dotted around in the grass underneath huge rain trees where monkeys play. A small passage leads to the relic chamber. At the cardinal points are four 'chapels' which were reconstructed in 1873, when renovation started. The restoration has flattened the shape of the dome, and some of the painting is of questionable style, but it remains a remarkably striking monument. Today, you may find watching the *dagoba* being 'whitewashed' an interesting spectacle.

BRAZEN PALACE

ⓘ *The site is open only on* poya *days.*

Follow the pedestrian walkway south towards to the Sri Maha Bodhi. Just before reaching the tree, you will see the many pillars of the Brazen Palace on your left. The name refers to the first monastery here and its now-disappeared roof, reputedly made of bronze. Built originally by Dutthagamenu, it was the heart of the monastic life of the city, the Maha Vihara. Described in the *Mahavansa* as having nine storeys, there were 1600 pillars, each just under 4 m high, laid out over an area 70 sq m. Above, each storey was supposed to have 100 windows, with 1000 rooms overall, the building adorned with coral and precious stones. This requires imagination these days, though now a wooden first floor has been erected, aiming to recreate the monastery's top storey. Originally destroyed by Indian invasion, the monastery was rebuilt several times, much of what is visible today being the reconstruction of King Parakramabahu I in the last quarter of the 11th century, making use of the remnants of former buildings.

SRI MAHA BODHI TREE

ⓘ *Rs 200. Shoes must be removed on entering the terrace – there is a booth at the eastern entrance.*

The 'Bo' ('Bodhi') tree or Pipal (*Ficus religiosa*) was planted as a cutting from the tree in Bodhgaya in India, under which Buddha found Enlightenment. It was brought by Emperor Asoka's daughter, the Princess Sanghamitta, at some point after 236 BC. Guardians have kept uninterrupted watch over the tree ever since, making it – all tourist literature will proudly tell you – the oldest historically authenticated tree in the world. Today, in keeping with tradition, it is the army who guard the tree, while the Director of the Peradeniya Botanical Gardens tends to its health. Nowadays, you can only see the top of the Bo tree, on the highest terrace, which is supported by an elaborate metal structure and surrounded by brass railings. There are other Bo trees around the Sri Maha Bodhi which are bedecked with colourful prayer flags and smaller strips of cloth which pilgrims tie in expectation of prayers being answered. In April a large number of pilgrims arrive to make offerings during the Snana Puja, and to bathe the tree with milk. Every 12th year the ceremony is particularly auspicious.

ARCHAEOLOGICAL AND FOLK MUSEUMS

This is a convenient place to visit these two museums, which are both worth a look around. The **Archaeological Museum** ⓘ *0800-1700, closed public holidays, small entry fee*, is in the old colonial headquarters. It is an excellent small museum, with a large collection from all over the island, including some beautiful pieces of sculpture and finds from Mihintale. It is well laid out, with occasional informative labels and some fascinating exhibits. There are statues from several sites, moonstones, implements, and a model of Thuparama *vatadage*. Outside in the garden, there are beautifully sculpted guard stones and an array of meticulously designed latrines. Separate latrine plinths were used for urinals, solid waste and bidets. Under each immaculately carved platform was a succession of pots containing sand, charcoal and limestone to purify the waste.

The nearby **Folk Museum** ⓘ *Tue-Sun 0900-1700, small entry fee*, is a collection that reflects rural life in the North Central Province, with a large display of handicrafts and vessels used by villagers in Rajarata.

THUPARAMA

Return to the Ruvanswelisiya *dagoba* to pick up your bike. Continuing north, turn left at the crossroads to the site's oldest *dagoba*, said to house the right collar-bone of the Buddha. Built by Devanampiya, the 19-m-high *dagoba* was originally in the shape of a 'paddy-heap' – its beautiful bell shape dates to renovation work completed in 1862. It is surrounded by concentric circles of graceful granite monolithic pillars of a *vatadage* which was added in the seventh century, possibly originally designed to support an over-arching thatched cover. It is a centre of active pilgrimage, decorated with flags and lights.

ABHAYAGIRIYA DAGOBA

Left from the first crossroads, 2 km north along Anulla Mawatha to the Abhagiriya Dagoba. First, a detour to the west takes you to the restored **Lankarama Dagoba**. Built in the first century BC it bears some similarities to the earlier Thuparama. Some columns remain of its *vatadage*.

ON THE ROAD
White lines

The ubiquitous *dagoba* is one of the most striking features of the island, ranging in size from tiny village structures to the enormous monuments at Ruvanwelisiya in Anuradhapura and Mahaseya at Mihintale. Even in nature the stone of the canonball tree fruit is a perfectly formed white *dagoba*.

There are of course many reasons why they stand out in a landscape: partly for their position, partly their size, but mostly for their colour – a dazzling white. Most are beautifully maintained and are often repainted before important Buddhist festivals.

It is no easy job to paint a large *dagoba*. A lime whitewash is used. Elaborate bamboo scaffolding cocoons the spire linked to the base by rickety bamboo ladders. Bamboo is ideal as it can be bent to conform to the shape of the dome and the lightness makes the ladders easily moveable. A team of about five painters assembles on the ladder which is about 20 m in height. Four men are deployed with ropes attached at the top and midpoints to give it some form of stability. At each stage, a painter is responsible for about 3 m of the surface in height, and an arm's width. The topmost 1.5 m of the painter's patch is covered first. Then he takes three steps down the ladder to cover the bottom 1.5 m. Once completed, the bamboo structure is moved an arm's width round and the whole process starts again.

You'll notice that not all the *dagobas* have yet been restored – their red brick or plain plastered surface are dull in comparison with those that have been returned to their original condition.

The Abhayagiriya Dagoba was the centre of one of Anuradhapura's largest and oldest monastic complexes. It is 400 m round and was supposedly 135 m high in its original form (part of the pinnacle has disappeared). It is now about 110 m high. Built in 88 BC by Vattagamani (and later restored by Parakramabahu I in the 12th century), it has two splendid sculpted *dwarapalas* (guardians) at the threshold. The *dagoba* and its associated monastery were built in an attempt to weaken the political hold of the Hinayana Buddhists and to give shelter to monks of the Mahayana school. It was considered an important seat of Buddhist learning and the Chinese traveller/monk Fa Hien, visiting it in the fifth century, noted that there were 5000 monks in residence. He also points out a 7-m jade Buddha, sparkling with gems, while the *dagoba* itself was said to have been built over a Buddha footprint.

ABHAYAGIRIYA (FA HIEN) MUSEUM
Abhayagiriya (Fa Hien) Museum, just south of the Abhayagiriya Dagoba, was built by the Chinese. The collection includes further examples of latrine plinths as displayed in the Archaeological Museum. There is also an extensive display detailing the excavation of the Abhayagiriya site.

RATNA PRASADA
To the west of the Abhayagiriya Dagoba are the ruins of the monastery. The area had once been the 'undesirable' outskirts of Anuradhapura where the cremation grounds were sited. In protest against the king's rule, an ascetic community of monks set up a *Tapovana* community (see box, page 50) of which this is an architectural example. This type of

monastery typically had two pavilions connected by a stone bridge within a high-walled enclosure which contained a pond. The main entrance was from the east, with a porch above the entrance. Here the Ratna Prasada, or 'gem palace', did not remain a peaceful haven but was the scene of bloody massacres when a rebellious group took refuge with the monks and were subsequently beheaded by the king's men. Their turn to have their heads roll in the dust followed another bloody revolt.

MAHASENA PALACE

The nearby Mahasena Palace has a particularly fine carved stone tablet and a beautifully carved moonstone, though the necessary protective railing surrounding it makes photography a little tricky. Note also the flight of steps held up by miniature stone dwarfs. You can return to the Archaeological Museum by taking the Lankarama Road to the south.

SAMADHI BUDDHA

Continue east from the Abhayagiriya Dagoba to this superb statue of the serene Buddha, probably dating from the fourth century AD. With an expression depicting 'extinction of feeling and compassion', some used to think the expression changes as the sun's light moves across it. Sadly though it has now been roofed to protect it from the weather.

KUTTAN-POKUNA

A road through the forest leads to these two ponds – restored eighth- and ninth-century ritual baths with steps from each side descending to the water. They were probably for the use of the monastery or for the university nearby. Though called **'twin' ponds**, one is more than 10 m longer than the other. You can see the underground water supply channel at one end of the second bath.

SOUTH TO JETAVARANAMA DAGOBA

There are two routes south from here. Sangamitta Mawatha leads back to the central area through the site of the 11th-century palace of **Vijayabahu I**, and close to the original **Dalada Maligawa** where the Tooth Relic was first enshrined when it was brought to Ceylon in AD 313. Only the stone columns remain. Alternatively, a 2-km cycle down Vata Vandana Para takes you straight to the vast Jetavanarama Dagoba.

JETAVANARAMA DAGOBA

This *dagoba*, looming impressively from the plain, is said to be the highest brick-built *dagoba* of its kind in the world. Started by King Mahasena (AD 275-292), its massive scale was designed in a competitive spirit to rival the orthodox Maha Vihara. The paved platform on which it stands covers more than 3 ha and it has a diameter of over 100 m. In 1860 Emerson Tennent, in his book *Ceylon*, calculated that it had enough bricks to build a 3-m-high brick wall 25 cm thick from London to Edinburgh, equal to the distance from the southern tip of Sri Lanka to Jaffna and back down the coast to Trincomalee. The *dagoba* is being renovated with help from UNESCO, though work periodically stops as there is a dearth of bricks.

The size of the image house here shows that Mahasena had an enormous Buddha image, similar to (though larger than) the one at Aukana, installed here facing the *dagoba*. There is a huge lotus pedestal, with large mortices for the feet of the statue. The image would have been destroyed by fire.

ON THE ROAD
Forest finery

The *Pansukulika* or *Tapovana* sect of ascetic Buddhist hermits who lived a simple life of deep meditation in forests and caves around the seventh to the 11th centuries are associated with Arankale, Mihintale and Ritigala. The monks were expected to wear ragged clothing and to immerse themselves in seeking the Truth, devoid of ritualistic forms of worship associated with Buddha images, relics and relic chambers. Such communities often won the admiration and support of kings, such as Sena I (AD 831-851).

The sites had certain features in common. There was a porched entrance, ambulatories, a water pool for cleansing and the *padhanaghara*. Another similarity was an open terrace, possibly intended as a 'chapter house' connected to a smaller section which was usually roofed. These 'double platforms' were aligned east to west; the two raised stone-faced platforms were connected by a narrow walkway or bridge. An interesting contradiction of the austere life was the beautifully carved latrines or urinal stones the monks used, examples of which can be seen in the Anuradhapura Archaeological Museum (see page 47).

JETAVANARAMA MUSEUM

① *0800-1700, closed public holidays. Small entry fee.*
This museum, well worth a visit, houses some interesting objects from the surrounding 120-ha site, including some fine guardstones and an amazingly intricate 8 mm gold chain with 14 distinguishable flowers.

TO THE LAKESIDE MONUMENTS

Continuing west across the main site towards Tissawewa, you might visit the Archaeological and Folk museums at this point (see above). West of here is the **Basawak Kulam tank**, the oldest artificial lake in the city, built by King Pandukabhaya in the fourth century BC. The dried-up southern side is good for walks and birdwatching, and there are excellent sunset views from the eastern shore.

Alternatively, head south to stop off for lunch or a drink at the **Nuwarawewa Rest House**. The Miraswetiya Dagoba is close by.

MIRISAWETIYA DAGOBA

This was the first monument to be built by Dutthagemunu after his consecration, enshrining a miraculous sceptre which contained a Buddha relic. The sceptre which had been left here by the king when he visited the tank, could not on his return be removed by any means. After a Chola invasion, the *dagoba* was completely rebuilt during the reign of King Kasyapa V in AD 930. Surrounded by the ruins of monasteries on three sides, there are some superb sculptures of *Dhyani* Buddhas in the shrines of its chapels.

TISSAWEWA AND ROYAL PARK

This tank was built by King Devanampiya Tissa, and was associated with the bathing rituals of newly crowned kings. You can walk/jog on the east and south sides along the raised tank *bund* and continue all round using local tracks on the west and a tarmac road on the north. The park just below the lake is very pleasant as it has few visitors. You can wander undisturbed across large rocks among ruined buildings and remains of bathing pools.

ISSURUMUNIYAGALA MONASTERY

① 0800-1930. Small entry fee. Ask for permission to take photos.

This small group of striking black rocks is one of the most attractive and peaceful places in town. It also has some outstanding sculptures. The temple, carved out of solid rock, houses a large statue of the reclining Buddha. There is a cleft in the rock which is full of bats and fascinating to watch. On the terraces outside is a small square pool. Don't miss the beautifully carved elephants, showing great individual character, just above the water level as if descending to it. The small **museum** is to the left of the entrance. Some of the best sculptures in Anuradhapura are now housed here, including perhaps the most famous of all – 'the lovers', which may represent Dutthagemunu's son Saliya and his girlfriend Asokamala, for whom he forsook the throne.

Behind the temple, you can climb up steps to the top of the rock above the temple to get a good view of the countryside and tank. Here there is a footprint carved into the rock, into which money is thrown.

NUWARA WEWA

Nuwara Wewa, which lies to the east of the New Town, is the largest of Anuradhapura's artificial lakes (1000 ha). It was probably built by Gajabahu I in the second century AD.

→ MIHINTALE

Mihintale (pronounced Mihin-taalay), named as Mahinda's Hill, is revered as the place where Mahinda converted King Devanampiya Tissa to Buddhism in 243 BC, thereby enabling Buddhism to spread to the whole island. The legend tells how King Tissa was chasing a stag during a hunting expedition. The stag reached Mihintale and fled up the hillside followed by the king until he reached a place surrounded by hills, where the animal disappeared and the frustrated king was astonished to find a gentle person who spoke to him the Buddha's teachings. It was Mahinda, Asoka's son, who had come to preach Buddhism and was able to convert the king along with 40,000 followers. As well as being important historically, it is an important religious site and a pleasant place to just stroll around away from the crowds at the more famous ancient sites. Mihintale town is little more than a junction and a few shops. It is however an important centre for pilgrims during the June festival.

APPROACH

Mihintale is close to the Anuradhapura–Trincomalee road. The huge *dagoba* can be seen from miles around, and is especially striking at night. At the junction with the village road, where you turn off for the main site, there are statues of six of the principal characters of the site. Follow the minor road leading to the site. On the right are the ruins of a ninth-century **hospital**, which appears to have had an outer court where medicines were ground and stored, and stone tanks for oil and herbal baths. The inner court appears to have had small treatment rooms. A 10th-century stone inscription mentions the use of leeches in treatment. There is a small **Archaeological Museum** *① close to the lower car park, free*, nearby. Displays include some terracotta dwarves, a couple of fine Ganadevi statues and a model of the middle chamber of the Mahaseya *dagoba*. There are some labels in English.

On the left at the foot of the steps, there is evidence of the **quincunx vihara** of a monastery (*arama*). You can avoid about half of the steps by driving round to the upper car park, which takes you straight to the second (refectory) level.

THE CLIMB

There are 1840 granite steps, some carved into the rock, to the top but they are very shallow and it is much less of a climb than it first looks. The width of the steps indicate the large number of pilgrims who visited the sacred site on special occasions in the past. The climb starts gently, rising in a broad stairway of 350 steps shaded by frangipani trees which lead to the first platform. Further steps to the right take you up to an open area with Kantaka Chetiya.

THE FIRST TERRACE

Kantaka Chetiya is the earliest *stupa* here. Excavated in 1932-1935, it had been severely damaged. Over 130 m in circumference, today it is only about 12 m high compared with its original height of perhaps 30 m. There is some unique stonework in the four projecting frontispieces at the cardinal points, especially to the eastern and southern points. Note the marvellously detailed friezes of geese, dwarves and a variety of other animals, flanked by *stelae* with floral designs. Around the Kantaka Chetiya are 68 caves, where the first monks here resided.

Returning to the first platform, steeper steps lead to a large refectory terrace. As you climb up (it takes under 10 minutes from the car park, at a gentle pace) you can see the impressive outer cyclopean wall of the complex. As an alternative to the steps to get to the refectory level, take a faint footpath to the left between the second and third flights. This crosses an open grassy area. Walk to the end and you will see the lake, green with algae. A path to the left takes you towards the **Giribandhu Chetiya Kiri Vehara**, though it is largely ruined and grassed over on the north side. You can look down on the lower car park and the quincunx. To the right, the path approaches the refectory from the rear and you pass a massive stone trough.

THE SECOND TERRACE

The Refectory Immediately on the left is the **Relic House** and the rectangular **Bhojana Salava** (Monks' refectory). There is a stone aqueduct and two granite troughs, one probably used for rice, the other for gruel. The square **Chapter House** or 'Conversation Hall' with signs of 48 pillars and a 'throne' platform, immediately to the north, is where the monks and lay members met. This has the bases of a series of evenly spaced small brick *dagobas*. At the entrance, stone slabs covered in 10th-century inscriptions on granite give detailed rules governing the sacred site.

The flat grassy terrace which can also be approached by car from the south up the old paved road or steps down from the Kantaka Chetiya, is dotted with trees and the outlines of three small shrines.

Sinha Pokuna (Lion Bath) To the west of the terrace, a short distance down the old road, this is about 2 m sq and 1.8 m deep and has excellent carvings in the form of a frieze around the bottom of the tank of elephants, lions and warriors. The finest, however, is the 2-m-high rampant lion whose mouth forms the spout. Water was gathered in the tank by channelling and feeding it through the small mystic gargoyle similar to the one that can be seen at Sigiriya.

The main path to the Ambasthala Dagoba, up the long flight of steps, starts by the 'Conversation Hall' in the square. After a five-minute climb a path leads off to the right, round the hillside, to the Naga Pokuna, which you can visit on the way back down (see below). Continuing to climb, you pass a beautifully inscribed rock on the right-hand side listing, in second-century AD script, lands owned by the king.

THE SACRED CENTRE
ⓘ *Rs 500 to enter and Rs 40 to leave your shoes.*

Ambasthala Dagoba At the top of the steps, you reach the ticket office, where you must leave your shoes (and hat). Straight ahead at the heart of the complex is the 'mango tree' *dagoba*, the holiest part of the site, built at the traditional meeting place of King Tissa and Asoka's son Mahinda. The monk in his office makes frequent loud-speaker announcements for donations from pilgrims – these donations have funded the erection of a large white Buddha statue on a rock overlooking the central area in 1991, up to which you can climb. The bronze Buddhas are gifts from Thailand.

Sela Cetiya A rock stupa at the site of the original mango tree has a replica of the Buddha's footprint. It is quite small and is surrounded a gilt railing covered in prayer flags, with a scattering of pilgrims' coins.

Mahinda's Cave A path leads out of the northeast corner of the compound between a small cluster of monks' houses down a rough boulder track to the cave, less than a 10-minute walk away. A stall selling local herbal and forest product remedies is sometimes set up halfway. The cave is formed out of an extraordinary boulder, hollowed out underneath to create a narrow platform at the very end of a ridge above the plain below. From the stone 'couch', known as **Mahinda's Bed**, there are superb views to the north across the tanks and forested plains of the Dry Zone. You have to retrace your steps to the Ambasthala compound.

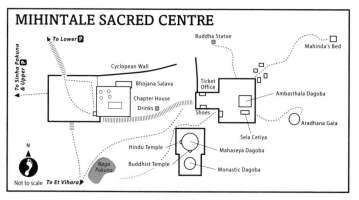

Aradhana Gala From the southeast corner of the compound a path with rudimentary steps cut in the bare granite rock leads to the summit of the Aradhana Gala (Meditation Rock). It is a very steep climb, and if you have no socks, very hot on the feet. A strong railing makes access quite secure. There is nothing much to see on the rock but there are superb views from the top, especially across the compound to the Mahaseya Dagoba, which is at the same height.

Mahaseya Dagoba A short flight of steep steps from the southwest corner of the compound, just beyond a small temple with a modern portrayal of Mahinda meeting King Tissa at the mango tree, leads up to the summit (310 m) with the Mahaseya Dagoba. According to legend this was built on the orders of King Tissa as a reliquary for a lock of the Buddha's hair or for relics of Mahinda. The renovated *dagoba*, which dominates the skyline, commands superb views back towards Anuradhapura to the southwest. Another monk may ask for donations here (anything above Rs 100 is recorded in a book).

On the south side of the main *dagoba* is a smaller brick *dagoba* while abutting it on its south side is a small Buddhist temple. To the west side is a Hindu temple with modern painted images of four Hindu deities: Ganesh, Saman, Vishnu and Kataragama.

DESCENT
Naga Pokuna After collecting your shoes, and immediately below the rock inscription (see above) is a small path which leads through cool forest to the Naga Pokuna. This 'Snake Pond', which has a five-headed cobra carving which you can still make out, is a 40-m pool carved out of solid rock which stored water for the monastery and, some believe, is where King Tissa would have bathed. At one end is a very small tank, now without water. Apparently this was where the Queen would bathe. It is a peaceful and beautiful place.

Et Vihara If you still have energy, a flight of 600 steps from the Naga Pokuna leads up to this inner temple, at the highest elevation in Mihintale. Though the small stupa is not very impressive, there are some magnificent views from here.

After descending and exiting the main complex, head west to the Kandy Road (accessible from either car park). Close to the junction are the remains of a monastery complex with two *dagobas*, of which the **Indikatu Seya** on a raised stone square platform to the north, is the larger. It shows evidence that the monks were devotees of Mahayan Buddhism in the ninth century. South of here, inscriptions in the **Rajagiri Lena** (Royal Rock Caves) suggest that they may represent the first living quarters of Sri Lanka's earliest Buddhist monks.

GOING FURTHER
Jaffna Peninsula

As the centre of Sri Lankan Tamil culture and, in peaceful times, the country's second most populous city, Jaffna was the greatest pawn, and the greatest victim, of the 20-year ethnic conflict of the north. Today, however, despite many houses remaining uninhabitable and mines rendering some areas inaccessible for years to come, many of the town's schools, temples, churches and mosques have been rebuilt – a testament to the spirit of this proud community, as well as to its support from abroad. With most of its heritage and 'sights' destroyed, Jaffna is no place for a holiday, but those who do make the trip are often unexpectedly charmed. The city can throw up some surprises from its lively festivals to its distinctive cuisine and famous ice cream parlours, and a wander through the market is not be missed.

→ ARRIVING IN JAFFNA

Getting there From Anuradhapura a car and driver to Jaffna takes 3½ hours; buses take five hours. The main bus stand is on Hospital Road, about 2 km west of Chundikuli, the main guesthouse and expat area. The bus route passes along Kandy Road – you can ask to be let off before the terminus. For those travelling from Colombo, by far the easiest (and most expensive) way is by air from Ratmalana Airport (see page 192). Expo Aviation and Helitours fly regularly to Palaly Airport (KKS) in the north of the peninsula. It is also possible to take the night train from Colombo to Vavuniya (see page 195) and then travel by bus to Jaffna. The buses between Vavuniya and Jaffna run regularly and there are long-distance buses from Colombo.

Getting around The city is quite spread out, and walking around it can be tiring in the heat. There is a good local bus network but cycling is the best way to get around. You may be able to borrow one from your guesthouse. Note that taking a three-wheeler here will be a lot more expensive than in other parts of the country, don't forget to bargain for your fare.

Best time to visit April to May can be unbearably hot when the southwest monsoon and heatwaves from South India conspire to drive up temperatures towards 40ºC. August to September is also very hot. December and January is the coolest time. The biggest festival is at Nallur in August.

Tourist information Further reading: Philippe Fabry, *Essential Guide for Jaffna and its region* (Negombo: Viator Publications, 2003).

HISTORIC CENTRE

Jaffna's 20-ha **Dutch fort**, built on the site of an earlier Portuguese building to control the trade route to India, was arguably once the strongest fortification in Asia. It was heavily damaged by shelling during the war but at the time of writing was under renovation and it was possible to walk around the ruins and watch the builders at work. Some of the original black coralline bricks remain and you can see what is left of the Groote Kerk.

Across the stadium to the east is the gleaming, restored Moghul-style **public library**. The original building was torched by an anti-Tamil mob in June 1981, tragically destroying almost 100,000 books and priceless *ola* leaf manuscripts. Thousands of volumes have been donated to the new library from abroad, particularly France and India. In the library garden is a statue of its founder, Reverend Long, said to have died on hearing the news of the original library's demise. Jaffna's restored **clocktower** reopened in June 2002, with clocks donated by HRH the Prince of Wales.

→ THE ISLANDS

The religious site of Nainativu (Nagadipa), sacred to both Buddhists and Hindus, is the only place in this area that receives a significant amount of visitors – the site is increasingly thronged with day-trippers from around the country. Kayts and Karainagar are linked to the mainland by separate causeways, while a third which cuts seemingly endlessly through dazzling blue sea, joins Kayts to Punguditivu, at the southwestern corner of which ferries can be caught to the outlying islands. The islands are rich in birdlife. Watch out for flamingos on the causeway to Kayts.

KAYTS
To the north of the island, the nearest to Jaffna town, is Kayts town, once a wealthy and sought-after area – look out for the ruins of beautiful villas lining the approach road. The road ends at a jetty for boats to Karaitivu Island. At the south of Kayts island, **Velanai** (or Chatty) is a popular beach.

KARAITIVU
At the north end of Karaitivu, is **Casuarina Beach**, the most popular in Jaffna, where swimming is safe in the calm, shallow waters. A few stalls sell drinks and snacks. The beach is so-called after the beefwood (*casuarina*) trees found here.

NAINATIVU
Accessed by ferry from **Punguditivu**, the tiny island of Nainativu has great religious importance to both Buddhists and Hindus. For the former it is **Nagadipa**, the point at which the Buddha set foot on his second visit to the island, four years after the first, in order to settle a quarrel between two Naga kings over a throne, said to be enshrined here. A *vihara*, with a restored silver *dagoba* and image house marks the spot. There is a bo tree opposite. The *vihara* is a 10-minute walk along the road leading left from the jetty point.

In a Hindu-dominated area however, the **Naga Pooshani Ambal Kovil** at the jetty point is the livelier temple, and can be the focus of a day-trip. Regular *pujas* are taken, with colourful processions, clattering drums, bells and pipes, and gasps as the inner sanctum of the temple is revealed. In its 15-day festival in June, a 30-m Ambal is paraded. In order to take advantage of Ambal's generosity, it is a good idea to arrive for the important *puja* at 1300, after which crowds of several hundred line up in the hall behind the temple for rice and curry, ladled out on to a banana leaf. Lunch is usually finished in time to catch the 1430 boat back to Pungudituvu.

DELFT
The windswept and bleak landscape of Delft, the outermost inhabited island, has been less affected by the conflict and contains various reminders of the Portuguese and Dutch periods. Famous for its wild ponies, which come from a Portuguese breeding stock, there are also the remains of a coral fort, fairly tumbledown but still recognizable, behind the hospital. South of the jetty is a single baobab tree and, further on, a large banyan, while at the southern tip the Quindah tower is an ancient navigational landmark.

ANURADHAPURA AND MIHINTALE LISTINGS

WHERE TO STAY

Anuradhapura

$$$$ Ulagalla Resort, Thirapanne,
23 km from Anuradhapura, T11-567 1000
(reservations), www.ulagallaresorts.com.
Some distance away from Anuradhapura
but the most luxurious hotel around.
25 tasteful a/c chalets with private
plunge pools, dotted throughout the
20-ha grounds which border Ulagalla
tank. Freshwater swimming pool, spa,
restaurants and activities such as kayaking,
horse riding and birdwatching. Electric
buggies will collect guests and ferry them
to the main house.
$$$-$$ Palm Garden Village,
Km 42 post, Puttalam Rd, Pandulagama,
2.5 km from the sites, T222 3961,
www.palmgardenvillage.com. 40 stylish
a/c rooms and 10 suites in upmarket
villas dotted around the gardens with
deer. Full facilities including large pool,
Ayurvedic centre, open-sided restaurants.

$$ Randiya, off JR Jaya Mawatha,
T222 2868, www.hotelrandiya.com.
Comfortable a/c rooms, standard or
deluxe, all with balcony in a modern
house. There's a pleasant restaurant
serving good food, excellent service. Can
arrange tours to Wilpattu National Park.
$ Milano Tourist Rest, 596/40, Stage One,
JR Jaya Mawatha, T222 2364, www.milano
touristrest.com. Modern house with
comfortable well-furnished rooms, fan or
a/c. Bathrooms are a bit of a let-down. Good
restaurant, bar, tours offered to Wilpattu
National Park (2-hr drive). Expensive bike
hire. Wi-Fi and terminals available.
$ Shalini, 41/388 Harischandra Mawatha
(opposite Water Tower Stage 1), T222 2425,
www.hotelshalini.com. 14 large, clean,
comfortable fan or a/c rooms, in modern
house, hot water, good food in attractive
roof-top restaurant, well kept, cycle hire,
free transfer from/to station, internet café.

RESTAURANTS

Anuradhapura

$ Casserole, above **Family Bakers**,
279 Main St, T222 4443. A/c offers welcome
respite from the heat, with good value
Chinese (set menus from Rs 300 upwards),
but has the atmosphere of a school gym
and staff are glum.

$ Shalini, 41/388 Harischandra Mawatha
(opposite Water Tower Stage 1), T222 2425,
www.hotelshalini.com. Terrace restaurant
in the tree-tops serving good-value food,
especially the rice and curry set menus.

HABARANA AND AROUND

Habarana is an important crossroads, with roads extending southwest to Colombo or Kandy, northwest to Anuradhapura and Jaffna, northeast to Trincomalee, and southeast to Polonnaruwa and Batticaloa. Tour groups often spend a night here, though apart from a scattering of hotels and rest houses and its accessibility, it has little to offer. It is, however, a good base for visiting a number of sights in the area including some of the region's most inspiring treasures. Most spectacular of all is the astonishing Sigiriya rock, atop which lie the remains of a sort of fifth-century playboy's palace, complete with pin-ups in the form of its famous frescoes of semi-clad women. No less remarkable are some nearby Buddhist sites: cave paintings at Dambulla; Aukana's sublime monolithic Buddha; and the ancient monastery at Ritigala, hidden deep within the jungle. Three national parks, around the tanks at Kaudulla and Minneriya, are close by though shop around for jeeps; elephant safaris are also available though they are expensive.

→ ARRIVING IN HABARANA

GETTING THERE

Habarana is a busy transport junction and is easily reached by bus from all directions. It takes two hours by bus from Anuradhapura; 1½ hours with a car and driver.

The train station is 2 km north of Habarana Junction and is on the Colombo–Batticaloa line. There are connections with Colombo, Trincomalee, Batticaloa and Polonnaruwa.

MOVING ON

If you have your own transport, it would be easy to combine the drive south with a stop at the **Dambulla** (see page 71) cave temples, and perhaps Aluwihare. There are regular buses from Habarana to Dambulla and Dambulla to **Kandy** (see page 81), but you would be hard pressed to travel to Dambulla, see the cave temples and travel on to Kandy in one day; an overnight stop in Dambulla would be a better option. To reach Aluwihare by public transport, take a Kandy-bound bus from Dambulla, which goes right past the entrance.

Note that buses passing through Habarana are very busy (particularly if heading north) and there may not be space for you and your bag. Unless travelling very light, try and catch the earliest bus of the day. The bus to **Trincomalee** (see page 77) is often full, so either arrange a private car (1½ hours) or take the bus from Anuradhapura (see page 43). It is possible to travel by train to Trincomalee but at the time of writing the only service was in the very early hours of the morning.

→ KAUDULLA NATIONAL PARK

ⓘ *The turn-off for the park is 17 km north of Habarana at Hatarasgoduwa from where it is a 5-km ride to the visitor centre. Jeeps from Habarana will usually charge Rs 4500 for a 3-hr 'safari', leaving 1500-1600. Entry costs US$15 plus service charge, tracker, etc. Best time to visit Aug-Dec.*

Sri Lanka's newest national park was opened to the public in September 2002, partly as another step in establishing protection for the elephants' ancient migration routes. It completes a network of protected areas around the Polonnaruwa area, comprising

Minneriya National Park, Minneriya-Giritale Nature Reserve and Wasgomuwa National Park to the south, and Flood Plains and Somawathie to the east and north. The 6936-ha park acts mainly as a catchment to the Kaudulla tank, which dates back to the 17th century. Its most prominent feature is its large herds of elephant (up to 250), which can be seen at the tank during the dry season when water is scarce elsewhere. The vegetation, which consists of semi-mixed evergreen, grasslands and riverine forest, supports a small population of leopard and sloth bear, while birdlife is excellent.

Outside the dry season, elephants are easier to see from the main Habarana–Trincomalee road (on the left coming from Habarana) than in the park itself. These are their preferred feeding grounds due to the lushness of the vegetation. Jeeps in Habarana are keen to take you to this area in these months but if you already have a vehicle there is little point getting a jeep since they feed very close to the road.

→ MINNERIYA NATIONAL PARK

ⓘ *26 km west of Polonnaruwa. The park entrance is at Ambagaswewa, east of Habarana on the Batticaloa Rd. Jeeps charge the same as to Kaudulla (see above). Park entry is US$15 plus service charge, tracker, etc. Best time to visit May-Oct. Keep a look out for wild elephants on the Minneriya–Giritale Rd, and don't drive this route at night.*

A sanctuary since 1938, Minneriya was upgraded to national park status in 1997. Here is King Mahasena's magnificent Minneriya tank (fourth century AD) covering 3000 ha, which dominates the park. It is an important wetlands, feeding around 8900 ha of paddy fields, and supporting many aquatic birds, such as painted storks, spot-billed pelicans, openbill storks and grey herons. At the end of the dry season there is little evidence of the tank which gets covered in weeds, the vegetation on its bed becoming a vital source of food for many animals. Around September and October, an influx or local migration of elephants takes place in a spectacular wildlife event. The high forest canopy also provides ideal conditions for purple-faced leaf monkey and toque monkey, while the short bushes and grasslands provide food for sambhar and chital. There are small populations of leopard and sloth bear. Mugger crocodiles and land and water monitors can also be seen.

→ HURULU ECO PARK

ⓘ *US$15 plus service charge.*

On the Habarana to Trincomalee road, Hurulu Eco Park is often suggested as an alternative when it's too wet to visit Kaudulla and Minneriya. Part of Hurulu Forest Reserve, which was designated as a biosphere reserve in January 1977, it is a good place to see elephants and for birdwatching. Taking up 10,000 ha of the 25,500-ha reserve, there are a number of waterways intersecting in the area there are plans to make a large tank from the smaller, abandoned tanks. Among the species living in the area are the turtle, Ceylon junglefowl, small populations of leopard and the rusty-spotted cat. Facilities are limited at the moment, but there are plans to develop the park for tourists and re-open some of the walking trails.

➜ RITIGALA

① You need your own vehicle to reach Ritigala. From Habarana, follow the A11 for 22 km west towards Maradankadawala, taking a right turn at Galapitagala for 5 km into the forest, then turn left along a track (suitable for a 2WD) for about 3 km where an ancient rock-cut path leads to the site. Park entry is Rs1500. There is a visitor centre where you can arrange a guide.

The 148-ha archaeological site is located within a 1570-ha Strict Nature Reserve, where wildlife includes elephants, sloth bear and leopard and varied bird life. The area, rich in unusual plants and herbs, is associated with the *Ramayana* story in which Hanuman dropped a section of herb-covered Himalaya here (see page 170).

The forest hermitage complex here was occupied by the ascetic *Pansakulika* monks. The structures found here include the typical double platforms joined by stone bridges, stone columns, ambulatories, herbal baths filled by rain water, sluices and monks' cells. There are many natural caves on the mountain slopes, some quite large, in which priests would meditate. Brahmi inscriptions here date the site from the third and second centuries BC.

As you enter the site, you will clamber over ruined steps leading down to the now overgrown two-acre bathing tank, the **Banda Pokuna**. Over an original stone bridge, follow a part-restored pathway, laid with interlocking ashlar, to the first major clearing, the monastery hospital, where you can see the remains of a stone bed, oil bath and medicine grinder. The next set of ruins is believed to be a library, now partly restored, perched atop a rock with magnificent views across to the jungle below. Beyond here, you come to the monastery, where you'll find the distinctive raised double-platforms, characteristic of Ritigala and other forest monasteries (see box, page 50). The platforms were probably for congregational use.

Platform 17 marks the end of the excavated territory – special permission is required from the Wildlife Department to venture further, and guides are in any case fearful of wild animals (workers have been maimed or killed in this area by elephants). Though in the Dry Zone, the Ritigala summit has a strange cool, wet micro-climate, with vegetation reminiscent of Horton Plains (see page 124).

➜ POLONNARUWA

Polonnaruwa, the island's medieval capital between the 11th and 13th century, is for many visitors the most rewarding of the ancient cities. Flowering principally under three kings over a short period of less than 100 years, it is, in contrast to Anuradhapura, historically as well as geographically compact, and so it feels easier to assimilate. Today, the ruins, built alongside the vast and beautiful Parakrama Samudra, stand witness to a lavish phase of building, culminating in the sublime Gal Vihara. In its imperial intentions, and the brevity of its existence, Polonnaruwa may be compared to the great Mughal emperor Akbar's city of Fatehpur Sikri, near Agra in India.

ARRIVING IN POLONNARUWA

Getting there Trains and buses arrive at Kaduruwela, 4 km east. From here, local buses run frequently to Polonnaruwa, or take a three-wheeler.

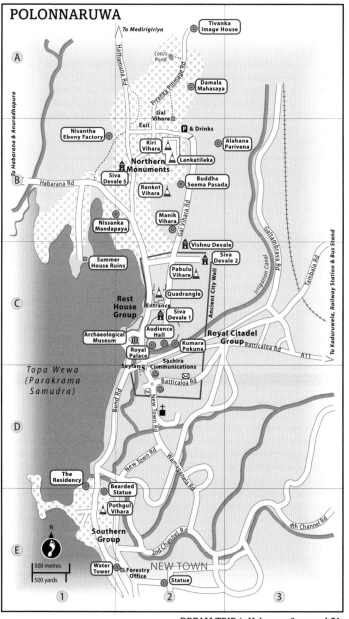

POLONNARUWA

To Medirigiriya

To Habarana & Anuradhapura

Hathamuna Rd

Tivanka Pirimage Rd

Tivanka Image House

Lotus Pond

Damala Mahasaya

Gal Vihara

Exit

P & Drinks

Nisantha Ebony Factory

Kiri Vihara

Lankatilaka

Alahana Parivena

Northern Monuments

Habarana Rd

Siva Devale 5

Rankot Vihara

Buddha Seema Pasada

Gal Vihara Rd

Manik Vihara

Nissanka Mandapaya

Vishnu Devale

Summer House Ruins

Pabulu Vihare

Siva Devale 2

Ancient City Wall

Rest House Group

Quadrangle

Entrance

Siva Devale 1

Irrigation Canal

Galtambrava Rd

Tambala Rd

To Kaduruwela, Railway Station & Bus Stand

Archaeological Museum

Audience Hall

Royal Citadel Group

Royal Palace

Kumara Pokuna

Battcaloa Rd

A11

Seylan

Sachira Communications

Topa Wewa (Parakrama Samudra)

Batticaloa Rd

New Town Rd

Bund Rd

Wamaganela Rd

The Residency

Bearded Statue

Pothgul Vihara

Southern Group

4th Channel Rd

N

500 metres
500 yards

Water Tower

Forestry Office

NEW TOWN

Statue

2nd Channel Rd

A   B   C   D   E

1   2   3

Moving on An alternative to returning to Habarana would be to spend the night in Polonnaruwa and take a bus directly to **Kandy** (see page 81) from here.

Getting around Under a hot sun the site is too spread out to walk around. Even if you have a car, cycling is the most practical and fun way to explore the town (available from most hotels), though take it easy as brakes are a luxury and the tracks are rough in places – you'll do well if you get round without a puncture. It is best to get your bearings before starting a tour. The ruins can be split broadly into five groups, though your ticket is only needed for three. Close to the entrance and within the old walls are the **Royal Citadel Group** to the south and the **Quadrangle** to the north. The **Northern Monuments**, which include the magnificent Gal Vihara, are spread out for 3 km north of here. Across the main road from the main site, close to the museum and bund is the small **Rest House Group**, and finally, the **Southern Group** is about 3 km south of town. The museum, unless you arrive early morning, is a good place to start. The entrance to the main site is 500 m from here though you may wish to see the Rest House Group first as it is closest to the museum. Once in the main site, there is a one-way route through the sacred site that is generally quite well signed.

Best time to visit As ever, early morning or late evening is best, to avoid the heat. To visit many sites you will need to remove your shoes – in the blazing sun the stones are scorching so taking socks is a good idea. Avoid visiting more remote ruins late in the day, as attacks on lone tourists have been known.

Tourist information Tickets are available from the counter at the Archaeological Museum, close to the rest house, which also acts as an information desk and sometimes sells maps of the city. Though the museum itself doesn't open till 0900, the desk is open from 0700. Tickets cost US$25. A book on Polonnaruwa is available from the bookshop for Rs 250.

BACKGROUND

The Sinhalese kings of Anuradhapura in AD 369 used Polonnaruwa as their residence but it did not rank as a capital until the eighth century. The Cholas from South India destroyed the Sinhalese Kingdom at the beginning of the 11th century and, taking control of most of the island, they established their capital at Polonnaruwa. In 1056 King Vijayabahu I defeated the Cholas, setting up his own capital in the city. It remained a vibrant centre of Sinhalese culture under his successors, notably Parakramabahu I (1153-1186) who maintained very close ties with India, importing architects and engineers, and Nissankamalla (1187-1196). The rectangular shaped city was enclosed by three concentric walls, and was made attractive with parks and gardens. Polonnaruwa owes much of its glory to the artistic conception of King Parakramabahu I who planned the whole as an expression and statement of imperial power. Its great artificial lake provided cooling breezes through the city, water for irrigation and at the same time, defence along its entire west flank. The bund is over 14 km long and 1 m high, and the tank irrigates over 90 sq km of paddy fields. Fed by a 40-km-long canal and a link from the Giritale tank, it was named after its imperial designer the Parakrama Samudra (Topa Wewa).

After Parakramabahu, the kingdom went into terminal decline and the city was finally abandoned in 1288, after the tank embankment was breached. Fortunately, many of the remains are in an excellent state of repair though several of the residential buildings remain to be excavated. In 1982 it was designated a World Heritage Site. The restoration at the site is by the UNESCO-sponsored Central Cultural Fund. Today it attracts numerous water birds, including cormorants and pelicans.

PLACES IN POLONNARUWA

Archaeological Museum ① *0900-1800. Entry is covered by the site ticket.* This is an excellent place to start a tour of the ancient ruins, and you may wish to return afterwards. In addition to the clearly presented exhibits found on site, and many photographs, there is also a well-written commentary on Sri Lanka's ancient history. Scaled down representations give you an idea of how the buildings would have looked during the city's prime. In the final (seventh) room, there are some extraordinarily well-preserved bronze statues.

Rest House Group Nissankamalla built his own 'New' Palace close to the water's edge in a beautiful garden setting. Today, the ruins are sadly in a poor state of repair. Just north of the rest house, beyond the sunken royal baths, are a stone 'mausoleum', the Audience Hall, and lastly the interesting Council Chamber which had the stone lion throne (now housed in the Colombo National Museum). The four rows of 12 sculpted columns have inscriptions indicating the seating order in the chamber – from the king at the head, with the princes, army chiefs and ministers, down to the record keepers on his right, while to his left were placed government administrators, and representatives of the business community. Across the water, to the northwest, the mound on the narrow strip of land which remains above flood water, has the ruins of the King Parakramabahu's 'Summer House' which was decorated with wall paintings.

Royal Citadel Group Cycle along the bund to the main road, where stalls sell drinks and snacks. The main entrance, for which you will need a ticket, is opposite, across the road. About 200 m south of the entrance (to the right as you enter), stands King Parakramabahu's Palace (Vejayanta Prasada). It is described in the Chronicles as originally having had seven storeys and 1000 rooms, but much of it was of wood and so was destroyed by fire. The large central hall on the ground floor (31 m x 13 m) had 30 columns which supported the roof. You can see the holes for the beams in the 3-m-thick brick walls. It has porticoes on the east and west and a wide stairway.

The Council Chamber (sometimes called Audience Hall) is immediately to its east. It has fine, partly octagonal, granite pillars and friezes of elephants, lions and dwarves, which follow the entire exterior of the base. Nearby, outside the palace wall, is the stepped Kumara Pokuna (Prince's Bath), restored in the 1930s. You can still see the spouts where the water is channelled through the open jaws of crocodiles.

Quadrangle Turning left from the entrance, you come first to the Siva Devale I, a Hindu Temple (one of the many Siva and Vishnu temples here), built in about AD 1200, which has lost its brick roof. An example of the Dravidian Indian architectural style, it shows exceptional stone carving, and the fine bronze statues discovered in the ruins have been transferred to the Colombo Museum.

Some 50 m further on, steps lead up to the **Quadrangle**, the highlight of the ruins within the ancient city wall. Though the structures here are comparatively modest in size, they are carved in fine detail. This is still regarded as a sanctuary and shoes and hats have to be removed.

The **Vatadage** ('hall of the relic') to the left as you enter the Quadrangle is a circular building with a *dagoba* on concentric terraces with sculptured railings, the largest with a diameter of 18 m. A superbly planned and executed 12th-century masterpiece attributed to Nissankamalla (1187-1196), the Vatadage has modest proportions but remarkably graceful lines. It was almost certainly intended to house the Tooth Relic. There are impressive guard stones at the entrances of the second terrace and wing stones with *makaras* enclosing lion figures. The moonstone to the north entrance of the top terrace is superb. The *dagoba* at the centre has four Buddhas (some damaged) with a later stone screen.

The **Hatadage**, with extraordinary moonstones at its entrance, is the sanctuary built by Nissankamalla and is also referred to as the Temple of the Tooth, since the relic may have been placed here for a time. See the Buddha statue here framed by three solid doorways, and then look back at one of the Buddha statues in the Vatadage, again beautifully framed by the doorways.

Gal Pota, to the east of the Hatadage, the 'Book of Stone' is to the side of the path and can easily be missed. According to the inscription it weighs 25 tons, and was brought over 90 km from Mihintale. It is in the form of a palm leaf measuring over 9 m by 1.2 m,

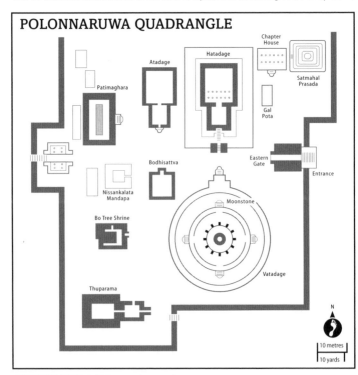

POLONNARUWA QUADRANGLE

over 60 cm thick in places, with Sinhalese inscriptions praising the works of the King Nissankamalla including his conquests in India. The **Chapter House** nearby dates from the seventh century. The ziggurat-like **Satmahal Prasada** (originally seven-storeyed) in the northeast corner, decorated with stucco figures, has lost its top level. The 9-m-sq base decreases at each level as in Cambodian *prasats*.

West of the Hatadage, the **Atadage** ('house of eight relics') was the first Tooth Relic temple, constructed by Vijayabahu when the capital was moved here. There are some handsome carved pillars. The ruins of the **Patimaghara**, west of here, reveal the remains of a reclining Buddha.

The **Bo Tree shrine** is to the west of the main Vatadage. The **Nissankalata** (Lotus Mandapa) nearby was built by King Nissankamalla (1187-1196) for a *dagoba*. This small pavilion has the remains of a stone seat (from which the king listened to chanting of scriptures), steps and a stone fence imitating a latticed wooden railing with posts. The ornamental stone pillars which surround the *dagoba* are in the form of thrice-bent lotus buds on stalks, a design which has become one of Sri Lanka's emblems. A statue of a *Bodhisattva* is to its east. The impressive **Thuparama**, in the south of the Quadrangle, is a *gedige* which was developed as a fusion of Indian and Sinhalese Buddhist architecture. This has the only surviving vaulted dome of its type and houses a number of Buddha statues. It has very thick plaster-covered brick walls with a staircase embedded in them. Exiting the Quadrangle by the same steps that brought you in, 500 m to the northeast are two temples which belong to different periods. If you walk past the **Pabulu Vihare**, a squat stupa up to the north wall of the ancient city, you come to one of the earliest temples with Tamil inscriptions, **Siva Devala 2**. Built of stone by the Indian Cholas in a style they were developing in Tamil Nadu (as at Thanjavur), but using brick rather than stone, it is almost perfectly preserved.

Northern monuments Beyond the original city wall, another group of scattered monuments stretches several kilometres further north. First, the **Alahana Parivena** (Royal Crematory Monastery) Complex, which was set aside by Parakramabahu, is worth exploring. The UNESCO restoration project is concentrated in this area. At the **Manik Vihara**, the squat cloistered stupa was restored in 1991. This originally housed precious gems.

The **Rankot Vihara**, further on, is the fourth largest *dagoba* on the island with a height of 55 m. It was built by Nissankamalla in the 12th century. Note the perfection of the spire and the clarity of the statues round the drum. The tall **Buddha Seema Pasada** was the Chapter House or convocation hall where you can still make out the central throne of the chief abbot, which was surrounded by monks' cells.

The large *gedige* **Lankatilaka** ('ornament of Lanka'), the image house with a Buddha statue, had five storeys. It has walls which are 4 m thick and still stand 17 m high, although the roof has crumbled. The design illustrates the development in thinking which underlay the massive building, for it marks a turning away from the abstract form of the *dagoba* to a much more personalized faith in the Buddha in human form. The building is essentially a shrine, built to focus the attention of worshippers on the 18-m-high statue of the Buddha at the end of the nave. Though built of brick and covered in stucco, the overall design of the building shows strong Tamil influence. The exterior bas-relief sculpture, most of which is impressively well preserved, sheds light on contemporary architectural styles. To the south of the Lankatilaka is a *madipa* with carved columns

Queen Subhadra is believed to have built the 'milk white' **Kiri Vihara** stupa next to it, so named because of its unspoilt white plaster work when it was first discovered. It remains the best preserved of the island's unrestored *dagobas*. The plasterwork is intact although the whitewash is only visible in place, such as around the relic box. There are excellent views from the Chapter House which has the foundations only just visible.

The **Gal Vihara** (Cave of the Spirits of Knowledge) is rightly regarded as one of the foremost attractions of Sri Lanka and has great significance to Buddhists. It forms a part of Parakramabahu's monastery where a Buddha seated on a pedestal under a canopy was carved out of an 8-m-high rock. On either side of the rock shrine are further vast carvings of a seated Buddha and a 14-m recumbent Buddha in *Parinirvana* (rather than death), indicated, in part, by the way the higher foot is shown slightly withdrawn. The grain of the rock is beautiful as is the expression. Near the head of the reclining figure, the 7-m standing image of banded granite with folded arms was once believed to be his grieving disciple Ananda but is now thought to be of the Buddha himself. The foundation courses of the brick buildings which originally enclosed the sculptures, are visible. Sadly, the presentation of the magnificent carved Buddhas is rather disappointing. An unattractive, protective canopy now shields the seated Buddha, which is caged in with rusty metal bars and a scratched plastic 'viewing window' making clear viewing and photography impossible.

A path continues north to rejoin the road. The **Lotus Pond**, a little further along, is a small bathing pool, empty in the dry season, with five concentric circles of eight petals which form the steps down into the water. The road ends at the **Tivanka Image House** where the Buddha image is in the unusual 'thrice bent' posture (shoulder, waist and knee) associated with a female figure, possibly emphasizing his gentle aspect. This is the largest brick-built shrine here, now substantially renovated (though work continues). There are remarkable frescoes inside depicting scenes from the *Jatakas*, though not as fine as those in Sigiriya. Under the 13th-century frescoes, even earlier original paintings have been discovered. The decorations on the outside of the building are excellent with delightful carvings of dwarves on the plinth. The image house actually has a double skin, and for a small tip the guardian will unlock a door about half way inside the building. You can then walk between the outer and inner walls. The passage is lit from windows high up in the wall. It is an excellent way of seeing the corbel building technique. The guardian may also unroll the painted copies of the frescoes, which eventually will be repainted onto the walls.

Southern Group This group is quite separate from the rest of the ruins, though it makes sense to start here if you are staying nearby. It is well worth walking or cycling down here along the bund as the view is lovely, though the main entrance is from the main road. You will first see the giant 3.5-m-high **statue** of a bearded figure, now believed to be King Parakramabahu himself, looking away from the city he restored, holding in his hand the palm leaf manuscript of the 'Book of Law' (some suggest it represents 'the burden of royalty' in the shape of a rope). Sadly, the statue is covered by an ugly canopy.

To its south is the **Pothgul Vihara**, which houses a circular *gedige* (instead of being corbelled from two sides), with four small solid *dagobas* around. The central circular room, with 5-m-thick walls, is thought to have housed a library.

Other places Once you've exhausted the ruins, a few peaceful hours can be spent cycling along the bund and attractive tree-lined **canals**, perhaps catching sight of a giant water monitor. The water system is so well planned it is hard to believe it is almost 1000 years old. Some 4 km south past the Southern Group along the east bank of the tank you come to a weir, a popular spot for bathing.

→ SIGIRIYA

The bloody history of the vast flat-topped 200-m-high 'Lion Rock' – a tale of murder and dynastic feuding – is as dramatic as its position, rearing starkly from the plain beneath. An exceptional natural site for a fortress, the rock dominates the surrounding countryside of the central forest and from the top offers views that stretch as far as the Dry Zone and south to the Central Highlands. Deriving its name (Sinha-Giri) from the lions which were believed to occupy the caves, for many visitors this impressive site is their favourite in the whole of Sri Lanka. The rewards of Sigiriya (pronounced See-gi-ri-ya), with its palace, famous frescoes and beautiful water gardens, justify the steep climb. Frequently labelled the 'Eighth Wonder of the World', it was designated a World Heritage Site in 1982.

ARRIVING IN SIGIRIYA
Getting there and around The main bus stop is close to the bridge by the exit (at the south of the rock) so those without their own transport have to undertake the 10-minute

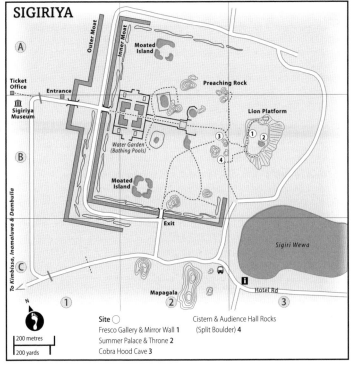

SIGIRIYA

Ticket Office
Entrance
Sigiriya Museum

Outer Moat
Inner Moat
Moated Island
Preaching Rock
Lion Platform

Water Garden (Bathing Pools)
Moated Island

Exit

Sigiri Wewa

To Kimbissa, Inamaluwa & Dambulla

Mapagala
Hotel Rd

N
200 metres
200 yards

Site ○
Fresco Gallery & Mirror Wall **1**
Summer Palace & Throne **2**
Cobra Hood Cave **3**

Cistern & Audience Hall Rocks
(Split Boulder) **4**

ON THE ROAD
Legends of Sigiriya

The romance of Sigiriya, the playboy's palace in the sky, has provided inspiration for many books, plays and even films, with more than one legend to explain its origins. All theories hinge around the cult of King Kasyapa.

The *Mahavansa* records that King Kasyapa (reigned AD 477-495) killed his father, King Dhatusena, by plastering him alive to a wall, in order to gain the throne, after which he lived in terror that his half brother, Moggallana, who had taken refuge in India, would return to kill him. He did come back, after 18 years, to find that Kasyapa had built a combination of pleasure palace and massive fortress. Kasyapa came down from the hill to face his half brother's army on elephant back. Mistakenly thinking he had been abandoned by his supporters, he killed himself with his dagger.

A conflicting, if equally bloody alternative theory, propounded by historian Senarat Paranavitana, is claimed to have been deciphered from inscriptions by a 15th-century monk. In this, Dhatusena is told that he can obtain imperial status by becoming a *Parvataraja*, or mountain king, ruling from a palace built on a rock summit. In the struggle for succession, Kasyapa on return from exile in India mistakenly attacks and defeats his father's army, believing it to belong to his brother, at which Dhatusena beheads himself. Remorseful as the cause of his father's death, Kasyapa, now king, attempts to put his father's dream into reality. In order to be accepted by overseas merchants, he proclaims himself as *Kubera*, the God of Wealth, and attempts to recreate his legendary palace on earth. He issues a gold coinage and establishes free ports, which accrue great wealth for the kingdom. In this theory Kasyapa dies in his palace after Moggallana persuades his wife to poison him.

walk round to the entrance (to the west) to buy their ticket (the track is signposted off the road 1 km west from the bus stand, past the rest house). Those visiting by car are dropped at the entrance – the driver will then drive round to the car park at the exit. Expect to be approached by guides as soon as you arrive, some of which can be very persistent. Be careful in Sigiriya at night, especially if you're a lone female.

Best time to visit Early morning is beautiful and the site is very quiet until 0730, but the late afternoon light is better for the frescoes. Avoid the high sun around noon. There can be long queues and the rock can be very crowded from mid-morning. If you wish to make an early start (avoiding groups which start arriving by 0800) buy your ticket the day before.

Tourist information The ticket office is near the entrance; entry costs US$30 (half price for children). It is advisable not to take food as the site is over-run by dogs which will follow you around. There is a road leading to the base of the rock for ease of access for disabled visitors. The **Centre for Eco-Cultural Studies (CES)** ① *T567 5523, www.cessrilanka. org*, is east of the bus station near the tank and should be able to provide more information about the flora and fauna in the area, and arrange tours.

Sigiriya, by RH De Silva, Ceylon, Department of Archaeology, 1971, is recommended reading for further background information.

BACKGROUND

Hieroglyphs suggest that the site was occupied by humans from times long before the fortress was built. The royal citadel, built between AD 477-485, was surrounded by an impressive wall and a double moat. As well as the palace, the city had quarters for the ordinary people who built the royal pavilions, pools and fortifications.

The engineering skills required to build the palace, gardens, cisterns and ponds become even more extraordinary when you realise that the entire site was built over a period of seven years and effectively abandoned after 18 years. For the famous frescoes Kasyapa gathered together the best artists of his day.

Water, a scarce commodity in the Dry Zone, was conserved and diverted cleverly through pipes and rock-cut channels to provide bathing pools for the palace above, and to enhance the gardens below with pools and fountains. The water pumps are thought to have been powered by windmills. On the islands in the two pools in the water garden near the entrance stood pavilions, while the shallow marble pools reflected the changing patterns of the clouds. Excavations have revealed surface and underground drainage systems.

When the citadel ceased to be a palace after Moggallana's reign, it was inhabited by monks till 1155, and then abandoned. It was rediscovered by archaeologists in 1828.

PLACES IN SIGIRIYA

Entering the site across the moat from the west, you will pass the fifth-century **water gardens** (restored by the Central Cultural Fund with UNESCO sponsorship) with walks, pavilions, ponds and fountains which are gravity fed from the moats as they were 1500 years ago. You can see the secret changing room doors. Legend states that Kaspaya used to watch his concubines bathe here from his palace.

A straight path leads through the group of four fountain gardens with small water jets (originally fifth century), some with pretty lotuses attracting a number of water birds. Finally you reach the flower garden with colourful beds and flowering trees. To the right as you walk up to the rock is a **miniature water garden**. The whole area (including the moat and drive) is immaculate. It is difficult to visualize the winter palace as there are no visible foundations.

THE ROCK

The top of the rock has a surface area of 1.5 ha. It is easy to forget that the site was in fact developed as a massive defensive fortress. Lookout points were located on ledges clinging to the rock. Steer clear of the aggressive monkeys in this area.

Base of the rock Before reaching the steps the path goes through the boulder garden where clusters of rocks, including the **preaching rock** with 'seats', are marked with rows of notches and occasional 'gashes'. These may have been used for decorating the area with lamps during festivals. To the right at the start of the climb, under a natural overhang, is the **Cobra Hood** rock which has a drip ledge inscription in Brahmi script dating from the second century BC. The floor and ceiling have lime plaster, the latter is decorated with paintings and floral patterns. A headless Buddha statue is placed horizontally. It is thought to have been a monk's cell originally. The **Cistern** and the **Audience Hall** rocks are parts of a single massive boulder which had split, and half of which had fallen away. The exposed flat surface had a 'throne' at one end and came to be called the Audience Hall while the upper part of the standing half retained the rectangular cistern. A second set of steps is under construction from the end of the new road to the Lion Terrace.

The climb This begins in earnest with steps leading through the Elephant Gate on well-maintained brick-lined stairways. These lead up to the second checkpoint immediately below the gallery containing the frescoes. Steps continue up to the **Fresco Gallery**, painted under an overhanging rock and reached by a spiral staircase which was built in 1938. A second staircase has been added to ease congestion. Of the original 500 or so frescoes, which vie with those in Ajanta in Western India, only 21 remain. They are remarkably well preserved as they are sheltered from the elements in a niche. In the style of Ajanta, the first drawing was done on wet plaster and then painted with red, yellow, green and black. The figures are 'portraits' of well-endowed *apsaras* (celestial nymphs) and attendants above clouds – offering flowers, scattering petals or bathing. Here, guides are keen to point out the girl with three hands and another with three nipples. Note the girls of African and Mongolian origin, proof of the kingdom's widespread trade at this time. Some paintings were destroyed by a madman in 1967 and you can see pictures of this in the small museum. You may photograph the frescoes but a flash is not permitted. Note that there is no entry to the frescoes after 1700.

Mirror wall Immediately beyond the foot of the spiral staircases the path is protected on the outer side by the 3-m-high, highly polished plaster wall believed to have been coated with lime, egg white and wild honey. After 15 centuries it still has a reflective sheen. Visitors and pilgrims (mostly between seventh and 11th century) wrote verses in Sinhalese – 'graffiti' prompted by the frescoes and by verses written by previous visitors. Some, today, find this section a little disappointing. Despite the threat of a large fine or a two-year jail sentence, there is plenty of modern graffiti to obscure the originals and it can be difficult to stop and study because of the pressure of people when the rock is busy. As you continue to climb, note the massive rock, close to the Guard House, wedged with stone supports which could be knocked out to enable it to crash on the enemy far below.

Lion Terrace Here, the giant plaster-covered brick paws of the lion become visible. Originally, the entire head and front part of the body would have awed visitors. Though the remainder of the structure has disappeared, the size of the paws gives some clue to the height of the lion's head. The terrace marks the halfway point of the climb where cool drinks are available and where many touts wait for customers. The wire cage is supposed to protect people from wild bees. You can see their nests under the metal staircase.

Final stairway The final stage of the ascent on the north ledge leads through the lion's paws to the top of the rock up the steep west and north sides. It is worth studying the remaining climb to the summit. You can clearly see the outline of small steps cut into the granite. The king was apparently scared of heights so these steps would also have been enclosed by a 3-m-high mirror wall. Here was the lion's gate after which the place is named: *Si* (shortened form of *Sinha*, lion) *Giriya* (throat). The stairway of 25 flights is mostly on iron steps with a small guard rail and is steep (particularly in one place where a small flight resemble a ship's ladder). Small children can find this quite frightening.

Summer Palace At the top are the ruins of the palace. The foundations reveal the likely size, surprisingly small when compared with the size of the stone throne underneath it, although it was only built for the king and queen. There was the granite throne, dancing terraces, a small pool fed by rain water, drinking water tanks, sleeping quarters of the concubines, a small flower garden and precariously positioned platforms for guards. If you walk to the sign on the west, there is a very good birds-eye view of the winter palace and its surrounding moat.

Descent Retrace your steps to the second checkpoint. Just below this, the path splits to the left from where you can get a view of the king's audience chamber and his anteroom. Once again, there is a huge throne in a semicircle where his advisors would sit – justice was swift and often brutal. Immediately below the audience chamber was another granite slab: this was the place of execution. Again to the left is the ante-chamber which was cooled by a tank of water cut into the rock above the ceiling. It too would have been covered in frescoes. Much of the construction is in brick, faced with lime plaster but there are sections built with limestone slabs which would have been carried up. The upper structures which have disappeared were probably wooden. Finally you exit through the cobra gate – a huge, overhanging rock.

OTHER SIGHTS
These include the **Mapagala Rock** with evidence of dressed stone work, a *dagoba* and other ruins on the roadside just over a kilometre away. **Pidurangala Royal Cave Temple** and Buddhist Meditation centre are 1.5 km away and signposted from the car park. The cave on the rock Pidurangala, where there had been an ancient monastery, still has a stupa with a 10th-century reclining Buddha and an inscription dating from the first century BC. These, and other finds of early settlement in **Rama Kale** nearby, point at the ancient nature of the spot chosen by Kasyapa for his palace fortress. The **Sigiriya Museum** ① *0830-1730 (last ticket 1700), closed 1st Mon of every month, price currently included in the Sigiriya ticket*, is the re-vamped archaeological museum. The empty echoing building may be off-putting but when entering the gallery the museum comes into its own. It showcases the history of the rock from its formation, to its use as a Buddhist monastery and palace. Archaeological finds are displayed and there is an interesting reproduction of the 'Golden Age' of Sigiriya, as well as translations of some of the graffiti from the mirror wall. The Fresco Gallery is of interest if you do not make it up the spiral stairs to see the originals. The museum also provides some tourist information on sights and accommodation.

→DAMBULLA AND AROUND

The richly painted cave temples at Dambulla, which lie atop a vast rocky outcrop, date to the first century BC and form one of Sri Lanka's World Heritage Sites (designated in 1991). Though the site is now privately run by wealthy monks, it is still considered to be part of the Cultural Triangle. Nearby, you can visit the massive rock-cut Aukana Buddha and the monastery at Sasseruwa, while Sigiriya rock is only 19 km away. Those heading to Kandy can visit the rock monastery at Aluwihare, near Matale, and the Nalanda *gedige* en route.

ARRIVING IN DAMBULLA

Getting there Dambulla lies almost in the dead centre of the country on an important junction of the Anuradhapura–Kandy and Trincomalee–Colombo roads and is well served by public transport.

Getting around Dambulla itself is tiny. The cave temples lie 2 km south of the junction (a short bus or three-wheeler ride). Most cheaper accommodation is strung out along the main road. The sights around Dambulla can be reached by bus, with the exception of Sasseruwa, where private transport is required.

Tourist information A Seneviratna, *Golden rock temple of Dambulla* (Colombo: Sri Lanka Central Cultural Fund, 1983) provides good background information. There is a good booklet in English and German.

BACKGROUND

Dambulla is sited on a gigantic granite outcrop which towers more than 160 m above the surrounding land. The rock is more than 1.5 km around its base and the summit is at 550 m. The caves were the refuge of **King Valagambahu** (Vattagamani Abhaya) when he was in exile for 14 years. When he returned to the throne at Anuradhapura in the first century BC, he had a magnificent rock temple built at Dambulla. The site has been repaired and repainted several times in the 11th, 12th and 18th centuries. In 2001, the temple authorities completed work on an enormous gold Buddha, which greets you from the car park.

The caves have a mixture of religious and secular painting and sculpture. There are several reclining Buddhas, including the 15-m-long sculpture of the dying Buddha in Cave 1. The frescoes on the walls and ceilings date from the 15th to 18th centuries. The ceiling frescoes show scenes from the Buddha's life and Sinhalese history. Cave 2 is the largest and most impressive, containing more than 150 statues, illustrating the Mahayana influences on Buddhism at the time through introducing Hindu deities such as Vishnu and Ganesh.

There is little evidence of monks who are housed in monasteries in the valley below where there is a monks' school. Some monasteries and sacred sites receive large donations from Buddhists overseas (particularly Japan) and so are not dependent on government sponsorship. Gifts and your entrance fee have provided the monks here with a 4WD and many other comforts not available to others of similar calling.

PLACES IN DAMBULLA

Buddhist Museum ⓘ *www.goldentemple.lk, 0730-2100, Rs 100 or free with a ticket to the caves.* Beneath the big gold Buddha, you reach the bizarre Buddhist Museum inside the Golden Temple (as distinct from the Rock Temple), through a fantastically gaudy dragon's mouth. Inside are exhibited statues gifted from around the Buddhist world, *ola* leaf manuscripts, copies of some of the cave paintings and other Buddhist objects. Its air-conditioning and piped music give it the atmosphere of a shopping mall.

Beside the museum, a flight of steps lead up into the Golden Temple, and you can climb the new Buddha, in a *dhamma chakka* pose.

The caves ⓘ *0730-1230 and 1300-1800 (last ticket 1730). Rs 1500 from the ticket booth at the entrance to the complex. Large bags and shoes are not allowed into the complex but they can all be left with the 'shoe keepers' (Rs 25). Hats must be removed and normal temple* *attire should be worn (cover knees, shoulders, etc). Carry a torch if you wish to view the cave paintings in detail. It is difficult to dodge the touts and beggars who line the steps leading to the caves, and the guides as they stand in the temple doorway. A good alternative to a guide is to buy the Rock Temple brochure from the Buddhist bookshop before starting the ascent.*

From the car park, it can be a hot and tiring climb. It is quite steep at first, almost 100 m across, at times, bare granite, after which there are about 200 steps in a series of 18 terraces, some longer and steeper than others. It is not too difficult to get to the top but try to avoid the heat in the middle of the day. In any case it is best visited in the early morning. There are panoramic views from the terrace of the surrounding jungle and tanks, and of Sigiriya. The caves are about halfway up the hill and form part of a temple complex.

There are five overhung cliff caves. Monastic buildings have been built in front, complete with cloisters, and these in turn overlook a courtyard which is used for ceremonial purposes and has a wonderful view over the valley floor below. Some of the other subsidiary caves which were occupied by monks contain ancient inscriptions in Brahmi.

Cave I (Devaraja-Viharaya) Contains the huge lying *Parinirvana* Buddha which is 14 m long and carved out of solid rock. The frescoes behind the Arahat Ananda (a disciple) are said to be the oldest in the site, though unrestored they lack the lustre of those in other caves. 'Devaraja' refers to the Hindu god Vishnu. The deity may have been installed here in the Kandyan period though some believe it is older than the Buddha images. There is a Vishnu temple attached.

Cave II (Rajamaha-Viharaya) This much bigger cave is about 24 sq m and 7 m high and was named after the two kings whose images are here. The principal Buddha statue facing the entrance is in the *Abhaya mudra*, under a *makara torana* (or dragon arch). The cave has about 1500 paintings of the Buddha – almost as though the monks had tried to wallpaper the cave. The paintings of his life near the corner to the right are also interesting – you can see his parents holding him as a baby, various pictures of him meditating (counted in weeks, eg cobra hood indicates the sixth week); some have him surrounded by demons, others with cobras and another shows him being offered food by merchants. The other historical scenes are also interesting with the battle between Dutthagamenu and Elara particularly graphic, illustrating the decisive moment when the defeated falls to the ground, head first from an elephant. Here, in the right-hand corner, you can see the holy pot which is never empty. Drips are collected into a bucket which sits in a wooden fenced rectangle and is used for sacred rituals by the monks.

Cave III (Maha Alut Viharaya) This cave is about 30 sq m and 18 m high. It was rebuilt in the 18th century and has about 60 images, some under *makara toranas*, and more paintings of thousands of the seated Buddha on the ceiling. This cave was a former storeroom and the frescoes are in the Kandyan style.

Cave IV (Pascima Viharaya or 'western' cave) The smallest cave and once the westernmost: it had the fifth cave constructed later to its west. It contains about 10 images though unfortunately the stupa here was damaged by thieves who came in search of Queen Somawathie's jewels. One image in particular, at the back of the cave, needed restoration. Unfortunately it is now painted in a very strong Marge Simpson yellow which jars with the rest of the cave.

Cave V (Devana Alut Viharaya) The newest, it was once used as a storeroom. The images here are built of brick and plaster and in addition to the Buddha figures, also includes the Hindu deities, Vishnu, Kataragama and Bandara (a local god).

Dambulla Museum ⓘ *Just south of the caves and Golden Temple. Open 0800-1600. Rs 400.* Don't be discouraged by the first small room, which has exhibits demonstrating how the Dambulla murals and frescoes were created. It may at first look like any local museum with bits cobbled together but climb the stairs for a well laid-out and informative exhibition on the history of Sri Lankan painting and the development of rock and wall art. The seven rooms lead visitors from the Primitive period right through to the 20th century, via the Classical period frescoes at Sigiriya, and murals from the Kandyan period. Exhibits are excellent reproductions on canvas of paintings from all over the island, bringing inaccessible frescoes and murals to people who would otherwise have little opportunity of seeing them.

AROUND DAMBULLA

Popham Arboretum ⓘ *2 km east of the caves, along Kandalama Rd towards the Kandalama Hotel, open 0600-1800, donation, ring in advance.* The only arboretum in the Dry Zone, it was set up by Sam Popham, a former tea planter, on his retirement in 1963. Originally planning on replanting, he discovered that clearing the scrub jungle enabled the native trees to seed and saplings to grow, and experimented on re-foresting with minimal human interference. The "Popham method" was a success and how over 70 tropical trees are preserved here, including ebony and satinwood. The woodland has been divided into blocks which are cleared at different times, and visitors have access via a set of well-maintained paths and can walk independently or organize a guided walk through the Bawa-designed visitor centre, which was Popham's house.

Aukana ⓘ *0700-1900. Rs 500 (includes photography). For those without their own transport, it is possible to get a bus to Aukana. There are occasional direct buses from Dambulla but more practical may be to take a bus to Kekirawa (45 mins), and change to a Galnewa bus, getting off at Aukana Junction. From here it is a 500-m walk to the site. From Anuradhapura, buses to Kekirawa take 1½ hrs. Aukana also lies on the Colombo–Batticaloa train line but trains stop more frequently at Kala Wewa (8 km from the site), where you can pick up a 3-wheeler who will 'go and come back'.* One of the island's most elegant and perfect statues, the Aukana Buddha, to the west of the large Kala Wewa tank, has gained even greater significance to Buddhists since the destruction of the similar (but much larger) statues at Bamiyan in Afghanistan (toponymical research suggests that in ancient times Bamiyan, in the region where Mahayana Buddhism originated, was known as Vokkana or Avakana). Here is a magnificent, undamaged 12-m-high free-standing statue of the Abhayamudra Buddha, showing superhuman qualities, carved out of a single rock. The right hand is raised toward the right shoulder with the palm spread, signifying a lack of fear, while the position of the left draws the worshipper to Buddha for release from earthly bonds. It has been ascribed to King Dhatusena (AD 459-477) who was responsible for the building of several tanks, including the one here. When you walk down to the base, note the small lotus flower in between the Buddha's feet. The carving is so perfectly symmetrical that when it rains the water drops from his nose down to the centre of the 10-cm flower.

Sasseruwa ⓘ *13 km west of Aukana. Rs 700. Allow 45 mins to explore – best visited early in the morning. Not accessible by public transport. The minor road from Aukana continues to the Sasseruwa via Negampaha, and the surface is poor.* This extensive complex has an ancient monastery site with more than 100 cave cells, remains of stupas, moonstones and inscriptions, and dates back to the second century BC. Here, too, there is a similar standing Buddha framed by the dark rock, though it is either unfinished or lacks the quality of workmanship. It was possibly carved at the same time as Aukana, although some believe it to be a later copy. One legend is that the two images were carved in a competition between master and student. The master's Buddha at Aukana was completed first, so the Sasseruwa statue was abandoned.

→ DAMBULLA TO KANDY

Nalanda ⓘ *49 km north of Kandy, 19 km south of Dambulla. Rs 500. There are frequent buses to Nalanda that run between Dambulla and Kandy, stopping near the turn off opposite the rest house.* This small reconstructed *gedige* (Buddha image house) shares some features in common with Hindu temples of southern India. Standing on the raised bund of a reservoir, it was built with stone slabs and originally dates from the seventh to the 10th centuries. Some tantric carvings have been found in the structure which combines Hindu and Buddhist (both Mahayana and Theravada) features. Note the *Karmasutra* bas-relief. It is the only extant Sri Lankan *gedige* built in the architectural style of the seventh-century Pallava shore temples at Mamallapuram near Chennai in India. The place is very atmospheric and has comparatively few visitors, which adds to its appeal. From the rest house where the bus drops visitors off there is a 1 km road leading east to the site.

Aluwihare ⓘ *32 km north of Kandy, 36 km south of Dambulla. Rs 200. Lying on a main tourist route, you will continually be asked for donations, which can get tiresome. Buses run between Matale and Dambulla and stop on the main road – the caves are on the west side. You can also take a 3-wheeler.* Aluwihare has the renovated ruins of ancient shrines carved out of huge boulders. In the first and second century BC, the site was associated with King Vattagamani Abhaya (103-77 BC). The *Mahavansa* (Buddhist chronicle of the island) was inscribed here in Pali. The original manuscript, inscribed on palm leaves prepared by 500 monks, was destroyed in the mid-19th century, and replacements are still being inscribed today. With the expectation of a 'contribution' to the temple (for which you are given a receipt) you are guided first into the small museum, where you will be shown the technique of writing on palmyra palm for a small donation.

The palmyra palm strips were prepared for manuscripts by drying, boiling and drying again, and then flattened and coated with shell. A stylus was used for inscribing, held stationary while the leaf was moved to produce the lettering or illustration (the rounded shape of some South Asian scripts was a result of this technology). The inscribed grooves would then be rubbed with soot or powdered charcoal while colour was added with a brush. The leaves would then be stacked and sometimes strung together and sometimes 'bound' between decorative wooden 'covers'.

The path up the boulders themselves is quite steep and can be slippery when wet (a newspaper cutting in the museum commemorates how the Duke of Edinburgh "nearly had a nasty fall" during the royal visit in 1956). Four of the 10 caves have ancient inscriptions. The curious 'Chamber of Horrors' has unusual frescoes vividly illustrating punishments doled out to sinners by eager demons, including spearing of the body and pouring of boiling oil into the mouth. The sculptures in another cave show torture on a 'rack' for the wrongdoer and the distress of having one's brains exposed by the skull being cut open. The impressive painted reclining Buddhas include one about 10 m long. There is a new construction showing plaster figures being gruesomely punished. It's very popular and if you want to step inside, show your ticket if you're asked to pay again. The stupa on top of the rock just beyond the cave temples gives fine views of the Dry Zone plains and pine covered mountains.

Matale ① *24 km north of Kandy, 44 km south of Dambulla. There are regular buses from Dambulla. Matale's railway station is in the centre of town 100 m east of the A9.* The small but bustling town surrounded by hills has some interesting short walks as well as some longer treks into the Knuckles Range (see page 90). The British built a fort here at the beginning of the 19th century (of which only a gate remains) while the branch railway line opened in 1880. Tour groups often stop at the Sri Muthumariamman Thevasthanam temple here.

A large number of **spice gardens** line the road north of Matale, as well as plantations of coffee, cocoa and rubber. While most are genuine, some so-called spice gardens which are open to visitors have very few plants and are primarily there to sell commercially grown spices and Ayurvedic herbal products.

GOING FURTHER
Trincomalee and around

After suffering tremendously during the civil war and being badly affected by the 2004 tsunami, Trincomalee today is once again attracting tourists. The largest city in Eastern Province, Trinco's fame – and perhaps one day its fortune – lies in its magnificent natural harbour, described by Nelson as the finest in the world. Fiercely contested for centuries, it was a crucial naval base for the British during the Second World War. Today, after a recent past it would rather forget, this dusty port is for most tourists the gateway to the magnificent deserted northern beaches. The city itself, a uniquely balanced ethnic blend, is also worth exploring.

Leaving Trincomalee city behind, most visitors take the route north to the famous white-sand beaches at Uppuveli and, especially, Nilaveli. As the area slowly begins to draw back tourists, resort hotels and guesthouses have renovated been and more are being built.

→ ARRIVING IN TRINCOMALEE

GETTING THERE
A car and driver from Habarana will take about 1½ hours. The bus takes around two hours but is often full; if you have a large bag it's best to catch the bus from its starting point in Anuradhapura (see page 44). The coastal route from Batticaloa is currently not recommended, although renovation work is underway, enquire locally. There is a daily train from Colombo via Gal Oya.

GETTING AROUND
The centre of Trincomalee is quite compact, though you will need to take a bus or three-wheeler to get to the beaches north of town. Orr's Hill, 15 minutes' walk from the centre, is the main expat area with NGO offices and the town's only luxury hotel. Kanniyai Hot Wells, the Commonwealth War Cemetery and the beaches north of Trinco can easily be visited from the city. From Trincomalee there are regular buses to Nilaveli and Uppuveli but many people decide to take a three-wheeler to their chosen hotel or guesthouse.

BEST TIME TO VISIT
Trincomalee and its surrounding beaches are best visited between April and October, when the area is at its driest. Between November and March, the east is sometimes battered by strong wind and rains, and the sea in unsuitable for swimming during these months.

→ PLACES IN TRINCOMALEE

The main town is built on a fairly narrow piece of land between Back Bay and the Inner Harbour, and, while much of the harbour remains off-limits, Fort Frederick provides the main point of tourist interest. At any one point it is only possible to see sections of the magnificent bay which gives the harbour its reputation, but there are some good views from Orr's Hill. One of the town's more unusual features is its many spotted deer which can be seen grazing throughout the city, including on the beach.

FORT FREDERICK
Situated on a rocky headland, this is still an active army base but visitors may enter. It is especially worthwhile to go up to the **Swami Rock** and the Konesvaram Temple built on

the cliffs high above the sea. The fort was originally built by the Portuguese in 1623 who destroyed the original and ancient Siva temple. Entering through the gate, which dates from 1676, a noticeboard on the left gives a short history of the fort's complex vacillating fortunes: it was continually handed back and forth between the Dutch, British and French, a result of wars in Europe, until finally taken by the British in 1796. It was christened Fort Frederick after the Duke of York, son of George III, who was stationed here.

Inside, in a cordoned-off military zone, there are two cannons, a howitzer and a mortar. To the right of the path is **Wellesley House**, which had a remarkable role in changing the course of European history. In 1800 the Duke of Wellington convalesced here from an illness after his South India campaign, missing his ship which subsequently went down with all hands in the Gulf of Aden. Nearby there are four British and Dutch gravestones from the early 18th century. Taking the left fork leads to a new standing Buddha, from where there are good views.

The modern Hindu **Konesvaram Temple**, one of the five most sacred Saivite sites in Sri Lanka, stands at the farthest end of **Swami Rock** in the place of the original. It has a lingam, believed to be from the original shrine, which was recovered from the waters below by a diver. Only a couple of stone pillars from the original temple have survived. The new temple is highly decorated and painted; regular services are held with the one on Friday evening particularly colourful. Leave your shoes at the entrance, for which a small donation will be requested. Go behind the temple to find '**Lovers Leap**', apparently so-called after the legend according to which the daughter of a Dutch official, Francina van Rhede, threw herself from the rock after her lover sailed away. The truth seems to be more prosaic than the fiction, however, for according to government archives she was alive and well when the Dutch memorial was placed here!

→ NORTH OF TRINCOMALEE

COMMONWEALTH WAR CEMETERY

At **Sampalthivu**, about 5 km north of Trinco, just before the road crosses the Uppuveli creek, is the Commonwealth War Cemetery. During the Second World War, Trinco was an important naval and air force base and the harbour was the focus of Japanese air raids in April 1942. Five Blenheim bombers were shot down, and the aircraft carrier *HMS Hermes*, along with the destroyer *Vampire* and corvette *HMS Hollyhock*, were sunk off Kalkudah and Passekudah bays to the south; many graves date from this time. As the island was a leave recuperation centre, still more died as a result of their wounds.

The cemetery was damaged by bombing during Sri Lanka's civil war in the late 1980s. The damaged headstones have now been replaced and the garden is beautifully maintained in the tradition of Commonwealth War cemeteries. HRH Princess Anne visited in 1995 and planted a *margosa* tree. The cemetery has great sentimental value for many whose families were stationed at the naval base, and a visit is a sobering experience for anyone. The custodian has a register of the graves and will show the visitor some interesting documents relating to Trincomalee.

UPPUVELI

For those without transport, Uppuveli Beach, 4 km north of Trinco, is probably a better option than its more famous northerly neighbour. It is more convenient for trips into town with buses and three-wheelers running regularly, and the main road is more accessible from the beach. While the scars from the war are still visible it is less obvious than at Nilaveli. The influx of tourists and the reopening of a major hotels has meant that parts of the beach, suitable for swimming from March to December, are now well maintained but during low season there can be a lot of debris and rubbish. Guesthouses may offer trips to the Hot Wells.

NILAVELI

Nilaveli, 16 km north of Trincomalee, is Sri Lanka's longest beach, and before the war was one of the island's most popular. It used to be a straight wide strip of inviting white sand, backed by screw pines and palmyras which provided shade, stretching for miles. Unfortunately, the tsunami which hit this area with incredible force not only destroyed homes, businesses and families, it also left its mark on the sand.

The beach's gentle waters are safe for swimming outside the period of the northeast monsoons. The collapse of tourism through the war years has taken its toll, though and there is still a visible military presence. However, tourists are returning and as their numbers rise, building and improvement work gets underway. Expect things to change rapidly here over the next few years.

Most visitors, especially those who stay in the northern part of the beach, take a trip to narrow **Pigeon Island**, just a few hundred metres offshore. It is covered with rocks but has some sandy stretches and offers snorkelling to view corals and fish. There is some good diving too. The island is named after blue rock pigeons which breed here (the island was once used by the British fleet for target practice). Their eggs are prized by Sri Lankans. There are no facilities and little shade, so go prepared and try to arrive early before it gets too busy. Hotels run trips to the island while local fisherman often approach tourists direct, undercutting hotel prices. The area around the **Nilaveli Beach Hotel** is the best place to leave from – trips are quickest and cheapest from here. Hotels can also arrange dolphin- and whale-watching trips (see below).

WHERE TO STAY

$$$$-$$$ Chaaya Blu, on beach 4.5 km north of Trinco, 600 m off road (and 300 m before war cemetery), T222 2307, www.chaayahotels.com. This hotel offers 79 rooms and beach chalets. 2 suites are also available (US$335). All rooms have sea views, a/c and Wi-Fi. There is a swimming pool, a dive centre, an exchange, bar and 2 restaurants. Popular with tour groups. Offers whale-watching trips, fishing, snorkelling and excursions to Mutur. Good location right on a curved bay.

$$ Welcombe, 66 Lower Rd, Orr's Hill, T222 3885, www.welcombehotel.com. Trinco's first luxury hotel is in an architecturally interesting boat design. Stylishly furnished and spacious rooms, all with balconies (those at 'stern' and 'bow' are best) and

harbour views, naval-themed wood-panelled bar, inviting pool.

$ Jaysh Beach Resort, 7/42 Alles Garden, next door to Lotus Park Hotel, T077-605 5821, jaymano@hotmail.co.uk. Clean a/c or fan rooms with verandas. Quiet and although not beachfront the sea is a quick walk down a side passage. Hot water can be arranged and meals are available. The manager spent years at sea and so has a supply of stories. Friendly and accommodating.

$ Palm Beach Resort, 12 Alles Garden, Nilaveli Rd, Uppeveli, T222 1250, lpalermi@hotmail.com. Friendly Italian-managed guesthouse offering a/c and fan rooms. Closed during the monsoon season (Nov to mid-Jan) and busy the rest of the time so book early.

HABARANA AND AROUND LISTINGS

WHERE TO STAY

Habarana

$$$ Cinnamon Lodge, T227 0011, www.cinnamonhotels.com. 150 tastefully decorated a/c rooms in bungalows, some are deluxe with tubs and TV, and 2 suites (US$498). Excellent facilities and lush grounds with woods, good pool, good service.

$$$-$$ Chaaya Village, T227 0047, www.chaayahotels.com. 106 a/c rooms in 'rustic' cottages (the deluxe ones have lake views), as well as 2 lodges. On the banks of the lake with extensive gardens. Excellent pool and good food. Popular with tour groups.

Polonnaruwa

$$ Sudu Araliya, near the Southern Group, T222 4849, www.hotelsuduaraliya.com. Attractive light open spaces, comfortable a/c rooms, with more being built shortly. TV, minibar, some rooms with tank view, bar, nice pool, herbal treatments available.

$ Siyanco, 1 Canal Rd, behind Habarana Rd, T222 6868, www.siyancotravel.com. Tucked away behind Habarana Rd. 19 a/c rooms that are clean and modern, although some are on the small side. Inviting restaurant, friendly and has a pool.

Sigiriya

$$$$ Vil Uyana (Jetwing), Inamaluwa, T492 3584, www.jetwinghotels.com. An artificially created wetland with 25 spacious chalets, some with private plunge pools and sunken baths, in a choice of 4 habitats (marsh, paddy, forest or lake). All have private decks for wildlife viewing. Beautiful infinity pool, and all facilities you'd expect. The walk to the main building can be hard going if you're not very mobile.

$$$ Sigiriya Village, Sigiriya, T228 6803, sigiriyavillage@sltnet.lk. Tastefully furnished standard or deluxe rooms with small terraces, large bathrooms, a/c, good open-sided restaurants, beautifully planted site with carefully landscaped gardens and theme clusters of cottages, each with its own colour scheme and accessories. Good Ayurvedic centre, own farm, friendly and efficient management. Internet access.

$ Flower Inn, Sigiriya, T567 2197. Family-run guesthouse with 3 rooms in the main house and newer ones at the back (cold water). Good food, friendly owner.

Dambulla

$$$$-$$$ Kandalama (Aitken Spence), head along Kandalama Rd for 4.5 km, take the right fork, T555 5000, www.heritance hotels.com/kandalama. Winner of many awards including Asia's 1st Green Globe. 152 plush a/c rooms in 2 wings, and luxury suites. Unique design by Geoffrey Bawa, built between a massive rock and peaceful tank and indistinguishable from its jungle surrounds. Resort-style complex with excellent cuisine and full facilities, 3 pools including one of the most spectacularly sited swimming pools in the world with crystal-clear water (filtration system based on ancient Sri Lankan technology). Magnificent views across undisturbed forest, magical details, exceptional service.

$$$$-$$ Amaya Lake, follow Kandalama Rd for 4.5 km, take the left fork, then follow the lake around for 4.6 km, T446 1500, www.amayaresorts.com. Variety of rooms including suites, chalets and clay eco-lodges (with TVs, DVD players and minibar) with a village theme. Good pool in large gardens, restaurant, Ayurvedic health centre, very attractive setting on the edge of the lake.

$$ Gimanhala Transit, 754 Anuradhapura Rd, 1 km north of Colombo Junction, T228 4864, gimanhala@sltnet.lk. Comfortable, clean a/c rooms, good restaurant overlooking lovely large and very clean pool. Bike hire, shop. Best of the town hotels, good value.

KANDY AND AROUND

Kandy, Sri Lanka's second largest city and cultural capital, stands both as one of the most important symbols of Sinhalese national identity, and as the gateway to the higher hills and tea plantations. Although it has a reputation as something of a tourist trap, and has a problem with touts, the clarity of the air and its verdant, hilly outlook around the sacred lake make it a pleasant escape from the heat of the coast. It is a laid-back place and many visitors base themselves here for a few days to explore the surrounding countryside.

Dotted around the lush Kandyan landscape are a number of important temples which make for a good day trip from the city. Thrill-seekers could head for the misty mountains of Knuckles, while for the green-fingered the magnificent botanical gardens at Peradeniya, arguably the finest of their kind in Asia, are an undoubted highlight.

➜ ARRIVING IN KANDY

GETTING THERE

From Habarana take the A6 to Dambulla and then the A9 south to Kandy (1½ hours). If travelling by public transport, there are regular buses (2¾ hours). Kandy is fairly easily accessible from all parts of the country. Some travellers head here immediately on arrival at the international airport (see page 190). Intercity buses leave every half an hour, taking 3½ hours. There are also direct buses from Negombo. From Colombo, there are government buses from the Central Bus Stand in the Pettah, or private buses from Bastian Mawatha.

MOVING ON

The A1 highway links Kandy and **Colombo** (see page 97) and though one of the island's busiest roads there's a lot to look at en route. Those without their own transport can take advantage of the frequent buses that ply the route, the Intercity buses are the fastest (three hours). Another popular option is to travel between Kandy and Colombo by train (2½ hours), as the scenery is superb. Choose an Intercity Express train and book your ticket in advance if you would like to sit in the observation carriage.

For those heading to the Central Highlands, a car and driver to **Nuwara Eliya** (see page 118) will take three hours. Alternatively, take the trian to Nanu Oya (6 km from Nuwara Eliya) and arrange to to be picked up from the station, or take a bus or taxi into town.

GETTING AROUND

The bus (Goods Shed) terminus and railway station are close to each other about 1 km southwest of the centre. A three-wheeler into town will cost around Rs 100; to the guesthouses in the Saranankara Road area south of the lake will cost up to Rs 150. Air-conditioned radio cabs are very convenient, safe and reliable; telephone T223 3322, tell them your location and allow 10 minutes.

Gopallawa Mawatha, the main road into town, is horribly choked with traffic, especially at rush hour. To avoid the fumes, it's a good idea to do as the locals do and walk north along the railway line into town. Local buses ply the routes to Peradeniya, Pinnawela and the surrounding sights.

BEST TIME TO VISIT

Kandy has a pleasant climate throughout the year, lacking the humidity of the coast. In July, **Esala Perahera** is a truly magnificent spectacle.

TOURIST INFORMATION

Hotel and guesthouse owners are usually the best source of information. There is a **Tourist Information Centre** ① *Headman's Lodge, 3 Deva Veediya (Temple St), T222 2661, Mon-Fri 0900-1645*, opposite the entrance of the Temple of the Tooth. There's also a very helpful tourist information office in the city centre shopping mall that can provide a free map of Kandy and information on buses, trains, sights, etc. See also www.kandycity.org.

→ BACKGROUND

Although the city of Kandy (originally Senkadagala) is commonly held to have been founded by a general named Vikramabahu in 1472, there was a settlement on the site for at least 150 years before that. On asserting his independence from the reigning monarch, Vikramabahu made Kandy his capital. He built a palace for his mother and a shrine on pillars. In 1542 the Tooth Relic was brought to the city, stimulating a flurry of new religious building – a two-storey house for the relic itself, and 86 houses for the monks. As in Anuradhapura and Polonnaruwa, the Tooth temple was built next to the palace.

Defensive fortifications probably came only when the Portuguese began their attacks. Forced to withdraw from the town in 1594, King Vimala Dharma Suriya set half the city on fire, a tactic that was repeated by several successors in the face of expulsion by foreign armies. However, he won it back, and promptly set about building a massive wall, interspersed with huge towers. Inside, a new palace replaced the one destroyed by fire, and the city rapidly gained a reputation as a cosmopolitan centre of splendour and wealth. As early as 1597 some Portuguese showed scepticism about the claims that the enshrined tooth was the Buddha's. In 1597 De Quezroy described the seven golden caskets in which the tooth was kept, but added that it was the tooth of a buffalo. The Portuguese were already claiming that they had captured the original, exported it to Goa and incinerated it.

By 1602 the city had probably taken the form (though not the actual buildings) which would survive to the beginning of the 19th century. The major temples were also already in place. Kandy was repeatedly attacked by the Portuguese. In 1611 the city was captured and largely destroyed, and again in 1629 and 1638, and the Tooth Relic was removed for a time by the retreating King Senarat. A new earth rampart was built between the hills in the south of the city. In 1681 there is evidence of a moat being built using forced labour, and possibly the first creation of the Bogambara Lake to the southwest, as a symbol of the cosmic ocean.

Vimala Dharma Suriya I had a practical use for the lake for he is said to have kept some of his treasure sunk in the middle, guarded by crocodiles in the water. It has been suggested that there was also a symbolic link with Kubera, the mythical god of wealth, who kept his wealth at the bottom of the cosmic ocean. Crocodiles are often shown on the *makara toranas* (dragon gateways) of temples.

A new Temple of the Tooth was built by Vimala Dharma Suriya II between 1687-1707, on the old site. Three storeys high, it contained a reliquary of gold encrusted with jewels. Between 1707-1739 Narendra Sinha undertook new building in the city, renovating the Temple of the Tooth and enclosing the Natha Devala and the sacred Bodhi tree. He

ON THE ROAD
Esala Perahera

Esala Perahera (procession), Sri Lanka's greatest festival, is of special significance. It is held in the lunar month of Esala (named after the *Cassia fistula* which blossoms at this time) in which the Buddha was conceived and in which he left his father's home. It has also long been associated with rituals to ensure renewed fertility for the year ahead. The last Kandyan kings turned the Perahera into a mechanism for reinforcing their own power, trying to identify themselves with the gods who needed to be appeased. By focusing on the Tooth Relic, the Tamil kings hoped to establish their own authority and their divine legitimacy within the Buddhist community. The Sri Lankan historian Seneviratne has suggested that fear both of the king and of divine retribution encouraged nobles and peasants alike to come to the Perahera, and witnessing the scale of the spectacle reinforced their loyalty. In 1922, DH Lawrence described his experience as "wonderful – midnight – huge elephants, great flares of coconut torches, princes... tom-toms and savage music and devil dances... black eyes... of the dancers".

Today the festival is a magnificent 10-day spectacle of elephants, drummers, dancers, chieftains, acrobats, whip-crackers, torch bearers and tens of thousands of pilgrims in procession. Buddhists are drawn to the temple by the power of the Tooth Relic rather than by that of the King's authority. The power of the Relic certainly long preceded that of the Kandyan dynasty. Fa Hien described the annual festival in Anuradhapura in AD 399, which even then was a lavish procession in which roads were vividly decorated, elephants covered in jewels and flowers, and models of figures such as Bodhisattvas were paraded. When the tooth was moved to Kandy, the Perahera moved with it.

Following the Tree Planting Ceremony (Kap), the first five days, **Kumbal Perahera**, are celebrated within the grounds of the four *devalas* (temples) – Natha, Vishnu, Skanda and Pattini. The next five days are **Randoli Perahera**. Torchlight processions set off from the temples when the Tooth Relic Casket is carried by the Maligawa Tusker accompanied by magnificently robed temple custodians. Every night the procession grows, moving from the Temple of the Tooth, along Dalada Veediya and DS SenanayakeMawatha to the Adahanamaluwa, where the relic casket is left in the keeping of the temple trustees. The separate temple processions return to their temples, coming out in the early morning for the water cutting ceremony. Originally, the temple guardians went to the lake with golden water pots to empty water collected the previous year. They would then be refilled and taken back to the temple for the following year, symbolizing the fertility protected by the gods. On the 11th day, a daylight procession accompanied the return of the Relic to the Temple. The **Day Perahera** continues, but today the Tooth Relic itself is no longer taken out.

You don't necessarily need to buy tickets to watch the processions since you can get good views by standing along the street. A good vantage point is that opposite or near to the Queens Hotel as much of that area is slightly better lit (the presidential vantage point is somewhere nearby) and can provide for slightly better photography.

established the validity of his royal line by importing princesses from Madurai, and set aside a separate street for them in the town.

Major new building awaited King Kirti Sri (1747-1782). He added a temple to Vishnu northwest of the palace, but at the same time asserted his support for Buddhism, twice bringing monks from Thailand to re-validate the Sinhalese order of monks. The Dutch, who captured the city in 1765, plundered the temples and palaces. The palace and the Temple of the Tooth were destroyed and many other buildings were seriously damaged.

Kirti Sri started re-building, more opulently than ever, but it was the last king of Kandy, Sri Vikrama Rajasinha (1798-1815), who gave Kandy many of its present buildings. More interested in palaces and parks than temples, he set about demonstrating his kingly power with an exhibition of massive building works. Once again he had started almost from scratch, for in 1803 the city was taken by the British, but to avoid its desecration was once again burned to the ground. The British were thrown out, and between 1809-1812 there was massive re-building. The palace was fully renovated and a new octagonal structure added to the palace, the Patthiruppuwa. Two years later the royal complex was surrounded by a moat and a single massive stone gateway replaced the earlier entrances.

In the west, Sri Vikrama Rajasinha built new shops and houses, at the same time building more houses in the east for his Tamil relatives. However, by far his greatest work was the construction of the lake. Previously the low-lying marshy land in front of the palace had been drained for paddy fields. Between 1810-1812 up to 3000 men were forced to work on building the dam at the west end of the low ground, creating an artificial lake given the cosmically symbolic name of the Ocean of Milk. A pleasure house was built in the middle of the lake, connected by drawbridge to the palace. By now the city had taken virtually its present form.

Rajasinha's rule had been so tyrannical however, violating religious laws and committing brutal murders, that the terrorized Kandyan aristocracy allied themselves with the British invaders, who garnered support for a war against the king promising to protect the people and their property. The final fall of Kandy to the British in 1815 signalled the end of independence for the whole island.

→ PLACES IN KANDY

The last bastion of Buddhist political power against colonial forces, the home of the Temple of the Buddha's Tooth Relic, and the site of the island's most impressive annual festival, Kandy is also the capital of the highlands. Its architectural monuments date mainly from a final surge of grandiose building by King Vikrama Rajasinha in the early 19th century. So extravagant were the edifices, and achieved only at enormous cost for the people of Kandy, that his nobles betrayed him to the British rather than continue enduring his excesses. The result is some extraordinary buildings, none of great architectural merit, but sustaining a Kandyan style dating back to the 16th century, and rich in symbolic significance of the nature of the king's view of his world.

The area with the Temple of the Tooth and associated buildings, a World Heritage Site, is the chief focus of interest. Sadly, it was the target of a bomb attack on 26 January 1998, which left over 20 dead. Security was upgraded and some roadblocks remain. Repairs to the extensive damage of the temple were completed in 1999.

TEMPLE OF THE TOOTH

ⓘ *Rs 1100. Cameras Rs 150 (video cameras Rs 300). Wear a long skirt or trousers and ensure shoulders are covered. Otherwise* lungis *(sarongs) must be worn over shorts. Remove shoes*

ON THE ROAD
Worship of the Tooth Relic

The eyewitness account of Bella Sidney Woolf in 1914 captures something of the atmosphere when the Tooth Relic could be viewed by pilgrims.

"The relic is only shown for royal visits or, on certain occasions, to Burmese and other pilgrims. If the passenger happens to be in Kandy at such a time he should try to see the Tooth, even though it may mean many hours of waiting. It is an amazing sight. The courtyard is crammed with worshippers of all ages, bearing offerings in their hands, leaves of young coconut, scent, flowers, fruit. As the door opens, they surge up the dark and narrow stairway to the silver and ivory doors behind which lies the Tooth.

The doors are opened and a flood of hot heavy scented air pours out. The golden 'Karandua' or outer casket of the Tooth stands revealed dimly behind gilded bars. In the weird uncertain light of candles in golden candelabra the yellow-robed priests move to and fro. The Tooth is enclosed in five Karanduas and slowly and solemnly each is removed in turn; some of them are encrusted with rubies, emeralds and diamonds.

At last the great moment approaches. The last Karandua is removed – in folds of red silk lies the wondrous Relic – the centre point of the faith of millions. It is a shock to see a tooth of discoloured ivory at least three inches long – unlike any human tooth ever known. The priest sets it in a golden lotus – the Temple Korala gives a sharp cry – the tom-toms and conches and pipes blare out – the kneeling worshippers, some with tears streaming down their faces, stretch out their hands in adoration."

and hats before entering (small fee for looking after your shoes). Museum, T223 4226, Rs 500, 0900-1700. The entrance to the complex is in Palace Square opposite the Natha Devala. It is best to visit early in the morning before it gets too busy with tourist buses and pilgrims. Whilst visiting, be sure to remember that the Temple of the Tooth (*Dalada Maligawa*) is a genuine place of worship and not simply a site of tourist interest.

The original temple dated from the 16th century, though most of the present building and the Patthiruppuwa or Octagon (which was badly damaged in the 1998 attack) were built in the early 19th century. The gilded roof over the Relic chamber is a recent addition. The oldest part is the inner shrine built by Kirti Sri after 1765. The drawbridge, moat and gateway were the work of Sri Vickrama Rajasinha. There is a moonstone step at the entrance to the archway, and a stone depicting Lakshmi against the wall facing the entrance. The main door to the temple is in the wall of the upper veranda, covered in restored frescoes depicting Buddhist conceptions of hell. The doorway is a typical *makara torana* showing mythical beasts. A second Kandyan-style door leads into the courtyard, across which is the building housing the Tooth Relic. The door has ivory inlay work, with copper and gold handles.

The **Udmale** (upper storey) houses the Relic. Caged behind gilded iron bars is the large outer *karandua* (casket), made of silver. Inside it are seven smaller caskets, each made of gold studded with jewels. Today the temple is controlled by a layman (the *Diyawadne*) elected by the high priests of the monasteries in Kandy and Asgiriya. The administrator holds the key to the iron cage, but there are three different keys to the caskets themselves, one held by the administrator and one each by the high priests of Malwatte and Asgiriya, so that the caskets can only be opened when all four are present.

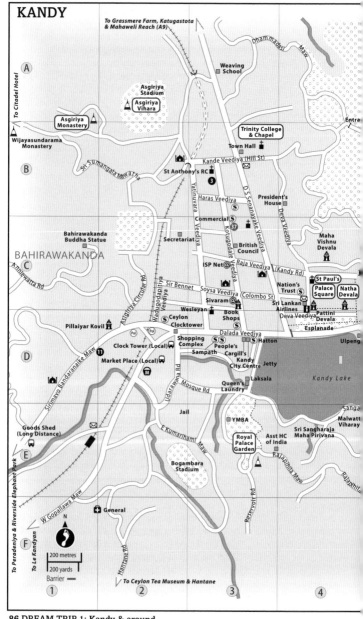

KANDY

To Grassmere Farm, Katugastota & Mahaweli Reach (A9)

To Citadel Hotel

Weaving School

Asgiriya Stadium
Asgiriya Vihara

Asgiriya Monastery

Wijayasundarama Monastery

Trinity College & Chapel

Entra

Sri Sumangala Mawatha

Town Hall

St Anthony's RC

Kande Veediya (Hill St)

Yatinuwara Veediya

Haras Veediya

President's House

D S Senanayake Veediya

Deva Veediya

Commercial

Maha Vishnu Devala

Bahirawakanda Buddha Statue

Secretariat

Kotugodala Veediya

British Council

BAHIRAWAKANDA

Amniewatta Rd

Asgiriya Circular Rd

Sir Bennet

Raja Veediya (Kandy Rd)

ISP Net@Veediya

Soysa Veediya

Wadugodapitiya Veediya

Nation's Trust

Sri Lankan Airlines

St Paul's
Palace Square
Natha Devala

Sivaram@

(Colombo St)

Deva Veediya

Pattini Devala

Pillaiyar Kovil

Wesleyan

Book Shops

Esplanade

Ceylon Clocktower

Dalada Veediya

Ulpeng

Sirimavo Bandaranaike Maw

Clock Tower (Local)

Market Place (Local)

Shopping Complex
People's
Sampath
Cargill's
Kandy
City Centre

Hatton

Kandy Lake

Udairawena Rd

Mosque Rd

Jetty

Queen's Laundry

Laksala

Sanga

Malwatt Viharay

Goods Shed (Long Distance)

Jail

E Kumariham Maw

YMBA

Royal Palace Garden

Sri Sangharaja Maha Pirivana

Asst HC of India

Bogambara Stadium

Reservoir Rd

Rajapihila Maw

Rajaphil

To Peradeniya & Riverside Elephant Park

W Gopallawa Maw

N

General

200 metres
200 yards
Barrier —

Hantane Rd

To Ceylon Tea Museum & Hantane

To Le Kandyan

(1) (2) (3) (4)

The **sanctuary** is opened at dawn. Ceremonies start at 0530, 0930 and 1830. These are moments when the temple comes to life with pilgrims making offerings of flowers amidst clouds of incense and the beating of drums. The casket is displayed for only a part of the day. The Relic itself for many years has only been displayed to the most important of visitors. You can join pilgrims to see the casket but may well have to overcome pushing and jostling by those desperate to see the holy object. There is a separate enclosure in front of the Relic, which wealthy Sri Lankans pay to go into. The hall behind the Tooth Relic sanctuary has a number of golden Buddha statues from Thailand and modern paintings depicting the Buddha's life and the arrival of Buddhism on the island.

The **Temple Museum** above is accessed from the rear. It contains bronze busts of the Kandyan kings, and displays some of their garments, as well as photocopies of documents detailing some of the history of the temple. There is also a gallery of photographs showing the extent of the damage to the temple in the 1998 bomb.

The **Audience Hall** was rebuilt in the Kandyan style as a wooden pillared hall (1784). The historic document ending the Kandyan kingdom was signed here, when the territory was handed over to the British. There is excellent carving on the pillars.

AROUND THE TEMPLE

Across from the complex is a working **monastery** and beyond its walls is **St Paul's Church** which was built in 1843 although the earliest minister, George Bisset, was here in 1816. The church was also damaged in the 1998 blast. Behind the temple, in the area of the Law Courts, you can watch lawyers in black gowns and white wigs going about their business in open-sided halls.

THE LAKE

On the lakeside, **Ulpenge**, opposite the Temple of the Tooth, was the bathing place of former queens and is now a police station. Further along to the east, is the **Buddhist Publications Society**, which has information on courses about Buddhism and meditation. The **Royal Palace Park (Wace Park)** ① *0830-1630, Rs 200*, is approached from the lake's southwest corner. There is a scenic 4-km path around the lake. Boat tours run from the jetty on the western side.

MALWATTE AND ASIGIRIYA VIHARAS

The 18th-century **Malwatte Vihara**, on the south side of the lake, where the important annual ordination of monks takes place in June, is decorated with ornate wood and metal work. Occasionally, a friendly monk shows visitors around the monastery and the small museum. This and the **Asigiriya Vihara** (northwest of town) are particularly important monasteries because of the senior position of their incumbents. The latter, which stands on a hill, has good wood carving and an impressive collection of old palm leaf manuscripts. There is a large recumbent Buddha statue and the mound of the old Royal Burial Ground nearby.

KANDY NATIONAL MUSEUM

① *Within the Queen's Palace, behind the Temple of the Tooth, T222 3867. Sun-Thu 0800-1700. Rs 500, children Rs 300, camera Rs 250.*

The collection traces a vivid history of the development and culture of the Kandyan Kingdom. It features jewels, armaments, ritual objects, sculptures, metalwork, ivory, costumes, games, medical instruments, old maps – an enormous range of everyday and exceptional objects. There is much memorabilia, and the attendants will attempt to explain it all, sometimes pointing out the obvious in expectation of a tip.

TUSKER RAJA MUSEUM

The much venerated elephant which carried the Tooth Relic casket in the Esala Perahera for many years, was offered to the temple by a pious Buddhist family when he was very young. Raja was 85 when he died in 1988. He was stuffed and placed in this separate museum north (left) of the Temple of the Tooth which is more easily visited before entering the temple.

ARCHAEOLOGICAL MUSEUM

① *Palace Sq. Wed-Mon 0800-1700. Free.*

Some good sculptures in wood and stone are housed in what remains of the old king's palace. The museum includes some architectural pieces, notably columns and capitals from the Kandyan kingdom, but the three dusty rooms are somewhat disappointing.

MUSEUM OF WORLD BUDDHISM

① *Behind the Temple of the Tooth, 0800-1900, Rs 500. Shoes must be removed before entering.*

A large two-storey museum dedicated to Buddhism. There are exhibits charting the history of Buddhism in Sri Lanka and also individual galleries dedicated to countries where Buddhism is the main religion. It's easy to tell those with the most money to put towards it, for example Japan. On display are photographs, statues of the Buddha and models of famous temples.

BRITISH GARRISON CEMETERY

① Donation expected.

To the right of the Kandy National Museum is a sign pointing the way to the British Garrison Cemetery. It is a short walk up the hill and here lie a number of colonial Brits. It was opened in 1822 until burials were all but banned in the 1870s. The cemetery was restored in the 1990s and is now a tranquil place to escape the bustle of Kandy town. The caretaker is very helpful and will show you around and point out the most interesting graves, such as the last recorded death of a European in Sri Lankan from a wild elephant.

UDAWATTEKELE SANCTUARY

① Rs 700. Kande Veediya, past the post office, leads to the entrance gate to the sanctuary.

Once the 'forbidden forest' of the kings of Kandy, this is now the city's lung. Previously reserved for the use of the court, the British cleared vast areas soon after arrival, though declared it a 'reserved' area in 1856. The sanctuary now covers 104 ha, and contains several endemic species of flora and fauna, with over 150 species of birds (including Layard's parakeet, Sri Lankan hanging parrot, barbets, bulbuls, bee-eaters and kingfishers), monkeys, squirrels and porcupines. There are also a number of meditation centres here. Some interesting legends are attached to the forest. Look out for the trail with stone steps leading down to a cove, the **Chittu Vishudi**. This is where King Vickramabahu was said to have hidden here when his palace was under siege. The pond is the original bathing place of the court. Gold coins are rumoured to be concealed by its murky waters. Myth has it that a serpent with glowing red eyes guards the treasure, which surfaces once a year. **Lady Horton's Drive** takes you into the tropical rainforest, and further east offers good views of the Mahaweli River.

TRINITY COLLEGE

Trinity College, which is approached from DS Senanayake Veediya, has a chapel with some beautiful paintings which makes a quiet diversion from the busy part of town. It is also worth exploring the school's archives.

→ SOUTH OF KANDY

CEYLON TEA MUSEUM

① 3 km south of town along Hantane Rd (past the hospital), T380 3284, www.ceylon teamuseum.com. Tue-Sat 0830-1630 (last tickets 1530). Rs 500.

Opened in December 2001, the government-backed Ceylon Tea Museum proudly claims to be the first of its kind in the world. Located in an old tea factory abandoned in 1986, it contains some impressive old machinery, polished up and laid out in manufacturing sequence, collected from various disused plantations around the highlands. The first floor holds the archive of James Taylor who set up the first tea plantation at Loolecondera in 1867, with some interesting curios such as the oldest extant packet of Ceylon Tea (still in its original packaging) and a photograph of the largest tea bush in the world, as well as a history of Thomas Lipton. The top floor has been converted into a restaurant and has a telescope for viewing the surrounding hills.

To the south, the **Hindagala Temple**, along the Galaha Road, has sixth-century rock inscriptions. The wall paintings date from different periods.

DUMBARA HILLS (KNUCKLES RANGE)

ⓘ *www.knucklesrange.org. Visiting hours 0600-1800. Rs 575, plus guide fees. Best time to visit Jan-Apr; be prepared for leeches.*

With peaks towering over above 1500 m and an annual rainfall range of 2500-5000 mm it follows that a wide variety of forest types would exist here from lowland dry patana to montane wet evergreen with their associated trees, shrubs, plants and epiphytes. These forests, in turn, harbour wildlife including leopard, sambar, barking deer, mouse deer, wild boar, giant squirrel, purple-faced langur, toque macaque and loris, as well as the otherwise rarely seen otter. More than 120 bird species recorded here include many endemic ones including the yellow-fronted barbet, dusky-blue flycatcher, Ceylon lorikeet, Ceylon grackle, yellow-eared bulbul and Layard's parakeet. In addition, endemic amphibians and reptiles include the Kirtisinghe's rock frog and leaf-nosed lizard, which are only found here.

The importance of the range as a watershed for the Mahaweli River and the Victoria reservoir has led the government to designate the area over 1500 m as a conservation area. Soil and water conservation have become critical issues because of the way the area has been exploited so far. Cardamom cultivation, the removal of timber and fuelwood,

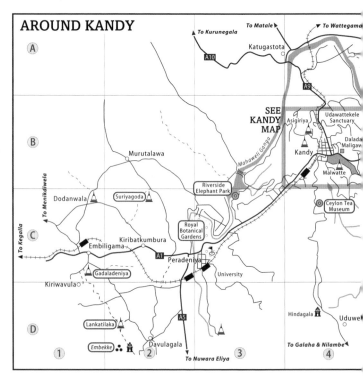

the use of cane in basket making and the production of treacle from kitul have all been sources of concern.

→ WEST OF KANDY

Beyond the wonderful botanic gardens at Peradeniya, is a group of 14th-century temples which display ancient artistic skills of the islanders. The traditions continue to be practised in the crafts villages nearby. If you have your own transport, you can combine a visit to the gardens and some temples with a visit to the Pinnawela Elephant Orphanage (see page 115). For a temple loop on foot, you could take the bus to Embekke, walk to Lankatilaka, finishing at Galadeniya, which is close to the main road.

PERADENIYA

ⓘ *Entry to the gardens is Rs 1100, students and children (under 12) Rs 550. A useful map is handed out with the tickets.*

Peradeniya is famous for its magnificent **botanic gardens** justly earning the town a place on most itineraries. Conceived originally in 1371 as the queen's pleasure garden, Peradeniya became the residence of a Kandyan prince between 1747 and 1782 where royal visitors were entertained. The park was converted into a 60-ha botanical garden in 1821, six years

after the fall of the last Kandyan king. There are extensive well-kept lawns, pavilions, an Orchid House with an outstanding collection, an Octagon Conservatory, fernery, banks of bamboo and numerous flower borders with cannas, hibiscus, chrysanthemums, croton and colourful bougainvillaea. The tank has water plants including the giant water lily and papyrus reeds. You will see unusual exotic species, especially palms (palmyra, talipot, royal, cabbage), and *Ficus elastica* (latex-bearing fig or 'Indian rubber tree' with buttress roots), an amazing avenue of drunken looking pines, and some magnificent old specimen trees. In all, there are about 4000 labelled species. A signboard at the entrance, with a map, features a numbered circuit from 1-30. The suggested route below closely follows this in reverse. It is best to keep to the paths to avoid the invisible large holes in the rough grass.

A suggested walk is to start at the **Spice Garden** (to the right of the entrance) which has many exotic spices (eg cardamom, cloves, pepper, vanilla). Follow the road to the right (east) to take in the **Orchid House**. Just off Palmyra Avenue there are Javanese

Almond trees with amazing roots. The palmyra leaf was used for ancient manuscripts. The **Cabbage Palm Avenue** from South America was planted in 1905. You can then walk along the **Royal Palm Avenue** (1885) – you will notice the fruit bats in quite large colonies hanging in many of the trees. This meets the **River Drive** which follows the course of the Mahaweli Ganga. Follow the drive to the **Suspension Bridge** which is about halfway around the River Drive and you can if you wish go back via the Royal Palm Avenue. This goes through the **Great Circle**, a large grassy central area around which a remarkably diverse list of dignitaries have planted further specimens. Alongside generations of English royalty, there are trees planted by Indira Gandhi, Yuri Gagarin, Marshal Tito, U Thant and Harold Macmillan. Between the Great Circle and the Great Lawn is the **Herbarium**. Try not to miss one of the rarest plants in the gardens – the Coco de Mer. You will find it on the path leading to George Gardner's monument. This is on your right as you return to exit (left as you enter the park). This plant has the largest and heaviest fruit (or nut) in the plant kingdom, weighing on average some 10-20 kg. They take between five and eight years to mature and are surprisingly productive. It is not unusual to have over 20 nuts on a tree. They are all carefully numbered. Native Coco de Mer are only found on Praslin, an island in the Seychelles. Carry on along this path to get to the **Memorial**, a dome shaped structure. George Gardner was Superintendent of the gardens from 1844-1849. From here you overlook the lily tank which is surrounded by giant bamboo, some 40 m tall (it grows at 2-3 cm a day).

Outside the gardens a bridge across the Mahaweli River takes you to the **School of Tropical Agriculture** at Gannoruwa, where research is carried out into various important spices and medicinal herbs as well as into tea, coffee, cocoa, rubber, coconuts and varieties of rice and other cash crops. The **Economic Museum** has botanical and agricultural exhibits.

Peradeniya is also the home of the **Sri Lanka University** (1942), built in the old Kandyan style in an impressive setting of a large park with the Mahaweli Ganga running though it and the surrounding hillocks. It is worth visiting the small teaching collection **museum** ① *in the Department of Archaeology, call ahead, T238 8345 ext 518.*

GADALADENIYA TEMPLE

① *Rs 200.*

The Buddhist temple is in a beautiful hilltop setting, built on a rock, 1 km from the main road. Built of stone, showing influence of Indian temple architecture, it has lacquered doors, carvings and frescoes and a moonstone at the entrance of the shrine. The brick superstructure, shaped like a stupa, has an octagonal base. The inscriptions on the rock by Dharmakirti date it to 1344. The principal gilded image of the Buddha (18th century, which replaced the original destroyed by the Portuguese) is framed by elaborate *makara* decoration. Unusually, there is also a shrine to Vishnu here. Outside, there is a covered stupa and a Bodhi tree. At **Kiriwavula village** nearby, craftsmen cast brass ornaments by the ancient lost-wax (*cire-perdu*) process. Some are for sale. Take a left turn off the A1 just after Pilimatalana.

LANKATILAKA MAHAVIHARAYA

The second monument of the group, 4 km away in Hiripitiya, sits on top of the rock Panhalgala. King Bhuvanekabahu IV (ruled 1341-1351) moved the Sinhalese capital from Kurunegala to Gampola nearby. When a monk reported the extraordinary vision of an elusive golden pot on the water of the tank here, the King saw this as a sign and had the temple built. He appears among the wall paintings.

The present two-storeyed blue-washed brick structure ⓘ *Rs 300*, was originally four storeys high. It was renovated and the tiled roof was added in 1845 after the two top storeys had fallen. If arriving on foot, you climb up a rock-cut stairway to the moonstone at the entrance, and the finely carved wooden doorway flanked by guardian *gajasinghas* (elephant-lions). The inner image house containing fine gold plated images of the Buddha is surrounded by a devale. The walls and ceiling have well preserved frescoes, some of the oldest and best examples of the Kandyan temple style. The west door has carved figures of Hindu gods (Saman, Skanda, Ganapathi and Vibhisena among others). There is a large rock inscription dating the temple to the thirteenth century. Craftsmen can be seen carving wood at the base of the rock.

EMBEKKE DEVALE

ⓘ *Rs 200.*

The Hindu devale, dedicated to God Kataragama (Skanda), is 1.5 km away along a track through pleasant cultivated fields. The temple with its sanctuary, Dancing Hall and the Drummers' Hall, is famous for its carved wooden pillars (which may have once adorned the Audience Hall in Kandy) with vibrant figures of soldiers, wrestlers, dancers, musicians, mythical animals and birds. You can see similar stone pillars at the remains of the old Pilgrim's Rest nearby. The patterned roof tiles are attractive too. The village has craftsmen working in silver, brass and copper.

SURIYAGODA VIHARE

If you have your own transport and wish to visit the Suriyagoda Vihare, turn off north from the A1 at Kiribatkumbura, signed to Murutalawa. The present 18th-century *vihara*, on a 15th-century site, has striking Kandyan wall paintings.

North of Embiligama (Km 105 post), the 17th-century **Dodanwala Temple** was built by Rajasinha II. It is where the king is believed to have offered the deity his crown and sword after defeating the Portuguese. From Embiligama, to reach the textile weaving village of **Menikdiwela**, after a short distance along the Murutalawa road take the left fork for 6 km.

MOVING ON
Kandy to Colombo

From Kandy, the route heads to Sri Lanka's buzzing capital, Colombo. The journey between Kandy and Colombo is described in Dream Trip 2, page 114. Many of the sights, such as Pinnawela Elephant Orphanage, can be visited as a day trip from Kandy.

KANDY AND AROUND LISTINGS

WHERE TO STAY

$$$$-$$$ Helga's Folly, 70 Frederick E de Silva Mawatha, T447 4314, www.helgasfolly.com. 40 individually decorated rooms in this eccentrically designed 'anti-hotel' full of character and quirkiness. The unique interior and exterior design ("the Salvador Dali of hotels") has to be seen to be believed. Set in quiet wooded hills, there's a stylish restaurant and a small pool (not well maintained). A long way from town but recommended for its imagination and romance.

$$$ Rangala House, 92b Bobebila, Makuldeniya, 1 hr from Kandy on a rough road, T240 0294, T077-600 4687, www.rangalahouse.com. A converted tea-planter's bungalow with beautiful views from the veranda. Close to the Knuckles Range and Corbett's Gap, there's excellent walking and birdwatching as well as a solar-heated swimming pool. Transport from Kandy is available and pick-ups from the airport arranged. The 3 rooms can be booked individually or there's a good discount for hiring the whole villa (US$290). British and Sri Lankan management. Excellent food. Minimum 2-night stay recommended.

$$ Amaya Hills, Heerassagala, 7 km southwest (near Peradeniya), T447 4022, www.amayaresorts.com. 100 very comfortable rooms including 4 excellent split-level suites (**$$$$**) in the most stylish hotel in Kandy based on a traditional Kandyan palace, good pool, popular **Le Garage** nightclub (Fri and Sat), Ayurvedic centre, excellent views, well run.

$ McLeod Inn, 65a Rajapihilla Mawatha, T222 2832, mcleod@sltnet.lk. 10 clean and pleasant rooms with hot water in the mornings and evenings, the 2 rooms with views are more expensive. The restaurant has the best view of any in this area (can be patronized by non-residents with advance notice). Very friendly and helpful. Popular so book in advance.

$ Sharon Inn, 59 Saranankara Rd, T220 1400, www.hotelsharoninn.com. 11 spotless rooms with balcony, restaurant, Wi-Fi, friendly, very popular.

RESTAURANTS

$$ Flower Song, 137 Kotugodalle Veediya (1st floor), T448 1650, www.flowerdrum.net. Open 1100-2230. Excellent Chinese, good portions. A/c.

$$-$ Devon, 11 Dalada Veediya, T222 4537. Open 0730-2000. The main restaurant has Sri Lankan rice and curry, Western dishes and Chinese. There is an excellent self-service area (open 1100-1900) for very cheap Sri Lankan/Chinese/seafood lunch and a fabulous bakery shop. Very popular with locals and tourists, waiters are miserable but the food is worth the scowls. There are other branches around town.

WHAT TO DO

Kandyan dancing is performed at various venues around town such as the **Kandyan Art Association** or the **Kandy Lake Club**. Most start around 1730 and performances last for 1 hr. These shows are heavily geared towards the tourist market.

Sri Lanka Trekking, T071-499 7666, www.srilankatrekking.com. Trekking trips into the Knuckles Range.

DREAM TRIP 2
Colombo→Kandy→Nuwara Eliya→Ella→Colombo
14 days

Colombo 1 night, page 97

Kandy 3 nights, page 81
Car and driver (3 hrs), bus (3 hrs)
or train (2½ hrs)

Nuwara Eliya 2 nights, page 118
Car and driver or bus (3 hrs), alternatively
take the train to Nanu Oya and arrange to
be picked up, or take a bus/taxi into town

Ella 3 nights, page 130
Car and driver (1 hr), bus (2½ hrs) or train
(2½ hrs, including getting from Nuwara
Eliya to the station at Nanu Oya)

Adam's Peak 1 night, page 138
This journey is much easier if you have your
own transport, car and driver (2½ hrs). See
'moving on' for details of public transport

Tea Trails 3 nights, page 141
You need your own transport to reach the
bungalows, or hire a taxi from Dalhousie or
Hatton (20-45 mins)

Colombo 1 night, page 97
To Kitulgala by car or taxi (45 mins), to
Colombo from Kitulgala (2 hrs). Buses from
Hatton to Colombo pass through Kitulgala

GOING FURTHER

Arugam Bay page 134
Car and driver/taxi from Ella (2½ hrs),
bus (4+ hrs) but you need to change at
Monaragala and head for Pottuvil and
from there take a 3-wheeler to Arugam Bay.

DREAM TRIP 2
Colombo→Kandy→Nuwara Eliya→Ella→Colombo

Head inland to escape the heat, and explore the tea plantations and misty peaks of the Hill Country. The journey begins in Colombo, offering the chance to hop on a train to Kandy, a scenic and very popular option. Home to the Temple of the Tooth and the island's most important Buddhist relic, Kandy was the last independent kingdom in Sri Lanka until it was signed over to the British in 1815. Today, it is a modern and bustling city packed with tourists, pilgrims and touts.

Nuwara Eliya is the next stop on this route. A former British Hill Station it is for many visitors something of a disappointment, as despite having a number of interesting colonial buildings it is not a step back in time. It looks much like many other Sri Lankan towns but there are tea factories nearby which can be visited, and is it the best base for a trip to Horton Plains to see the spectacular view from World's End. A side trip to Ella to enjoy the laidback atmosphere, stunning scenery and walking trails is recommended, before doubling back to Dalhousie for an ascent of Adam's Peak. During the pilgrimage season, join the faithful as they climb the steps at night to reach the summit in time for sunrise.

Those with their own transport, and time to relax, may want to stay at one of the luxury Tea Trails bungalows for a few days. Learn about tea processing, hike or bike in the surrounding countryside or enjoy an in-room spa treatment. Whitewater rafting can also be arranged from the bungalows, or this route passes through Kitulgala, the main rafting base on the island, on the way back to Colombo.

It is possible to extend this trip by travelling further east from Ella to Arugam Bay, best know as a surfing destination and a vibrant and fun place to visit during the season.

COLOMBO

Sprawling, choked with traffic and invariably chaotic, Colombo, like most large Asian cities, may not be to everyone's taste. As Sri Lanka's commercial capital and its only conurbation, the city centre was an obvious target for Tamil separatists and saw occasional curfews and a high military presence during troubled times. Today, however, firmly fixed on the future, investment is flowing in and this characterful and diverse city is buzzing with a new found energy.

Although Colombo's origins pre-date the arrival of the Portuguese, culturally and architecturally it appears a modern city, with few established tourist sights. Close to the enormous harbour, to which Colombo owes its pre-eminence, the banking centre of Fort houses some impressive red brick and whitewashed buildings, which give an impression of its colonial origins. To the east are the narrow lanes of the bustling Pettah district with its atmospheric and colourful bazaars and some reminders of the Dutch period.

Increasingly the heart of modern Colombo lies to the south of the old centre, where the city's wealthy young elite rub shoulders in the fashionable boutiques and restaurants of Kollupitiya and Bambalapitiya, while the broad avenues and elegant villas of Cinnamon Gardens nearby reveal the city's most exclusive residential district. Inland from here, or south to the predominantly Tamil suburb of Wellawatta, brings you to a more 'local' Colombo. Alternatively, the pleasant colonial resort of Mount Lavinia with its narrow strip of beach is only a 30-minute train ride away from the centre, and a laid-back alternative base for exploring the city.

→ ARRIVING IN COLOMBO

GETTING THERE

Air Almost all international visitors to Colombo arrive by air at **Bandaranaike International Airport** at Katunayake, about 30 km north of the city and 6 km from Negombo, www.airport.lk. Available at the airport are regular buses to Colombo's Bastian Mawatha Stand in the Pettah; catch the free shuttle from outside Arrivals to where the buses leave from. There are also pre-paid taxis (Rs 2550 depending on which part of town you're heading to) and more expensive air-conditioned taxis (from Rs 2805), which can be arranged from the taxi service counter. A breakdown of fares is available at www.airport.lk/getting-arround/taxi-rates.php and includes prices to reach other destinations such as Kandy and Hikkaduwa. Taxis are also available from the travel agent counters.

Trains leave from **Katunayake Train Station**, which is about 1 km from the airport. From here suburban commuter trains run north to Negombo (15 minutes) and south to Colombo (1¼ hours). Trains run infrequently but there are plans for 15-minute shuttles.

It is also possible to rent a car at the airport, though rates tend to be steep and it usually pays to shop around in Colombo. Moreover, if you wish to self-drive a Sri Lankan Recognition Permit is needed to accompany International Driving Permits, so it may not be possible to drive immediately. These are available from the AA or the Department of Motor Traffic in Colombo (see page 193). Domestic air passengers arrive at **Ratmalana Airport** to the south of the city; see Transport in Sri Lanka, page 192, for details of domestic flights.

Bus Government and private buses run to and from Colombo from virtually every significant town in Sri Lanka. There are three bus stands, all close to each other, 1 km east

ON THE ROAD
I'm in heaven ... Colombo Seven

Even more than London, Colombo's citizens define their city by its postcodes. Aside from recognizing the snob value of having an office in Colombo 1 or a residence in Colombo 7 (and being suitably impressed), having a grasp of the most important postcodes will help you find your way around the city.

Colombo 1	Fort	Colombo 9	Dermatagoda
Colombo 2	Slave Island	Colombo 10	Maradana
Colombo 3	Kollupitiya	Colombo 11	Pettah
Colombo 4	Bambalapitiya	Colombo 12	Hultsdorf
Colombo 5	Havelock Town	Colombo 13	Kotahena
Colombo 6	Wellawatta	Colombo 14	Grandpass
Colombo 7	Cinnamon Gardens	Colombo 15	Mutwal
Colombo 8	Borella		

of Fort station in the Pettah. There are regular bus services along Galle Road to Colombo's southern suburbs, where many visitors choose to stay.

Train Nearly all of Sri Lanka's railway lines originate in Fort Railway Station at the southwestern corner of the Pettah (Colombo 11), which is within walking distance of the major hotels in Fort. There are regular services from Kandy, main tourist areas in the highlands, Anuradhapura, west and south coast beach resorts and Trincomalee on the east coast.

MOVING ON

The busy A1 highway connects Colombo and **Kandy** (see page 81) and there are regular buses between the two cities. The journey (see Colombo to Kandy, page 114) takes about three hours and traverses the coastal plain, passing through lush scenery: paddy fields interspersed with coconut and areca nut palms, bananas and pineapples. A number of visitors choose to take the train to Kandy (2½ hours); book your ticket at the railway station in the Pettah. Ensure that you catch an Intercity service as they're faster, and if you want a seat in the observation car or on one of the 'luxury coaches' buy your ticket a few days in advance as there is only one service a day offering these options. Others just have standard first class carriages.

For those heading to **Uda Walawe National Park** (see page 153), take a bus to **Ratnapura** (see page 148, three hours) and then either a taxi (1½ hours) or a bus to Embilipitiya (2½ hours). Alternatively, a car and a driver will take you from the capital to Uda Walawe in about 2½ hours.

GETTING AROUND

Although the city is quite spread out, it is fairly simple to get your bearings. If you venture beyond Fort you will need transport to explore. Many three-wheelers now have meters but you may have to ask them to turn it on. If you choose to travel in one without a meter bargain hard and try and pick it up away from the main tourist areas. Radio cabs are a reliable alternative and quite affordable if you can share one. Some streets in Fort, around the president's house and major banks, are blocked or have strict security checks so it is sometimes impossible for transport to take the most obvious route. The **Colombo City Tour**

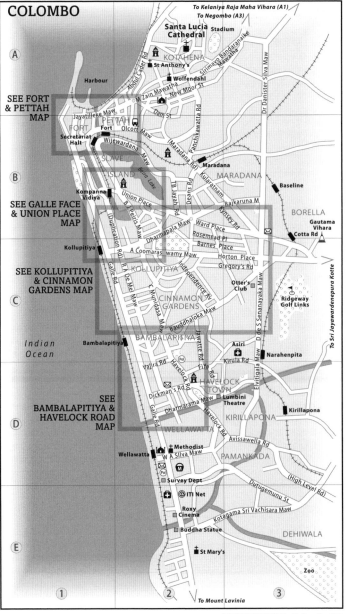

COLOMBO

To Kelaniya Raja Maha Vihara (A1)
To Negombo (A3)

Santa Lucia Cathedral

Stadium

(A)

KOTAHENA

Sirimavo Bandaranaike Mawatha

St Anthony's

Wolfendahl

Harbour

N Zain Mawatha

New Moor St

Dam St

Dr Danister Silva Maw

SEE FORT & PETTAH MAP

Jayatilleke Maw.

FORT

Fort

Olcott Maw.

PETTAH

Panchikawatta Rd

Secretariat Halt

Wijewardana Maw.

(Maradana Rd)

Maradana

SLAVE

(B)

ISLAND

Beira Lake

T B Jayah

Kularatnam

MARADANA

Baseline

Kompanna Vidiya

Union Place

Deans Rd

Rajkaruna M.

Lynsey Rd

BORELLA

SEE GALLE FACE & UNION PLACE MAP

Duplication Rd

B Peiris Maw.

Dharmapala Maw.

Ward Place

Rosemead Pl

Gautama Vihara

Cotta Rd

Kollupitiya

A Coomaraswamy Maw.

Galle Rd

Barnes Place

Horton Place

SEE KOLLUPITIYA & CINNAMON GARDENS MAP

Indian Ocean

(C)

R A De Mel Maw.

C W W Kannangara Maw.

KOLLUPITIYA

Independence Av.

Gregory's Rd

Otter's Club

Ridgeway Golf Links

To Sri Jayawardenepura Kotte

CINNAMON GARDENS

Bauddhaloka Maw.

BAMBALAPITIYA

Bambalapitiya

Jawatte Rd

Asiri

Narahenpita

Vajira Rd

Havelock Rd

Fife

Kirula Rd

Elvitigala Maw.

D de S Senanayaka Maw.

SEE BAMBALAPITIYA & HAVELOCK ROAD MAP

Dickman's Rd

Lumbini Theatre

HAVELOCK TOWN

Kirillapona

Galle Rd

Dharmarama Maw.

Havelock Rd

Avissawella Rd

WELLAWATTA

KIRILLAPONA

PAMANKADA

Wellawatta

Methodist

W A Silva Maw.

Dutugemunu St

(High Level Rd)

Survey Dept

@ ITI Net

Kotagama Sri Vachisara Maw.

Roxy Cinema

Buddha Statue

DEHIWALA

(E)

St Mary's

Zoo

(1)   (2)   (3)

To Mount Lavinia

ⓘ www.colombocitytour.com, US$30, children US$22, is easily recognizable by its red double decker buses, but currently this isn't a hop-on/hop-off service and it only runs at weekends.

ORIENTATION

If you are going to spend any time here, it pays to become familiar with the city's postcodes, by which areas are often referred (see box, page 98). The main coastal road, Galle Road, which leads to Galle and beyond, is the spine of the city, and many of the areas of interest lie on it or within a few kilometres inland. Officially the city's centre, and the area from which all suburbs radiate, is **Fort**, containing the harbour, the president's house and banks, and to the south some of the most exclusive hotels. East is the busy bazaar of the **Pettah**, which contains the main train and bus stations, and which turns into **Kotahena**. South of Fort is **Galle Face Green**, a popular place for a stroll, which soon becomes **Kollupitiya**, a wealthy shopping area with many excellent restaurants. Inland, and separated from Fort and the Pettah by Beira Lake, is **Slave Island** and the busy thoroughfare of Union Place. South of here (and inland from Kollupitiya) is leafy **Cinnamon Gardens**, the most exclusive area of Colombo, with the city's biggest park, main museums and some attractive guesthouses, so many visitors choose to stay here. To the east is **Borella**. Back on the coast, Galle Road continues south to **Bambalapitiya**, another shopping area but progressively less exclusive, which is parallel to **Havelock Town**. Further south is **Wellawatta**, a large Tamil area, then **Dehiwala** (not strictly speaking part of Colombo), which houses Colombo's zoo. Then you reach **Mount Lavinia**, a traditional bolt-hole from the city for both locals and tourists, see page 185. Yet none of these areas constitute Sri Lanka's administrative capital, which was moved to **Sri Jayawardenepura Kotte**, 11 km southeast of Fort, in 1982.

TOURIST INFORMATION

The **Sri Lanka Tourist Board** ⓘ 80 Galle Rd, Col 3, T243 7059, www.srilanka.travel, Mon-Fri 0830-1615, Sat 0830-1230, has free literature in English (and some in German, French, Italian, Swedish and Japanese) and will arrange guides, though not much information on transport. They usually keep the leaflets behind the counter so you will have ask for what you want. There is also an information counter at Bandaranaike Airport, T245 2411. **Railway Tourist Office** ⓘ Fort Station, Col 11, T244 0048, offers friendly advice to anyone planning a rail journey. They will suggest an itinerary, book train tickets and hotels, and arrange a car with driver. Some may find their sales techniques a little pushy. Special steam train excursions are offered on the *Viceroy Special* (usually groups of 30 are required for a two-day one-night trip to Kandy).

Travel Lanka is a free monthly tourist guide available at larger tourist offices and in major hotels. It has some useful information and listings for Colombo and the main tourist areas, though much is out of date. If the copy on display in the tourist office is months out of date ask for the more recent edition, it's usually tucked away in a cupboard.

→ BACKGROUND

Sheltered from the southwest monsoon by a barely perceptible promontory jutting out into the sea, Colombo's bay was an important site for Muslim traders long before the colonial period. Its name derives from 'Kotomtota', or port to the kingdom of Kotte founded in 1369, close to present-day Sri Jayawardenepura Kotte, see page 108.

However, Colombo is essentially a colonial city. Soon after arrival in Sri Lanka, the Portuguese set up a fortified trading post in modern-day Fort, captured in 1656 by the

Dutch. The canals constructed to link up the coastal lagoons are a lasting legacy, as well as the churches and mansions of the Pettah, Kotahena and Hultsdorf. Colombo's rise to pre-eminence however did not start until the 19th century and the establishment of British power. When the British took control of Kandy and encouraged the development of commercial estates, the island's economic centre of gravity moved north, thereby lessening the importance of Galle as the major port. The town became the banking and commercial hub and benefited from its focal position on the rapidly expanding transport system within the island. From 1832 the British encouraged the rapid development of a road network which radiated from Colombo. In the late 19th century this was augmented by an expanding rail network. Since independence Colombo has retained its dominant position.

→ THE CITY

Colombo is a modern city with plenty of buzz but few 'must-see' sights. Its historical centre is the colonial Fort, which combined with a visit to the hectic bazaar and Dutch period legacy of the Pettah area to its east, can make for an interesting walking tour. Most of the rest of the city's sights are spread out in the southern suburbs, where the attractive wide boulevards of Cinnamon Gardens, the city's most exclusive district, are a highlight. Here you can visit the city's principal park and museums, and perhaps even more enticingly, sample some of the fare that is fast making Colombo one of the culinary capitals of Asia.

FORT AREA

Lying immediately south of the harbour, the compact fort area, historically Colombo's commercial centre, is a curious blend of old and new, modern tower blocks rubbing shoulders with reminders of its colonial past. It can be a quiet place outside office hours. Because it houses the president's residence and the principal banking area, it was a separatist target during the war and remains the only road-blocked area of the city with continued high security. Though it houses many fine British colonial buildings (many of which are boarded up), little remains from either the Portuguese or Dutch periods, and the last traces of the fort itself were destroyed in the 19th century.

The **Grand Oriental Hotel** is a good place to start a tour. Formerly the first port of call for all travellers arriving by steamship, it was once the finest hotel in Colombo. It used to be said that if you waited long enough in its hall, you would meet everyone worth meeting in the world. It is rather faded now, but you can get fascinating views of the harbour area from the hotel's fourth-floor restaurant. Next door to the hotel, if you walk along the pavement next to the checkpoint, is the simple but very peaceful **St Peter's Church** which was once part of the Dutch governor's residence. **York Street**, Fort's main shopping area, runs due south of the hotel, passing the brick-built colonial-era department stores of **Cargill's** and **Miller's**.

To the east on Bristol Street is the central YMCA, next to the Moors Islamic Cultural Home. Across Duke Street is the Young Men's Buddhist Association. The shrine houses a noted modern image of the Buddha.

Sir Baron Jayatilleke Mawatha, once the main banking street, stretches west of York Street. Nearly all the buildings are in red brick. At the western end of Chatham Street to the south, past the Dutch period Fort Mosque, is the **Lighthouse Clocktower**. A modern clocktower (with Big Ben chimes) takes its place. The northern end of Janadhipathi Mawatha, which includes the **president's house** (*Janadhipathi Mandiraya*), is normally closed to the public.

Heading south along Janadhipathi Mawatha, a quite different, more vibrant Fort comes into view. The 1960s **Ceylon Continental Hotel** has magnificent views along the coast to Mount Lavinia, while on Bank of Ceylon Mawatha is Fort's modern day commercial hub, the twin steel and glass towers of the 39-floor **World Trade Center** (1991), Sri Lanka's tallest building, along with some other high-rise offices. Over the road is the restored **Old Dutch Hospital**, a complex of cafés, restaurants and shops (including a branch of **Barefoot**). To the south, opposite the Galadari Hotel, the colonial **Old Parliament House** is now used as the president's secretariat.

North down Chaithya Road will lead you past the lighthouse and under the legs of the **Sambodhi Chaitya Temple**. There are great views from the top of the temple, but photography is currently not allowed. The road leads to the **Maritime Museum**, which was once a Dutch Prison, and inside are various sailing and trade related artefacts. At the time of writing it was not possible to go any further and you had to double-back the way you came.

THE PETTAH AND KOTAHENA
To the north and east of Fort Station is a busy market area with stalls lining Olcott Mawatha and Bodhiraja Mawatha, making pedestrian movement slow and tedious at times. The

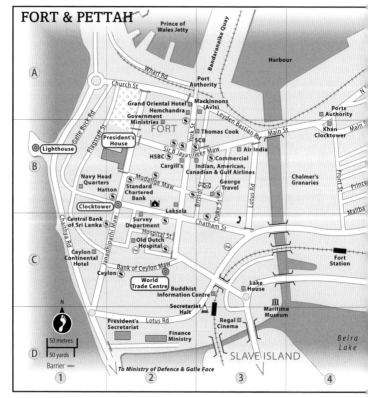

central area of the Pettah, with many wholesale outlets, bounded by these two roads as well as Main Street and Front Street, is frantic, dirty and noisy, the cries of the traders mingling with the endless traffic horns. It is fascinating and enervating in equal measure. Specialist streets house craftsmen and traders such as goldsmiths (Sea Street), fruit and vegetable dealers (the end of Main Street) and Ayurvedic herbs and medicines (Gabo's Lane). In the market area to the north, Arabs, Portuguese, Dutch and British once traded. Today, most of the traders are Tamil or Muslim, as evidenced by the many *kovils* and mosques.

About 100 m northeast of Fort Railway Station at the south western edge of the Pettah, the **Dutch Period Museum**, ① *Prince St, T244 8466, Tue-Sat 0900-1700, Rs 500, children Rs 300, camera Rs 250,* was originally the residence of the Dutch governor, Thomas van Rhae (1692-1697); it was sold to the VOC (Vereenigde Oostindische Compagnie or Dutch East India Company) before becoming the Colombo seminary in 1696. Then in 1796 it was handed over to the British who turned it into a military hospital and later a post office. It has now been restored and offers an interesting insight to the Dutch period. The museum surrounds a garden courtyard and has various rooms dedicated to different aspects of Dutch life including some interesting old tombstones. Upstairs, several rooms display Dutch period furniture.

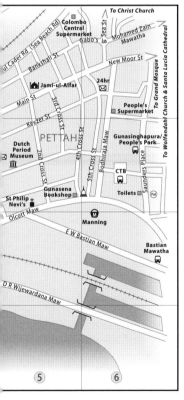

To the north, halfway along Main Street on the left-hand side after 2nd Cross Street is the **Jami-ul-Alfar Mosque** with its interesting white and red brick facade but little of architectural interest inside. At the eastern end of Main Street, Mohamed Zain Mawatha (once Central Road) goes east from a large roundabout, just north of the market, and you enter **Kotahena**. A left turn off Mohamed Zain Mawatha immediately after the roundabout leads to a right fork, Ratnajothi Saravana Mawatha (formerly Wolfendahl Street). At the end (about 500 m) is the **Wolfendahl Church**. Built in 1749 on the site of an earlier Portuguese church, it is prominently placed on a hill, where its massive cruciform shape stands out, commanding a view over the harbour. Its Doric facade is solid and heavy, and inside it has many tombstones and memorial tablets to Dutch officials. It is the most interesting surviving Dutch monument in Sri Lanka. Some 200 m to the south in New Moor Street is the **Grand Mosque**, a modern building in the style, as one critic puts it, of a "modern international airport covered in metallic paint".

About 1 km to its northeast is **Santa Lucia**, the Roman Catholic cathedral, in

ON THE ROAD
Slave Island

The high rise hotels and offices that occupy the northward jutting peninsula in Beira Lake facing the fort show no trace of the earlier uses of what was known as Slave Island. 'Island' was a misnomer, but slaves played a very real part in the colonial history of Colombo.

During the Dutch period this tongue of open land was known as Kaffir Veldt. The Kaffirs – Africans from the East Coast around Mozambique – were brought to Sri Lanka for the first time by the Portuguese from Goa in 1630. When the Dutch ousted the Portuguese they made use of the slave labour force to build the fort in Colombo, when there may have been 4000 of them. Their numbers grew, but after an unsuccessful insurrection in the 18th century the Dutch authorities decided to insist that all slave labour must be identifiably accommodated. The Kaffir Veldt was the nearest open space on which special shanty houses could be built, and a nightly roll call would be held to ensure that every slave was there.

By 1807, the number of slaves had fallen to 700, though the British did not abolish slavery in Sri Lanka until 1845. Nonetheless, the name Slave Island has persisted.

some people's eyes the most remarkable church building in Sri Lanka. It is a huge grey structure with a classical facade and a large forecourt, begun in 1876, and completed in 1910. Inside are the tombs of three French bishops but little else of interest. The Pope conducted a service here during his visit in 1994. **Christ Church**, the Anglican cathedral back towards the harbour, is a kilometre northwest of here and is the main church in a diocese that dates from 1845.

Also in the Pettah are three modest Hindu temples, of little architectural interest, but giving an insight into Hindu building style and worship. Perhaps the most striking is that of **Sri Ponnambula Vanesvara** at 38 Sri Ramanathan Road. The *gopuram* (gateway) has typical sculptures of gods from the Hindu pantheon. A Siva lingam is in the innermost shrine, with a Nandi bull in front and a dancing Siva (*Nataraja*) to one side.

GALLE FACE, UNION PLACE AND BEIRA LAKE

Heading south from Fort past the **Ceylon Continental Hotel** and Old Parliament, you reach **Galle Face Green**, to the south of the mouth of the canal feeding Beira Lake. Originally laid out in 1859, the area has been redeveloped and, green once more, is a pleasant place to wander and very popular with Sri Lankans. There are lots of food stalls and hawkers selling knick-knacks, kites and children's toys. **Speaker's Corner** is at its southwestern corner opposite the historic **Galle Face Hotel**. Be on guard for pickpockets and touts, especially at night when the whole area comes alive.

Cross Galle Road, and then the canal, and head into **Slave Island** (see box, above). On Kew Street, near the **Nippon Hotel**, city tours often visit the **Sri Siva Subharamaniya Kovil**, with its enormous colourful *gopuram*. Along Sir James Pieris Mawatha to the south is **Beira Lake**, where the endangered spot-billed pelican can be seen. At its northern end along Navam Mawatha is an important commercial zone, with some restaurants and bars, and a pavement leads some of the way around the lake. It is possible to hire out a **swan pedalo** ① *Rs 100, children Rs 50 for 30 mins*, for a trip around a section of the lake. There are jetties to two tiny islands, one a park, the other the tranquil **Seema Malakaya**, designed for meditation by Geoffrey Bawa with various Buddha statues. It belongs to the **Gangaramaya Temple** to the east, which has an interesting selection of rare curios, including an impressive set of gold Buddhas and some intricate carved ivory on show. You might also see the temple elephant shackled up in the grounds. The temple comes alive during the **Navam Perahera** in January.

KOLLUPITIYA, CINNAMON GARDENS AND BORELLA

Inland and parallel with Galle Road runs RA de Mel Mawatha (formerly Duplication Road), built up all the way south. Kollupitiya and, further south, Bambalapitiya have some of Colombo's best shopping areas, with some upmarket boutiques, notably **Barefoot**, see page 113. Wealthy locals also flock to the numerous excellent restaurants.

East of Kollupitiya station, Ananda Coomaraswamy Mawatha leads to the most prestigious residential area of Colombo, **Cinnamon Gardens** – widely referred to by its postal code, Colombo 7 – where cinnamon trees used to grow during colonial times. Broad roads and shaded avenues make it a very attractive area, more reminiscent of Singapore than South Asia, though an increasing number of offices and government buildings have moved here in recent years from Fort. Its centrepiece is the attractive **Vihara Mahadevi Park** ⓘ *0600-1800, approach from the northeast, opposite the Town Hall,* with the museums and

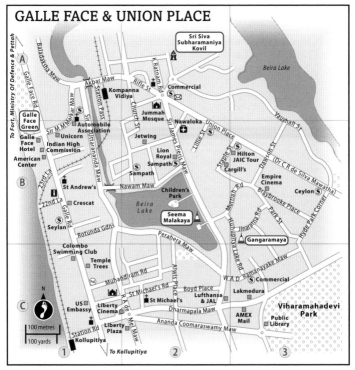

art gallery to its south. The park was re-named after the mother of the King Dutthagamenu. Early morning is an excellent time to visit. In the southwest is a **botanical garden** with a range of tropical trees including a Bo tree, ebony, mahogany, *sal* and lemon eucalyptus which attract a wide variety of birds. There is also an enormous profusion of climbing and parasitic plants as well as rare orchids. The park is particularly colourful in the spring. You may catch sight of elephants which are bathed in the water tank to the southwest. A series

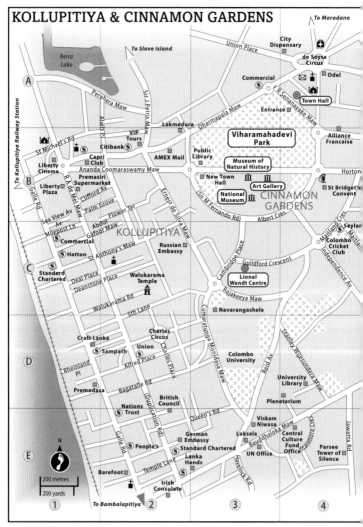

KOLLUPITIYA & CINNAMON GARDENS

of rectangular lakes to the east of the park leads to a golden statue of the seated Buddha. The white cupola of the impressive **Town Hall** stands out on Kannangara Mawatha to the northeast corner of the park. It was completed in 1927. At the De Soysa Circus roundabout is an equally interesting red-brick building, the **Victoria Memorial Rooms**, built in 1903.

In **Borella**, the suburb east of Cinnamon Gardens, the modest shrine room of the **Gautama (Gotami) Vihara** contains impressive modern murals depicting the life of the Buddha by the Sri Lankan artist George Keyt, painted in 1939-1940.

The **National Museum** ① *8 Marcus Fernando Mawatha (Albert Crescent), T269 4768, Sat-Thu 0900-1830 (last entry 1730), closed public holidays, Rs 500, children Rs 300, cameras Rs 250, video cameras Rs 2000*, has a statue of Sir William Gregory, governor 1872-1877, in front of the imposing facade. Opened in 1877, it has a good collection of paintings, sculptures, furniture, porcelain and Kandyan regalia. The library houses a unique collection of over 4000 *ola* (palm manuscripts) – an extremely rich archaeological and artistic collection. Very well labelled and organized, a visit is an excellent introduction for a tour of Sri Lanka. Exhibits include an outstanding collection of 10th- to 12th-century bronzes from Polonnaruwa, and the lion throne of King Nissankamalla, which has become the symbol of Sri Lanka. The ground floor displays Buddhist and Hindu sculptures, including a striking 1500-year-old stone statue of the Buddha from Toluvila. Other exhibits include ancient jewellery and carvings in ivory and wood, and there are superb scale reproductions of the wall paintings at Sigiriya and Polonnaruwa.

The **Natural History Museum** ① *entered via the National Museum or from A Coomeraswamy Mawatha, T269 4767, daily 0900-1700 (last entry 1630), closed public holidays, Rs 300, children Rs 150, cameras Rs 250, video cameras Rs 2000, or as a combined ticket with the National Museum*, is a Victorian-style array of ageing stuffed animals and lizards in formaldehyde, although the scope is quite impressive. The 'applied botany' section introduces you to how various industries work, such as rubber, timber, tea and coconut (note the 13 different types), while there is also a collection of fossils found in Sri Lanka dating back to the Pleistocene Age. Overall, it's a little disappointing. The **National Art Gallery**, next door, a one-room collection by Sri Lankan artists.

A little further south, the **Lionel Wendt Centre** ⓘ *19 Guildford Cres, Mon-Fri 0900-1245 and 1400-1700, Sat-Sun 1000-1200 and 1400-1700*, is a registered charity fostering the arts in Sri Lanka. Local artists are supported with temporary exhibitions, while there is a permanent exhibition of Wendt's pictures. Plays and dance recitals are also performed here.

The well-presented **Bandaranaike Museum** ⓘ *Bauddhaloka Mawatha, 0900-1600, closed Mon and poya holidays*, is housed inside the massive and imposing Bandaranaike Memorial International Conference Hall (BMICH), built by the Chinese government. As well as commemorating the life and times of the assassinated prime minister, with some interesting letters, diaries and personal effects on display, it offers a useful insight into Sri Lanka's steps into post-colonial nationhood. Opposite the BMICH is a replica statue of the Aukana Buddha.

→ NORTH AND EAST OF THE CITY

KELANIYA

Some 13 km northeast from Fort, across the Kelaniya River, is the **Raja Maha Vihara**, the most visited Buddhist temple in Sri Lanka after the Temple of the Tooth in Kandy. In the 13th century Kelaniya was an impressive city but for Buddhists its chief attraction today is the legendary visit of the Buddha to the site. The *Mahavansa* recorded that the original stupa enshrined a gem-studded throne on which the Buddha sat when he visited Sri Lanka. Ultimately destroyed by the Portuguese, the present *dagoba* is in the shape of a 'heap of paddy'. The first city on the site was believed to have been built by King Yatala Tissa. According to legend this was destroyed by a flood from the sea which was a punishment given to the king for mistreating the Buddhist *sangha*. He tried to placate the sea by setting his daughter afloat on a golden boat. Having drifted ashore in the south of the island she married King Kavan Tissa, and became the mother of one of Sri Lanka's great heroes, King Dutthagemenu. The city is subsequently believed to have been destroyed by Tamil invasions, and was only re-built in the 13th century by King Vijayabahu.

The present temple, which dates to the late 19th century, is set amongst attractive frangipani trees and has an impressive bell-tower. There is a famous image of the reclining Buddha, but there are also many images of Hindu deities. **Duruthu Perahera** each January draws thousands of pilgrims from all over the island. Take a Biyagama bus from Bastion Mawatha. They leave every half an hour and the trip takes 20-30 minutes.

SRI JAYAWARDENEPURA KOTTE

Built in the shadow of the modern city of Colombo, most government offices have relocated in this new artificially planned capital 11 km southeast, but Colombo still retains its importance as the commercial capital. The decision to put the new 'parliament' here was based partly on the fact that the site was formerly the almost sacred territory of Kotte, the ancient capital of Sri Lanka under Alakeswara who built a large fortress and defeated the Tamil leader Chakravarthi. Parakramabahu VI (ruled 1412-1467) transformed the fortress into a prosperous modern city, building a magnificent three-storey temple to hold the Tooth relic which he had placed within several bejewelled gold caskets. However,

ON THE ROAD
Grand designs

In May 2003, Sri Lanka mourned the death of Geoffrey Bawa, the island's best known, most prolific and most influential architect. Amongst his many projects Bawa was the creative visionary behind some of the Sri Lanka's most spectacular hotels, from the austerity of the 1-km-long camouflaged jungle palace of Kandalama near Dambulla, to the colonial-influenced lighthouse at Galle. He also constructed Sri Lanka's first purpose-built tourist complex, the Bentota Beach in 1968.

Bawa's work blends traditional Sri Lankan architecture and use of materials with modern ideas of composition and space. Hallmarks include a careful balance, and blurring of the boundaries, between inside and outside, the creation of vistas, courtyards and walkways that offer a range of perspectives, and an acute sensitivity to setting and environment. His work builds on Sri Lanka's past, absorbing ideas from the west and east, while creating something innovative and definably Sri Lankan.

Born in 1919 to wealthy parents, Bawa went to England in 1938, where he studied English at Cambridge and took up law. Soon tiring of this, he spent some years drifting and it was not until 1957 that he qualified as an architect. On his return to Ceylon, he gathered together a group of talented young artists who shared his interest in the island's forgotten architectural heritage, including batik artist Ena de Silva and designer Barbara Sansoni. The prolific practice he established set new standards in design over the next 20 years for all styles of buildings, from the residential and commercial to the religious and the educational.

Bawa's fame was sealed in 1979 when he was invited by President Jayawardene to design the new parliament building in Kotte. The result, which required the dredging of a swamp to create an artificial lake and island, itself symbolizing the great irrigation of the ancient period, was a series of terraces with copper domed roofs rising from the water, with references to monastic architecture, Kandyan temples and South Indian palace architecture, all within a Modernist framework. Other high profile buildings followed including the Ruhuna University near Matara, dramatically arranged on two rocky hills overlooking the ocean.

In 1998 he suffered a massive stroke. Although it rendered him paralysed his colleagues completed his projects with a nod of assent or shake of the head from the bed-ridden master. In the same year he was honoured privately by his friend the Prince of Wales who snuck away from the official 50th anniversary celebrations to pay him tribute; official recognition followed in 2001 when he was awarded the prestigious Chairman's Award for Lifetime Achievements by the Aga Khan.

subsequent weak rulers left the city relatively defenceless and it fell easy prey to the Portuguese. They destroyed the city so that there are no traces of its former glory left. Some panels from the old temple can be seen in the National Museum.

The impressive **Parliament Building** itself was designed by the renowned modern Sri Lankan architect Geoffrey Bawa, see box, above. It stands in the middle of a lake surrounded by parkland but is not open to the public.

The **Gramodaya Folk Arts Centre** has craftsmen working with brass, silver, leather, coir and producing jewellery, pottery, natural silk, lace and reed baskets. There is a craft shop and a restaurant serving Sri Lankan specialities. Ask the tourist office for details.

The drive from Colombo's Fort area through the suburbs takes about 30 minutes. Buses run from the city or you can take a three-wheeler.

BAMBALAPITIYA AND HAVELOCK TOWN

South of Kollupitiya, Bambalapitiya extends south along Galle Road. This is a busy shopping area with two popular indoor malls at Majestic City and Liberty Plaza and some enticing eateries, but few interesting sights although the **Vajirarama Temple**, whose missionary monks have taken Buddhism to the west, is worth a look. To the east, south of Bauddhaloka Mawatha, **Havelock Road**, lined with some more excellent restaurants, is another traffic-filled thoroughfare, stretching south to Havelock Town. The **Isipathanaramaya Temple**, just north of Havelock Park, is famous for its beautiful frescoes.

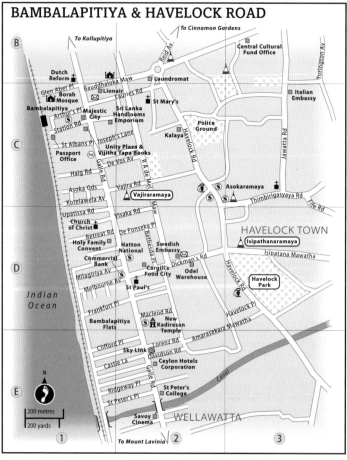

BAMBALAPITIYA & HAVELOCK ROAD

WELLAWATTA AND DEHIWALA

South of Bambalapitiya, Wellawatta is the last busy suburb within the city limits. Home to many of Colombo's Tamils (and sometimes called 'Little Jaffna' as a result), it has a bustling charm away from the pretensions of wealthier suburbs further north.

Near the busy bazaar of Dehiwala, the **Subbodaramaya Temple** is a Buddhist complex with a shrine room dating from 1795. There is the usual *dagoba*, a Bo-tree and also a 'Seven-Week House' which illustrates the weeks following the Buddha's Enlightenment. There are several Buddha statues, some well-preserved wall paintings and woodcarvings but the most arresting figure is the supremely serene 4.5 m-reclining Buddha with eyes set in blue sapphires.

Dehiwala Zoo ① *A Dharmapala Mawatha (Allan Av), 10 km southeast of the centre, T271 2751, 0830-1800, Rs 2000, children Rs 1000, Rs 250, video camera Rs 2000,* is often very crowded during holidays and weekends. The 22 ha of undulating grounds is beautifully laid out with shrubs, flowering trees and plants, orchids, lakes and fountains. There are more than 3000 animals from all around the world, including big cats, crocodiles, bears and so on. The aquarium has over 500 species of fish. The zoo is particularly noted for its collection of birds – there is a large walk-in aviary for Sri Lankan species. Sea-lions perform at 1600 and a troupe of trained elephants, around 1630. By Asian standards, the animals are well housed, though some, such as the big cats, have insufficient space. You can reach the zoo on bus Nos 100 or 155 to Dehiwala Junction and walk the last kilometre or take bus No 118. There are also trains to Dehiwala Station but it is easier to come by three-wheeler.

MOVING ON
Mount Lavinia

Just 12 km south of Fort, Mount Lavinia is a popular base for visitors wishing to explore Colombo by day then escape the noise and congestion of the city by night. The area is described in Dream Trip 3, see page 185.

COLOMBO LISTINGS

WHERE TO STAY

$$$$ Casa Colombo, 231 Galle Rd, Col 4, T452 0130, www.casacolombo.com. 12 spacious suites in a boutique hotel, ranging in size and layout, and each individually decorated. Stylish mix of old and new, 200-year-old mansion with colonial touches, designer furniture, flatscreen TVs, free Wi-Fi, etc. Attentive service, pool, spa, dining areas and bar.

$$$$-$$$ Cinnamon Lakeside, 115 Sir CA Gardiner Mawatha, Col 2, T249 1000, www.cinnamonhotels.com. Slightly north of Galle Face in Slave Island, 340 rooms and suites, good restaurants, beautiful pool, nightclub.

$$$$-$$$ Colombo Hilton, 2 Sir Chittampalam A Gardiner Mawatha, Col 2, T249 2492, www.hilton.com. 387 rooms, best views in the city, all facilities including 6 restaurants, 4 bars, pool, Wi-Fi, leisure centre. There is another Hilton hotel, the **Colombo Residence**, 200 Union Pl, T534 4644, www.hilton.com, which is smaller and popular with families.

$$$$-$$$ Galle Face Hotel, 2 Galle Rd, Col 3, T558 5858, www.gallefacehotel.com. Originally built in 1864 and re-designed by Geoffrey Bawa (see box, page 109), probably the most atmospheric place to stay in Colombo. Room price varies and there are 2 wings, Regency and Classic. Avoid rooms overlooking Galle Rd, as these can be very noisy. Carefully maintained colonial atmosphere, with beautiful furniture. Friendly staff, 'superb' service,

30-m saltwater pool overlooking the Indian Ocean; the **Verandah** bar is the best in Colombo for a sunset drink. Very competent travel desk. At the time of writing, the Classic wing was closed for renovations and was not set to reopen for some time.

$$$$-$$$ Tintagel, 65 Rosemead Pl, Col 7, T460 2122, www.tintagelcolombo.com. This 10-room boutique hotel from the owners of the **Paradise Road** franchise, used to be the home of the Bandaranaike family, a political dynasty in Sri Lanka. SWRD Bandaranaike was shot here in 1959. The suites are as stylishly decorated as one would expect, and each are individual. There is a restaurant and bar, pool and free 3-wheeler to other Paradise Rd properties. Staff are excellent.

$$ Renuka and **Renuka City**, 328 Galle Rd, T257 3598, www.renukahotel.com. Twin hotels with 81 comfortable a/c rooms aimed mainly at business travellers, with TV, fridge and Wi-Fi. Small pool, basement **Palmyrah** restaurant recommended for Sri Lankan curries (see Restaurants, below). Good location.

$ YWCA, 7 Rotunda Garden, T232 8589, natywca@sltnet.lk. The best are the large double rooms with balcony, but cheaper accommodation with shared bathroom also available (Rs 550). Clean, very central, breakfast included in the price. Has an old-fashioned, institutional feel but good value. Couples accepted but not single men.

RESTAURANTS

$$$ Chesa Swiss, 3 Deal Pl, off RA de Mel Mawatha, Col 3, T257 3433. Open 1900-2300, closed *poya* days. Excellent Swiss food, though at a price.

$$$ Il Ponte, **Ginza Hohsen** and **Curry Leaf** restaurants, **Colombo Hilton**, see Where to stay, above. For 1st-class Italian, Japanese and Sri Lankan cuisine.

$ Crescat Food Court, (next to **Cinnamon Grand**). Not the most authentic surroundings (self-service in Western-style shopping mall basement) but a good way to sample a wide range of Asian cuisines. Wi-Fi available.

$$$ Gallery Café, 2 Alfred House Rd, Col 3, T258 2162, gallerycafe@paradiseroadsl.com.

Open 1000-2400. Once the office of famed Sri Lankan architect Geoffrey Bawa, see box, page 109 (his old work table is still there), exclusive setting with unbeatable ambience, minimalist chic decor, good fusion food, fabulous desserts and cakes, excellent wine list. Book in advance.

$$$-$$ The Colombo Fort Cafe, Ministry of Crab and **Heladiv Tea Club**, Dutch Hospital, Bank of Ceylon Mawatha. A couple of options in this precinct of shops and eateries. Come for a refreshing ice tea and cake and use the free Wi-Fi at the **Heladiv** or if staying in Fort come down here for dinner or an evening drink.

$$$-$$ Cricket Club Café, 34 Queen's Rd (near British Council), Col 3, T150 1384. Open 1100-2300. International range of dishes, many named after famous cricketers (such as Murali's Mulligatawny or Gatting's Garlic Prawns), in a cricket-lover's heaven, though shows other sports on TV too. Local and touring teams usually visit. Good bar popular with expats.

$$$-$$ Palmyrah, Hotel Renuka, see Where to stay, above. Open 0700-1430, 1900-2200. Widely praised for its Sri Lankan food and Jaffna specialties, it also serves Western and South Indian dishes. Attentive service, popular, try the hoppers. Recommended.

$$ 7 Degrees North, Cinnamon Lakeside, see Where to stay, above. Tapas and cocktails overlooking the lake, or Mediterranean cuisine by the pool. Live music at weekends, good atmosphere.

Cafés

Barefoot Garden Café, 706 Galle Rd, Col 3, T255 3075. Daily 1000-1900. Wonderfully chic terrace café serving light meals, sandwiches and cakes in frangipani gardens next to shop and art gallery.

Coco Veranda, 32 Ward Pl, Col 7. 0800-2330. An attractive café with free Wi-Fi serving good coffee and tea, as well as sandwiches, burgers and the like.

Perera & Sons, 17 Galle Rd, Col 3, T232 3295. Cakes, snacks, breads, mainly takeaway but some tables. Other branches around the city, 24 Deal Pl, Col 3; 2 Dharmapala Mawatha; off Pieris Maw, Col 2, and on Havelock Rd.

SHOPPING

Barefoot, 704 Galle Rd, Col 3, T258 9305, www.barefootceylon.com. Very popular shop with tourists and wealthy locals. Started by Barbara Sansoni, the artist, it's the place to pick up excellent handloom fabrics, home furnishings, batiks and clothes. Also sells toys and books.

Crescat, Galle Rd, Col 3 (next to Cinnamon Grand). A small but upmarket shopping mall, brighter than the others. Internet café, **Dilmah Tea**, **Mlesna**, and branch of **Vijitha Yapa** bookshop. Foodcourt and supermarket in the basement.

Mlesna Tea Centre, 44 Ward Pl, Col 7, T269 6348, www.mlesnateas.com. Excellent range of teas, pots, etc. Several branches over town at **Hilton**, **Crescat**, **Liberty Plaza**, **Majestic City** and at the airport.

Odel, 5 Alexandra Pl, Lipton Circus, Col 7, T268 2712. A classy department store that sells clothes, shoes, soaps, cosmetics, jewellery, music and homewares, and has cafés, including **Delifrance** and a sushi bar.

Paradise Road, 213 Dharmapala Mawatha, Col 7, also Gallery Shop at **Gallery Café** (1000-2230). Kitchen accessories, candles, beautiful leather diaries, address books, etc, well-made sarongs. For larger pieces, including furniture visit **Paradise Road Design Ware House**, 61/3 Ward Pl, Col 7, T269 1056.

COLOMBO TO KANDY

Taking 11 years to complete, the trunk road from Colombo to Kandy was the first modern road to be opened in Sri Lanka in 1932, when the first mail service ran between the two cities. Tour groups invariably stop to visit the baby elephants at Pinnawela, but there are some lesser known sights along this busy route that are well worth a digression. Barely free of Colombo's suburbs, the road passes near the impressive temple at Kelaniya, the island's most popular, just 13 km from Colombo (see page 108). Although the road route is quicker, the train often gives better views, the last hour rattling through stunning scenery.

SAPUGASKANDA

Situated on a low hill, there are beautiful views from the terrace of the small stupa here, but the temple is famous for its murals, which show the arrival of the Burmese saint Jagara Hamuduruvo in Sri Lanka. It's 3 km along a side road off the main A1.

HENERATGODA BOTANICAL GARDENS

ⓘ *0730-1700. Rs 600, students Rs 400.*

These beautiful gardens are particularly famous as the nursery of Asia's first rubber trees introduced from the Amazon Basin more than a century ago. Several of the early imports are now magnificent specimens. No 6, the first tree planted, is over 100 years old, but the most famous is No 2 because of its remarkable yield. The trees include *Hevea brasiliensis*, *Uncaria gambier*, rubber producing lianas (*Landolphia*), and the drug *ipecacuanha*. A female of the Coco de Mer was imported from the Seychelles and bore fruit in 1915. Turn off just before Yakkala.

BANDARANAIKE FAMILY HOME AND MEMORIAL

The road passes through Yakkala, and then by the former estate of Sir Solomon Dias Bandaranaike, aide de camp to the British governor at the time of the First World War. His son, Solomon Western Ridgway Dias Bandaranaike, became prime minister of independent Ceylon in 1956 but was assassinated in 1959. His widow, Sirimavo Bandaranaike, succeeded him becoming the world's first female prime minister. They are buried together at the memorial here. Their daughter, Chandrika Kumaratunga, was elected president in 1994. The family home, where visitors such as King George V and Jawaharlal Nehru stayed, is nearby, though it is private. The Bandaranaike memorial is by the side of the road at Nittambuwa, 39 km from Colombo. A broad walkway, about 10 m wide and 100 m long and flanked by frangipanis, leads to a raised plinth with five stone pillars behind it, the whole surrounded by a coconut grove. On the other side of the road, on a small hill, is a monument to Bandaranaike Senior.

PASYALA

The area around Pasyala is noted for its *plumbago* (graphite) mines, betel nuts and above all, cashews. This is western edge of the Central Highlands massif. Passing through **Cadjugama** ('village of cashew nuts'), you will see women in brightly coloured traditional dress selling cashew nuts from stalls lining the road. Sadly, the cashews offered here are not always of the highest quality – they are often 'seconds'. Inspect and taste before you buy.

WARAKAPOLA AND AMBEPUSSA

This is a convenient and popular stop en route to Colombo. The busy little village of **Warakapola** provides an outlet for locally made cane baskets and mats in its bazaar. It is also a popular halt for those with a sweet tooth searching for sesame seed *thalagulis* which are freshly made at **Jinadisa's** shop, among others.

Ambepussa's rest house is claimed to be Sri Lanka's oldest, built in 1822, and is a popular lunch stop. About 1.5 km behind the rest house, near the Devagiri Vihara, is a series of caves which at one time formed a hermitage.

DEDIGAMA

Near Ambepussa, a turn off takes you to the two 12th-century *dagobas* at Dedigama, built by King Parakramabahu I, who was born here. One has 10 relic chambers, including one a lower level. A gem-studded golden reliquary has also been found here. The nearby **museum** ① *Wed-Mon*, is worth visiting.

KEGALLA TO KANDY

Kegalla is a long straggling town in a picturesque setting. Most visitors take a detour here towards Rambukkana for the Pinnawela Elephant Orphanage (see below). The route to Kegalla is very beautiful and the vegetation stunningly rich. About 1 km before Mawanella, a town surrounded by spice plantations, a sign points to the place where **Saradial** ('the local Robin Hood') lived, where there is a small monument. You then pass through **Molagoda**, a village devoted to pottery with both sides of the road lined with shops displaying a wide range of attractive pots. At the top of the Balana Pass is a precipice called **Sensation Point**.

At the Km 107 mark is an outdoor museum displaying the original equipment used to lay the Colombo–Kandy road, such as steamrollers and bitumen boilers. Next to the museum is a replica of the 300-year-old Bogoda Bridge (see page 129).

The railway goes through two tunnels to Peradeniya, where the road crosses the Mahaweli Ganga, Sri Lanka's longest river, and into the city.

PINNAWELA

Pinnawela, 6 km off the main Kandy–Colombo road, is the home of one of the most popular stops on the tourist circuit, the famous elephant orphanage. A number of spice gardens line the road. While most visitors are en route between Kandy and Colombo, travellers who choose to spend a night are delighted by the peace and beauty of this place with its river and jungle orphanage. The village becomes an oasis of natural quietness as calm descends when the tourist groups leave.

PINNAWELA ELEPHANT ORPHANAGE

① *T226 6116, www.elephantorphanage.lk. 0830-1800. Rs 2000, children Rs 1000. Video camera Rs 500 (professional Rs 1500). There is a ticketing area just down from the car park. Retain your ticket as may be checked again on the way to the elephant bath.*

The government-run elephant orphanage is a must for most visitors, although some may want to wait and see elephants in the wild. It was set up in 1975 to rescue four orphaned baby elephants when they could no longer be looked after at Dehiwala Zoo. Now there are almost 90, the largest group of captive elephants in the world. The animals, some only a few weeks old, very hairy and barely 1 m high, are kept in parkland where they are nursed by adult elephants. There has been a successful captive breeding project, which at the time of visiting had produced 22 second generation births.

The elephants, which roam freely in parkland, are 'herded' just before being taken to the feeding sheds, when they are very photogenic. They may occasionally 'charge', so to avoid getting hurt stand well back. The feeding, usually around 0915, 1315 and 1700, is done in a couple of large sheds. Each baby elephant is shackled and then bottle-fed with copious amounts of milk (if visitors pay an additional Rs 250 they can hold the bottle). Adults, which need around 250 kg of food each day, are fed mainly on palm leaves. Two special farms run by the National Zoological Gardens meet part of their needs. After feeding they are driven across the road, down to the river. You can usually watch them bathing there for an hour or so at 1000 and 1400, and sometimes being trained to work. For a good view of the bathing, go down early, buy a drink and secure a table at the **Elephant Park Hotel** terrace.

Although the park has capacity for 100 elephants, the authorities are realizing that the programme cannot last forever in its current format. Since the elephants become so used to humans, it is impossible for them to be released back into the wild. Previous efforts have resulted in them returning to villages to find food. Another problem has been the lack of facilities and the proximity of humans to elephants to tourists, some of whom fail to realise that the elephants are still, at least in part, wild. This has led to a couple of incidents.

There is scope for up to 10 **foreign volunteers** to work at the orphanage, on programmes lasting from two weeks to three months. If you're handy with a shovel, contact **i-to-i** ① *www.i-to-i.com*, or the **National Zoological Gardens** ① *T011-276 1554, zoosl@slt.lk*, for further information.

MILLENNIUM ELEPHANT FOUNDATION

① *Hiriwadunna, Randeniya, T226 5377, www.millenniumelephantfoundation.com, 0800-1700, Rs 600.*

This registered charity, formerly Maximus Elephant Foundation, a member of WSPA, cares for elderly and disabled elephants. There are currently eight elephants living here, aged 21-65, but numbers fluctuate. Pooja is the youngest elephant and was born here in 1984, the others are retired working animals. The scheme also runs a mobile veterinary unit, established in 2000, which provides healthcare across the country for domesticated and wild elephants. You can help bathe and feed the elephants and also go on rides around the grounds. As at the elephant orphanage, foreign volunteers can help with the project, and there is also an 'adopt an elephant' scheme: for US$35 (under 16s US$25) you can adopt an elephant for a year. Apply direct for voluntary work placements for up to three months. Unfortunately, concerns have been raised recently about the conditions the elephants are kept in and visitors have reported being hassled for tips by the mahouts.

MOVING ON
To Kandy

Once you arrive in Kandy (see Dream Trip 1, page 81) there is plenty to see and do. It's recommended that you spend three nights here, exploring the city and surrounding area, before continuing the route south to the Central Highlands.

CENTRAL HIGHLANDS

Steep mountain passes snake up through the brooding highland landscape south of Kandy, reaching their pinnacle in the Peak Wilderness Sanctuary, where the plateau of the Horton Plains represents the island's last stretch of high montane forest. It was not until the 19th century, and the coming of the British, that wild and impenetrable rainforest gave way to the familiar, intensively cultivated tea plantations of today. The British legacy has lingered longer here, most notably in the anachronistic hill station of Nuwara Eliya, nicknamed 'Little England'. Equally distinctive is the Indian Tamil culture, which dates back to the same era when migrant plantation workers were brought in from southern India. But the area's greatest appeal lies in the natural beauty of its scenery, carved by mountain streams and powerful waterfalls, and its cool, crisp air.

→ KANDY TO NUWARA ELIYA

By either rail or road, the journey up into the Central Highlands offers some spectacular views, climbing through tea estates and passing nearby some magnificent waterfalls. From Kandy, the direct route to Nuwara Eliya is along the A5. Start by crossing the Mahaweli Ganga, passing through Peradeniya and then follow the river valley to the pleasant town of Gampola, a mediaeval Sinhalese capital. The Niyamgampaya *vihara* which has some interesting stone carvings, is built on the original 14th-century temple which was mostly built of brick and wood and largely disappeared.

From Gampola a road leads off towards the Ginigathena Pass for the alternative Adam's Peak route through the tea estates of the Hatton-Dickoya region (see page 139), but most people continue on the more direct A5. Shortly after Gampola the road crosses the river and starts the long climb of almost 1000 m up through some of the highest tea gardens in the world to Nuwara Eliya.

Pussellawa is a busy shopping centre and has a rest house where you can stop for a meal or a drink. The tea gardens begin just below Pussellawa. The craggy hill **Monaragala** appears to the south. Legends tell that this is where King Dutthagamenu hid in a rock while escaping from his father, who had imprisoned him.

Some 5 km later the road passes the Helbodda Oya River. By **Ramboda**, you have climbed to 1000 m. There is a fine 100-m waterfall with a twin stream on the Puna Ela, a tributary of the Mahaweli River, just off the road which can be seen from the bazaar. It may be possible to visit the **Rang Buddha Tea Estate**.

After 54 km from Kandy the road climbs through a series of hairpins to the **Weddamulla Estate**, with great views to the west over Kothmale Reservoir. The area is covered with pine trees and ferns.

The 415-ha **Labookellie Estate** ① *T052-223 5146, free*, one of the island's largest, follows the twisty road for miles along the hillside. Teams of women pluck the tea on fairly steep slopes, picking in all weathers – they use plastic sacks as raincoats. The women labourers are all Tamils, descendants of the labourers who migrated from Tamil Nadu before independence. They are keen to pose for photographs, and as they earn very little, tipping is customary. The tea factory, an enormous corrugated iron building, welcomes visitors to drop in to the delightful tea centre and sample a free cup of tea, indulge in a piece of chocolate cake, and perhaps to buy a packet or two of tea though there is no pressure to do so. The tour is quite informative – all stages of the process from picking, drying, oxidation and grading are shown if you go in the morning. There are free guided tours of the factory, available in English, German, French and Italian, which run every 20 minutes.

From the Labookellie Estate it is a short climb through more tea gardens to the narrow pass above Nuwara Eliya, and the road then drops down into the sheltered hollow in the hills now occupied by the town.

→NUWARA ELIYA

Nuwara Eliya (pronounced Noo-ray-lee-ya) is one of those curiosities of history – a former British hill station. Vestiges of colonial rule are found everywhere, from the fine golf course threading through town to the creaking grand hotels, complete with overboiled

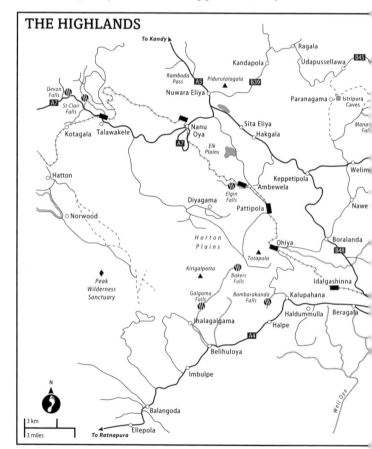

THE HIGHLANDS

vegetables and leaky roofs. Today, Sri Lanka's highest (and coolest) town remains a popular escape from the plains at long weekends and especially during the April 'season'. Visitors respond to Nuwara Eliya's fading appeal in different ways, some delighted by the tongue-in-cheek revelry in its colonial past; others are turned off by the town's lack of civic pride, depressed by its English climate (nights can get very cold), or simply confused by its archaism. For most though Nuwara Eliya represents nostalgic fun. This is also excellent walking country and a useful base for visiting Horton Plains.

ARRIVING IN NUWARA ELIYA

Getting there Those with their own transport should note that the road from Kandy is a series of hairpin bends, though the tea plantation scenery is breathtaking. There are regular buses between Kandy and Nuwara Eliya and the journey takes about three hours. Buses arrive in the centre of town.

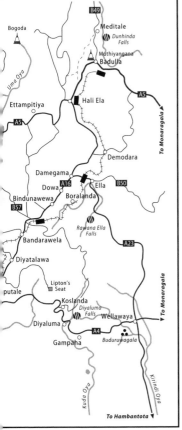

The train from Kandy is a scenic though time-consuming alternative to the bus. Booking is essential for the first class carriages, observation car or a seat in one of the 'luxury' coaches (which have air conditioning), especially during busy periods. During the pilgrimage season it is often full as far as Hatton. Nuwara Eliya's nearest train station is 6 km away at Nanu Oya, a short bus or taxi ride away (avoid the touts who will offer free transport provided you go to a hotel of their choice – buses are always available and most hotels will arrange for taxis to collect you if contacted in advance). Ask to be dropped near the Town Hall if you are planning to stay in the southern part of town where most of the hotels are clustered up the hillside opposite the racecourse.

Moving on There are about five buses a day between Nuwara Eliya and **Ella** (2½ hours, see page 128) and regular services to Badulla. The journey is slightly quicker if you have your own transport (one hour). It's also possible to take a train from Nuwara Eliya's closest station, Nanu Oya, to Ella (2½ hours). There are a couple of trains a day stopping at Haputale and Badulla. Again, if you want to travel first class, consider buying your ticket in advance. For Nuwara Eliya to **Adam's Peak**, see page 139.

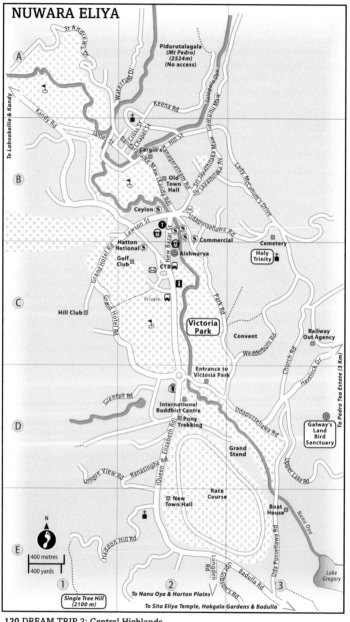

NUWARA ELIYA

Pidurutalagala
(Mt Pedro)
(2524m)
(No access)

To Labookellie & Kandy

St Andrew's Dr

Waterfield Dr

Kandy Rd

James St

Keena Rd

Badulla Chapel St

Hill St

Badulla Ke Maw (Kandy Rd)

Cargill's

Old Town Hall

Ceylon $

Lawson St

Hatton National $

New Bazaar St

Pol

Udapussellawa Rd

Commercial $

@ Aishwarya

Holy Trinity

Cemetery

Golf Club

Grand Hotel Rd

CTB

Private

i

Hill Club

Victoria Park

Convent

Railway Out Agency

Wedderburn Rd

Church Rd

Havelock Dr

To Pedro Tea Estate (3 Km)

Entrance to Victoria Park

Glenfall Rd

International Buddhist Centre

Pony Trekking

Udapussellawa Rd

Galway's Land Bird Sanctuary

To Galway's

Grand Stand

Unique View Rd

Ranasinghe Rd

(Queen Elizabeth Rd)

Upper Lake Rd

New Town Hall

Race Course

Boat House

Nanu Oya

Haddon Hill Rd

Longden Rd

Gibson's Rd

Badulla Rd

Uva Pussellawa Rd

Lake Gregory

N

400 metres

400 yards

Single Tree Hill
(2100 m)

To Nanu Oya & Horton Plains

To Sita Eliya Temple, Hakgala Gardens & Badulla

ON THE ROAD
A superior cup

Many concur that Sri Lankan tea, with its fine, rich flavour and bright, golden colour, is the best in the world. After textiles, tea remains Sri Lanka's second biggest export, and you will notice the distinctive cropped bushes all across the hill country. Although introduced by the British, the tea industry is a source of immense national pride, and recent years have seen some ingenious methods of capitalizing on the country's heritage. Near Nuwara Eliya, an old factory has been converted into a magnificent hotel, retaining its original features, while the world's first tea museum is open up near Kandy. A visit to a working tea factory is also recommended.

Tea famously originated in China (though one legend suggests it was introduced by an Indian missionary) but it was not until 1833 that the Chinese monopoly on exporting tea was abolished, and the East India Company began to grow tea in Assam in India. In Sri Lanka, the first tea bushes were planted in 1849 by James Taylor on a cleared hill slope just southeast of Kandy. It was an attempt at experimenting with a crop to replace the unfortunate diseased coffee. The experiment paid off and Sri Lanka today is the world's third biggest producer of tea, and the largest exporter, with a 20% share of global demand. The bushes now grow from sea level to the highest slopes, though the lush 'low-grown' variety lacks the flavour, colour and aroma which characterize bushes grown above 1000 m. The slow-growing bushes at greater heights produce the best flavour and aroma when picked carefully by hand – just two leaves and bud.

The old 'orthodox' method of tea processing produces the aromatic lighter coloured liquor of the Golden Flowery Orange Pekoe in its most superior grade. The fresh leaves are dried by fans on 'withering troughs' to reduce the moisture content and then rolled and pressed to express the juices which coat the leaves. These are then left to ferment in a controlled humid environment in order to produce the desired aroma. Finally the leaves are dried by passing them through a heated drying chamber and then graded – the unbroken being the best quality, down to the 'fannings' and 'dust'.

The more common 'crushing, tearing, curling' (CTC) method produces tea which gives a much darker liquor. It uses machinery which was invented in Assam in 1930. The process allows the withered leaves to be given a short, light roll before engraved metal rollers distort the leaves in a fraction of a second. The whole process can take as little as 18 hours. Despite its name and heritage, the Ceylon tea industry (as it is still called) has lost some of its dominance in the world market, cheaper producers having wrestled away traditional export markets. Britain, for example, which once absorbed 65% of total production, now only represents 3%, importing much of its lower grade tea from East Africa. Today Russia and the Middle East are the industry's biggest customers. In recent years however, privatization and advances in production techniques have improved yields, and producers have responded to trends in the market, beginning to embrace the vogue for green, organic and flavoured teas.

Getting around The town is fairly compact, so it is easy to get around on foot but carry a torch at night to avoid holes in the pavement leading to the sewers.

Best time to visit The town really comes alive during the April 'season' (see box, page 122) though accommodation is very expensive and hard to find at this time. It

ON THE ROAD
Blooms, bets and beauty pageants

Throughout April, and particularly over Sinhalese and Tamil New Year, Nuwara Eliya is invaded by the Colombo set. A banner across the road proudly announces "Nuwara at 6128 ft: Welcome to the salubrious climate of Nuwara Eliya: cultured drivers are welcomed with affection"!

For several weeks, the normally sedate town throngs with visitors. Many come for a day at the one of the five races, beloved by all betting mad Sri Lankans, which culminate in the nine-furlong Governor's Cup. Motor racing also draws the crowds. Over 100 Formula Three cars hare around the hills at the Mahagastota Hill Climb, while the Fox Hill supercross at the nearby Diyatalawa circuit can be very exciting. Back in town, there are dances and beauty pageants, all culminating in the judging of the all-important flower show at the end of the month.

The town of course gets packed. Prices become inflated (tripled) and it is virtually impossible to find accommodation. Stallholders, mostly selling food and drink, pay vast amounts of money to rent a pitch alongside the main road by Victoria Park. Most hotels run all night discos (the best is said to be at the Grand Hotel) and the crowds roam the streets for much of the night.

is often cold at night, especially during January and March, when there may be frosts, though these are also the driest months.

Tourist information Tourist information is available at www.nuwaraeliya.org.

BACKGROUND

In 1846, when Samuel Baker first visited the semi-enclosed valley surrounded by hills on the west and overlooked by Pidurutalagala, the island's highest peak, he singled it out as an ideal spot for a hill country retreat. Today, with its television aerials, the highest on the island, and modern hotels, golf course and country walks, his rural idyll has been brought into the modern world.

'The City of Light' was a favourite hill station of the British and it still retains some distinctive features. The main street is the usual concrete jungle of small shops with the pink post office being an obvious exception. One of the distinctive features of Baker's plans was the introduction of European vegetables and fruit. Flowers are extensively cultivated for export to Colombo and abroad. The road out of Nuwara Eliya towards Hakgala passes through intensively cultivated fields of vegetables and a short walk up any of the surrounding hillsides shows how far intensive cultivation methods have transformed Nuwara Eliya into one of Sri Lanka's most productive agricultural areas.

The key to Nuwara Eliya's prosperity lay in the railway connection from Colombo to the hills. The line was extended from Talawakele to Nanu Oya in 1885, and a very steep narrow gauge line right into Nuwara Eliya was opened in 1910, but subsequently closed to passenger traffic in 1940 as buses began to provide effective competition.

Without the pretensions or political significance of the Raj hill stations in India, Nuwara Eliya nonetheless was an active centre of an English-style social life, with country sports including hunting, polo, cricket and tennis. It has retained all the paraphernalia of a British hill station, with its colonial houses, parks, an 18-hole golf course and trout streams (there are brown trout in the lake for anglers). The real clue to its past perhaps lies in its extensive private gardens where dahlias, snap-dragons, petunias and roses grow amongst well-kept lawns.

PLACES IN NUWARA ELIYA

There are attractive walks round the small town, which has lawns, parks, an Anglican church and the nostalgic **Hill Club**. To the south of town are the racecourse and Lake Gregory (about 1 km from the town centre), for which boats which can be hired and where there are lakeside paths.

Nuwara Eliya is popular birdwatching country, and there are two excellent areas close to town. **Galway's Land Bird Sanctuary** ① *0600-1730, Rs 100*, covers 60 ha to the north of Lake Gregory, while in **Victoria Park** ① *centre of town, 0700-1830, Rs 60, children Rs 30*, 38 species have been identified. The park is pleasant, well kept and provides a welcome escape from the congested New Bazaar. Take care when walking along the outside of the park where the metal fence is in poor repair and has some sharp, rusty spikes.

Pidurutalagala (Mount Pedro), the island's highest peak at 2524 m, has recently reopened to the public and offers great views. There's a car park and refreshment kiosk, but a security pass is required to travel the last 100 m or so to the top. A popular walk around Nuwara Eliya is up to **Single Tree Hill**, at 2100 m, and a path to it winds up from Haddon Hill Road, beyond **Haddon Hill Lodge** (southwest of town), towards the transmission tower, through cultivated terraces and woods. The path then follows the ridge towards the north, through Shantipura, a small village and the island's highest settlement, eventually returning close to the golf course. This walk gives excellent views across Nuwara Eliya and beyond and takes three to four hours.

Pedro Tea Estate ① *Boralanda, T222 2016*, 3 km away, still uses some original machinery and is less commercialized than other estates. There are some very pleasant walks through the plantations here, especially down to the tank and to Warmura Ella (ask at the Tea Centre). The estate can be visited on a Boralanda bus or it is a taxi ride away. Alternatively, for those feeling active it is a very attractive walk. The **Tea Factory**, at Kandapola, which, as well as having been innovatively converted into an award-winning hotel (see page 127), still retains a small working unit, is well worth a visit. The original oil driven engine, now powered by electricity, is still in place and switched on occasionally. It is a 30-minute taxi ride away and is a good place for lunch. **Labookellie Tea Estate** is only 15 km away (see page 117).

AROUND NUWARA ELIYA

On the route to Hakgala Gardens you pass **Sita Eliya Temple**, a temple to Rama's wife which is thought to mark the spot where she was kept a prisoner by King Ravana. There are magnificent views.

Hakgala Botanical Gardens ① *www.botanicgardens.gov.lk/hakgala, 0800-1700, Rs 1100, students/children Rs 500*, is 10 km from Nuwara Eliya. Established in 1861, it is located within a Strict Natural Reserve, and was once a Cinchona plantation. This delightful garden is now famous for its roses. The name Hakgala or 'Jaw Rock' comes from the story in the epic *Ramayana* in which the Monkey god takes back a part of the mountainside in his jaw when asked by Rama to seek out a special herb. There are monkeys here which are quite used to visitors. The different sections covering the hillside include a plant house, Japanese garden, wild orchid collection, old tea trails, arboretum, fruit garden, rock garden and oaks. Buses bound for Welimada or Bandarawela pass the entrance.

Horton Plains (see below) can be visited on a day trip if you have a car, but involve an early start (breakfast at 0600) as the plains have a reputation for bad weather after midday.

Randenigala Reservoir is good for birdwatching and in the early morning, elephants. It can easily be visited as a day trip, but is also a good camping spot.

→ HORTON PLAINS NATIONAL PARK

The island's highest and most isolated plateau is contiguous with the Peak Wilderness Sanctuary. Bleak and windswept, the landscape is distinctive and unlike any other on the island. It has been compared to both the Scottish Highlands and the savannah of Africa. Most people come on a day trip to see the spectacular views from the sheer 700-m drop at World's End though there is more to see within the sanctuary. In recent years, park fees have spiralled and budget travellers are increasingly choosing to forego a visit.

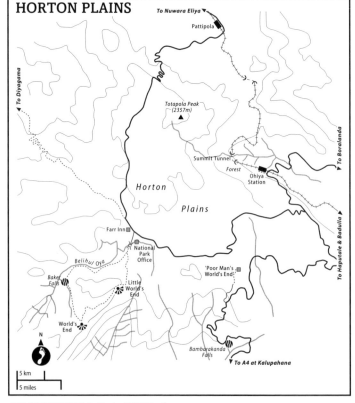

HORTON PLAINS

To Nuwara Eliya ▼
Pattipola

To Diyagama ◀

Totapola Peak
(2357m) ▲

To Boralanda ▶

Summit Tunnel
Forest
Ohiya Station

Horton

Plains

To Haputale & Badulla ▲

Farr Inn
National Park Office

Belihul Oya

'Poor Man's World's End'

Baker Falls
Little World's End

World's End

Bambarakanda Falls
To A4 at Kalupahana ▼

N

5 km
5 miles

ARRIVING IN HORTON PLAINS NATIONAL PARK

Getting there Horton Plains is accessible by car from Nuwara Eliya and the journey takes around 1½ to two hours. Ohiya, 11 km away, is the nearest train station from which you can take a taxi or walk to the park entrance. By train, Haputale (see page 132) is the closest base for a day trip though World's End will probably have clouded over by the time you arrive. If you are prepared to hire transport, Nuwara Eliya may be the most convenient option for day trips. Many guesthouses and hotels organize tours. Trekkers can come from Talawakale on the Agrapatana–Diyagama track or from Belihuloya via Nagarak, though this requires serious preparation.

Getting around Horton Plains is unique amongst Sri Lanka's national parks in that independent walking is permitted. Keep to the footpaths, especially if misty. A number of people go missing each year.

Best time to visit The best months to visit are April and August. The winter months tend to be the driest, with the best visibility, though can be very cold. The weather can be foul at any time and it gets cold at night so come prepared. For World's End it is essential to arrive by 0930-1000, after which the area usually clouds over for the day. Avoid visiting at weekends and public holidays when it can be very noisy and busy.

Tourist information Entry fees are US$30, children US$15. There is a **visitor information centre** ① *at Farr Inn, 0600-1830*, where information on the park's flora and fauna is displayed and an expensive café.

BACKGROUND

Horton Plains' conservation importance lies in its role as the catchment area of most of the island's major rivers. Covering 3160 ha, the area was declared a national park in 1988, though had received some protection since 1873 when logging above 1500 m was prohibited. The plains are named after former British governor Sir Robert Horton.

There is a mixture of temperate montane forest and wet patana grassland. The prominent canopy tree is the keena, its white flowers contrasting with the striking red rhododendrons lower down, which makes them in some ways reminiscent of a Scottish moor. In other ways, the gently undulating grassland has an almost savannah-like feel with stunted forest on the hill tops. There is widespread concern about the condition of the forest which appears to be slowly dying. Blame seems to be attached to the acidification of rain.

The bleak and windswept area harbours many wild animals, including a few leopards though no longer any elephants. You may see sambar (sambhur), especially at dawn and dusk close to the entrance, and possibly toque macaques, purple-faced leaf monkeys and horned lizards. Wildlife has suffered at the hands of tourism though, with visitors' discarded plastic bags responsible for the death of large numbers of sambar. There is a rich variety of hill birds, and a number of endemics, including the dull blue flycatcher, Sri Lanka white-eye, and yellow-eared bulbul as well as a good range of butterflies. Some are disappointed by how difficult it is to see the wildlife; it is not impossible to visit and spot little more than the invasive crow. However by being attentive and patient an interesting variety of flora and fauna can be observed.

PLACES IN HORTON PLAINS NATIONAL PARK

Most people will take the well-trodden 4.5-km bridle path to **World's End**, returning in a loop via the scenic **Baker Falls**. The walk takes three to four hours and it is essential to visit early in the morning before the mists close in, after which only a wall of cloud is visible.

World's End The 4.5-km walk takes from 40 minutes to 1½ hours depending on how many times you stop to admire the view. You cross a small stream with lots of croaking frogs before passing across the grassland and then descending a few hundred metres through the forest. You first come to Little (or Small) World's End (2.5 km), a mere 260-m cliff overlooking a ravine (more a wide valley) with a tiny village 700 m below. You can look along the sheer cliff face to the big green rock which marks (Big) World's End about 1 km away. The path continues another 2 km up the escarpment to the astonishing (Big) World's End, a spectacular precipice with a 1050-m drop. On a clear day, you can apparently see the coast, but more realistically, it is the blue-green lake of the Samanala Wewa reservoir project. Once at Big World's End, take the small path up the hill. After only a few yards, there is a split in the rock which gives an excellent view of the valley below.

Baker's Falls Return to the main path, and a track drops down to a valley along which a 2-km walk leads to a small forested escarpment. A climb and then a scrambling descent (very slippery for the last few metres so take care) take you to the picturesque Baker's Falls. The water here is deliciously cool and refreshing, though it is said to be unsafe to swim. From Baker's Falls it is an easy 3-km walk back along the river, passing the attractive **Governor's Pool** (again prohibited to swim) on the way.

CENTRAL HIGHLANDS LISTINGS

WHERE TO STAY

Nuwara Eliya

$$$$-$$$ Tea Factory (Aitken Spence), Kandapola, T222 9600, www.heritance hotels.com. Winner of numerous awards, including UNESCO Heritage Award. This superbly inventive conversion of an old British factory retains many of its original features. The 57 comfortable rooms (the best are on the top floor), including 4 suites, are set amidst a 10-ha tea plantation with magnificent views. There are 2 restaurants (eat at the 'TCK6685' restaurant – in a railway carriage), a 9-hole putting green, horse riding, games and a gym. Highly recommended for its setting and originality.
$$$-$$ The Grand, Grand Hotel Rd, T222 2881, www.tangerinehotels.com.

156 rooms in 2 wings – the Golf Wing is larger, carpeted and more comfortable than the Governor Wing – and 2 presidential suites, in a Victorian former governor's residence with considerable colonial character. Facilities include 2 restaurants (1 ballroom-sized, catering for package tour buffets), shops, foreign exchange and a gym. Efficient but can lack the personal touch. Popular with tour groups.
$ The Trevene, 17 Park Rd, T222 2767, thetrevene@yahoo.com. Colonial bungalow, family-run, 10 clean rooms, those at the front are larger and have fireplaces and period furniture. Internet, bike hire, good food, can arrange tours but enquire elsewhere regarding public transport.

RESTAURANTS

Nuwara Eliya

$$$ Hill Club, Grand Hotel Rd, up the path from **The Grand**, T222 2653. Oozing colonial atmosphere and a unique dining experience, especially if you choose to eat in the formal dining room (for which you'll need to have/ borrow a jacket and tie) rather than the casual one. Courteous service. Recommended though some feel the 'tongue-in-cheek fogeyism' has gone a bit too far.

$$ Grand Indian, The Grand, see Where to stay. Excellent Indian restaurant open for lunch and dinner, serving curries, thalis and a wide selection of breads. Recommended.
$$ Milano, 24 New Bazaar St, T222 2763. Halal restaurant, tasty seafood, Chinese and Sri Lankan, good portions, tempting watalappam dessert, sales counter, no alcohol. Several similar restaurants nearby.

WHAT TO DO

Nuwara Eliya

Nuwara Eliya Golf Club, T052-222 2835. Beautiful and superbly maintained par 70 golf course.

ELLA AND AROUND

East of the Central Highland ridge are the picturesque hills of Uva Province. In contrast to the comparatively recently populated highland region, Uva, which stretches across the plains as far south as Kataragama, is sometimes held to be the original home of the Kandyan civilization, whose people would have used the river valleys draining into the Mahaweli Ganga as a natural migration route into the hills. Protected from the Wet Zone rains by the highland massif, it has a sunny, dry climate and a relatively bare landscape. In the hills there are impressive waterfalls and some of the best views on the island.

South of the provincial capital Badulla, whose festival draws Buddhist pilgrims from across the island, the climate of the triangle formed by Ella, Haputale and Welimada is regarded by many Sri Lankans as the most favourable on the island. This is marvellous walking country, where views, particularly at Ella and Haputale, formed by spectacular 'gaps' in its precipitous ridges come without the price tag of Horton Plains. There is a wonderful circular route from Nuwara Eliya which makes for a rewarding day tour, or there are plenty of attractive places to stay if you don't want to rush.

→ ARRIVING IN ELLA

GETTING THERE

From Nuwara Eliya, the A5 goes southeast across Wilson's Plain and then east towards Badulla. At Hali-Ela, the A16 heads south down to Ella. By car the journey takes about an hour; the bus or train take about 2½ hours (including getting from Nuwara Eliya to the station at Nanu Oya).

MOVING ON

The drive from Ella to **Dalhousie** (the most practical base for climbing Adam's Peak, see page 139) should only take a couple of hours or so and passes through some beautiful countryside. If travelling by public transport, take a train from Ella back towards Nanu Oya or a bus back to Nuwara Eliya, and from there travel on to Hatton. At Hatton either jump on a bus to Dalhousie (frequent during pilgrimage season) or arrange a three-wheeler.

→ NUWARA ELIYA TO BADULLA

From Nuwara Eliya, the A5 goes southeast across Wilson's Plains then east to Badulla. This is the market garden area where carrots, bean, brassicas and many other fresh vegetables are grown, much of it for export to the Middle East. Some 10 km past the Hakgala Botanical Gardens (see page 123) is a superb view southeast across the hills of Bandarawela and over the baked plains of the east coastlands. The road passes through **Keppetipola**, where you can pick up information about local attractions, as it drops rapidly through to Welimada on the Uma Oya River.

Istripura Caves, north of Welimada, are a pot-holer's delight. They are reached by a path from Paranagama, which is 10 km along the road north from Welimada. The maze of damp caves holds a large lake.

From Welimada, a right turn on to the B51 leads to Bandarawela (see page 131) past terraced fields of paddy and across occasional streams. At Hali-Ela, the A5 goes to Badulla. This area is already in the rain shadow of the hills to the west, sheltered from the

The area of open scrub around the coastal *lewayas* offers great opportunities for birdwatching with the added bonus of being able to spot the odd elephant and basking crocodile. The salt pans attract vast numbers of migratory shore birds, accommodating tens of thousands at any one time, making it the most important wetlands in Sri Lanka outside the Northern Province.

Much of the park boundary is contiguous with the A2, so you do not necessarily need to go in to appreciate the wildlife. Before the park, the **Malala Lagoon**, reached by following the Malala River from the main road, is a birdwatchers' paradise, where you might also see crocodiles. The **Karagan**, **Maha** and particularly **Bundala** *lewayas* are also excellent for shore-bird enthusiasts.

The **reserve** itself consists of a series of shallow lagoons which are surrounded by low scrub which is really quite dense. Tracks go through the bush and connect each lagoon. The sanctuary skirts the sea and it is possible to see the lighthouse on the Great Basses some 40 km away to the east. Bundala is particularly rewarding for its winter migrants, which arrive chiefly from Eastern Europe. From September to March, you can see abundant stints, sand pipers, plovers, terns, gulls and ducks. The migrants join the resident water birds – pelicans, herons, egrets, cormorants, stilts and storks – contributing to an extraordinarily variety. In the scrub jungle, you may also come across elephants (though often difficult to see), jackals, monkeys, hares (rare and carry a Rs 1000 fine for killing!) and, perhaps, snakes. The beaches attract olive ridley and leatherback turtles which come to nest here.

TISSAMAHARAMA AND AROUND LISTINGS

WHERE TO STAY

Tissamaharama

$$$ The Safari (CHC), Kataragama Rd, T223 7201, www.ceylonhotels.lk. 53 a/c rooms, some with lake views. Excellent location next to Tissa Wewa, with nice pool overlooking the tank. Restaurant and open-air bar.

$$ Priyankara, Kataragama Rd, T223 7206, www.priyankarahotel.com. 26 clean a/c standard and deluxe rooms, all with private balcony overlooking paddy fields. Inviting pool, bar, good restaurant with wide wine selection, pleasant atmosphere, friendly staff.

$ Elephant Camp Guest House, Kataragama Rd, opposite **The Safari**, T072-493 4992, jayathunga.herath@yahoo.com. Family-run guesthouse offering 5 clean a/c and fan rooms with individual outdoor seating areas. Excellent food, small garden, friendly hosts. Recommended.

Yala West (Ruhuna) National Park

$$$$ Cinnamon Wild, Kirinda, T223 9450, www.cinnamonhotels.com. This hotel has the quality you would expect from the **Cinnamon** brand and is found near the park and Kirinda beach. Choose from the 60 jungle chalets or 8 beach chalets (with sea views), all with balconies. There's an observation deck bar, a restaurant serving good food and a pool that will be a welcome relief after a day bouncing around in a jeep.

RESTAURANTS

Tissamaharama

$$ Refresh, Kataragama Rd, Akurugoda, T223 7357. A branch of the excellent Hikkaduwa-based restaurant, offering a wide variety of good food. Portions are large. Very popular with tourists, overpriced and a little self-satisfied.

WHAT TO DO

Leopard Safaris, 45 Ambagahawatta, Colombo Rd, Katunayake, T077-731 4004, www.leopardsafaris.com. Based near Colombo, offers excellent tented safaris in Yala National Park.

SOUTH COAST

The outstandingly beautiful 80-km stretch of road between Tangalla and historic Galle is one of the most scenic routes in the country. Less package oriented than the west coast, the spectacularly scenic bays and beaches of the south coast are a magnet for independently travelling sun and sea worshippers, with fewer crowds and some good-value accommodation. Tangalla, Unawatuna, and, increasingly, Mirissa, are the main beaches here, each with long sweeps of fine sand; while city life focuses on Matara and particularly Galle, whose colonial origins provide some historical interest. While you could pass along the south coast in under four hours, those with the time might easily spend a week here, hopping from village to village and enjoying the laid-back lifestyle.

→TANGALLA

Travelling west from Tissamaharama, the landscape changes over just a few kilometres from comparatively barren to the lush vegetation of the Wet Zone. Tangalla (pronounced Tunn-gaa-le), famous for its turtles, is an attractive fishing port with a palm-fringed bay. The town suffered damage during the tsunami but there are still a few distinctive colonial buildings and a picturesque *ganga*. The surrounding bays have some of the best beaches in the southern coastal belt. Even though there are a growing number of hotels and guesthouses, the beach remains quiet despite good sand and safe swimming (when the sea is not rough). There isn't an enormous amount to see or do here except lie on the beach, but it does make a useful base for visiting the turtles at Rekawa, and the magnificent Mulgirigala Rock Temple.

ARRIVING IN TANGALLA
Getting there Buses from Tissa take about 1½ hours to reach Tangalla and they run nearly every half an hour. If driving, follow the coastal A2 road.

Moving on Ideally, travel the coast road in your own transport so you can stop anywhere that takes your fancy. You can hire a three-wheeler to make the journey if you don't have a car and driver or alternatively, take a Colombo-bound bus (you may have to change at Matara). Some buses have scheduled stops in **Mirissa** (see page 168), but make sure the driver knows where you want to get off.

PLACES IN TANGALLA
There is a **Dutch fort** standing on the slope above the bay. Built of coral with two bastions in opposite corners, it was turned into a jail after a report in 1837 declared it was in sound condition and able to safely hold up to 100 men. The exterior has now been covered over by cement.

There are some lovely **beaches** with visitors having a choice of three main areas to stay. The settlements of **Goyambokka** and **Pallikaduwa** are on a series of bays to the south of town, and have clean and secluded beaches.

In **Tangalla town**, there are a couple of hotels near the harbour including the **rest house**. The cove in front of is fairly sheltered so is consequently quite busy. The quietest location is probably **Marakolliya** to the north. **Medilla Beach** is lined with budget guesthouses, hotels and restaurants. Some luxury accommodation has been built at **Rekawa**, 4 km east.

AROUND TANGALLA

Mulgirigala ⓘ *16 km north of Tangalla, Rs 200, take a bus to Beliatta, then change to a Wiraketiya-bound bus or alternatively jump in a 3-wheeler*, is a monastic site situated on an isolated 210-m-high rock. It was occupied from the second century BC and was again used as a place of Buddhist learning in the 18th century. In 1826, George Turnour discovered the *Tika*, commentaries on the *Mahavansa*, here. This allowed the ancient texts, which chronicle the island's history from the third century BC, to be translated from the original Pali to English and Sinhala.

Although not a citadel, it is in some ways similar to Sigiriya. At the base of the rock there are monks' living quarters. The fairly steep paved path goes up in stages to the main temple and image house at the top. Along the way there are three platforms. The first platform has the twin temple, Padum Rahat Vihara, with two 14-m reclining Buddhas, images of Kataragama and Vishnu among others and a Bodhi tree. The wall paintings

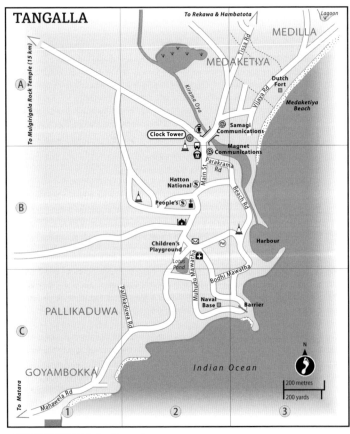

ON THE ROAD
Endangered turtles

Five of the world's seven species of turtle, the green, leatherback, olive ridley, loggerhead and the hawksbill all come ashore to nest on the beaches of Sri Lanka. All are listed by the World Conservation Union (IUCN) as either threatened or endangered. Despite the measures taken by the government, marine turtles are extensively exploited in Sri Lanka for their eggs and meat. In addition, turtle nesting beaches (rookeries) are being disturbed by tourism-related development, and feeding habitats, such as coral reefs, are being destroyed by pollution, especially polythene bags, and unsustainable harvesting. Around 13,000 turtles each year are caught, not always accidentally, in fishing gear while the illegal 'tortoise shell trade' continues to encourage hunting of the highly endangered hawksbill turtle's carapace.

Tourism has proved a double-edged sword in the fight to save the turtles. Since the early 1980s, the government has encouraged the setting up of tourist-friendly turtle hatcheries along the coast, from Induruwa on the west coast to Yala in the southeast, though the Wildlife Department acknowledges that these sometimes do more harm than good. In 1993, the Turtle Conservation Project, www.tcpsrilanka.org, was set up dedicated to pursuing sustainable marine turtle conservation strategies through education, research and community participation. It currently runs tourism projects at Rekawa, Kalpitiya and Kosgoda, and education schemes for school children.

inside illustrate the *Jatakas* while the ceiling has floral decorations. The small second platform has a *vihara* with another Buddha (reclining) with two disciples. The murals show Hindu gods including Vishnu and Kataragama and the nine planets, and elsewhere, scenes from the Buddha's life. The third has four cave temples and a pond with a 12th-century inscription. The Raja Mahavihara with a fine door frame, has several statues and good wall paintings (though they are not as fine as at Dambulla), some partially hidden behind a cabinet which hold old *ola* manuscripts. The little cave temple, **Naga Vihara**, to the far left has a small door with a painted cobra – a cobra shielded the Buddha from rain when meditating, so is considered sacred and worthy of protection. The cave is believed to be a snake pit, so take care. The final climb is steeper. You pass a Bodhi tree believed to be one of 32 saplings of the second Bodhi tree at Anuradhapura, before reaching the summit with a renovated stupa, image house and temple.

Rekawa Beach ① *4 km east of Tangalla, then 3 km along Rekwara Rd from Netolpitiya Junction, www.tcpsrilanka.org, Rs 1000, from 1900, if no turtles show up it's possible to negotiate a refund, 3-wheelers from Tangalla charge around Rs 1500 including waiting, no facilities*, is said to be where up to 75% of Sri Lanka's female green turtles nest. A 'turtle night watch' takes place each night, run by a local community tourism project which employs ex-poachers as tourist guides (see box, above). Visitors are encouraged to observe the females laying their eggs and returning to sea. The turtles could arrive at any time (often after midnight) so be prepared for a long wait. You will first visit a small 'museum' hut, where you can read about the turtles, and then be led on to the beach by a watcher. No flash photography or torches are permitted on the beach, but you might need one to navigate the dirt track.

MAWELLA

Mawella, 6 km west of Tangalla, has remained one of this stretch of coastline's best-kept secrets. It has a 3-km-long, very wide beach, avoids the busy main road, and offers safe swimming. It's easy to miss – turn off the main road at the **Beach Cottage** sign.

KUDAWELLA

The natural blowhole at Kudawella, also known as **Hummanaya** ① *Rs 200*, due to the 'hoo' sound that you hear, is one of the more bizarre attractions in Sri Lanka and worth the detour during the monsoon season. The water spray can rise to 25 m when the waves are strong. Take care when clambering on the rocks as they are wet and slippery in places. It is best to avoid weekends and go during school hours. The blowhole doesn't always 'perform' and is disappointing out of season, so check locally before making the trip. The blowhole is 1.5 km off the main road. If travelling by bus, ask the driver to drop you off at the turn-off. The route to the blowhole is well signposted by the Elephant House.

DIKWELLA AND WEWURUKANNALA

The marvellous bays and beaches continue across to Matara. There are some established resort hotels at the village of Dikwella offering diving and watersports in the bay, while 2 km inland at Wewuurukannala is **Buduraja Mahawehera** ① *Rs 100, a guide will approach*. The statues, tableaux and Buddhist temple are in a complex which has an impressively tacky 50-m-high seated Buddha statue with a 'library' at the back. Some 635 paintings in cartoon strip form depict events from the Buddha's life covering every square centimetre of the interior. The artists are from all over the world but retain the same style throughout. There is also a garish 'Chamber of Horrors' with depictions of the punishments meted out to sinners, including some frighteningly graphic life-size models. One critic describes the site as looking "more like an airport terminal than a temple".

DONDRA

Dondra or Devinuwara (the British renamed the town as they couldn't pronounce it), which means 'City of Gods', is a fishing village famous for its Vishnu temple. The original temple, one of the most revered on the island, was destroyed by the Portuguese in a brutal attack in 1588. **Devi Nuwara Devale** retains, however, an ancient shrine possibly dating to the seventh century AD, which maybe the oldest stone built structure on the island. The modern temple, to the south, has old columns and a finely carved gate. Even today the Buddhist pilgrims continuing the ancient tradition venerate Vishnu of the Hindu trinity.

Some 2 km south of the town, the 50-m-high **lighthouse** (1889) on the southern promontory at Dondra Head marks the southernmost point of Sri Lanka.

WHERAHENA

About 5 km east of Matara, a turning leads to this modern **Buddhist sanctuary** ① *donation and tip for the guide*, which has a 40-m six-storey-high painted Buddha statue. Much older is the *vihara*, whose 600 m of tunnels are lined with some 20,000 friezes, some dating back to Portuguese times. **Perahera** takes place in November/December full moon.

Matara (pronounced locally as Maa-tre) is the south's second biggest town, after Galle. It is also an important transport hub, with the terminus of the railway line and an enormous bus station. Locals will tell you that the city is better than Galle as it has two Dutch forts to Galle's one. Though busy and full of traffic, it does have a rich history, and the old town with its narrow streets and colonial buildings is a pleasant place to explore. In the old marketplace you might still see the local wooden hackeries (oxcarts) that are sometimes used for races. Today, Ruhuna University, 3 km east, attracts students to the town. Matara is also famous for its musical instruments, especially drums, and you can pick up some good batik. Though the beach is attractive the waters are too rough for comfortable bathing much of the year. At **Polhena**, south of the town, is a good coral beach protected by a reef which offers year-round swimming and some excellent snorkelling opportunities. There are also some good-value guesthouses, a pleasant alternative to staying in Matara town.

GETTING THERE
There are hourly bus departures from Tangalla to Matara and the journey takes about an hour.

MOVING ON
There are regular buses from Matara to **Mirissa** (see page 168). It is also possible to get a Colombo-bound train from Matara and get off in **Weligama** (see page 168) or **Galle** (see page 173).

PLACES IN MATARA
An important Dutch possession on the south coast, controlling the trade in cinnamon and elephants, Matara was well fortified. **Star Fort**, which is faced with coral, was built in 1763. It has a moated double-wall and six points, and was designed to house ammunition, provisions and a small garrison. The gateway that shows the VOC arms and date is particularly picturesque. As in Galle, the Dutch government has recently invested money in restoring the fort, formerly a library. Across the **Nilawala Ganga** from the fort, on the left-hand side is a gleaming and impressive **mosque**, a replica of the Meeran Jumma Masjid in Galle.

The **Main Fort**, south of the *ganga*, consists of a single rampart from which guns were fired. Its inadequacy as a defence was revealed during the 'Matara rebellion' of 1762, when a Kandyan army managed to take the town by bombarding it with cannonballs that simply went over the wall. The Dutch retook the town the following year, and built the more successful **Star Fort** ① *generally closed, but the caretaker will show you around*, to defend the town against siege from the river. Near the main bastion is the British clocktower (1883).

North of here, on Beach Road, is **St Mary's Church**. The date on the doorway (1769) refers to the repair work after the 'Matara rebellion'. Close by is St Servatius College, one of Matara's two exclusive public schools, whose most famous son is Sri Lankan batting hero and former cricket captain Sanath Jayasuriya.

Of all the south coast beach resorts to have developed in recent years, Mirissa, with its beautiful wide stretch of golden sand backed by luxuriant vegetation, has received the greatest attention. For the moment the plaudits seems justified, as so far this relaxed little village, has been more sensitively developed than Hikkaduwa or Unawatuna, with the intrusion of guesthouses and restaurants on to the beach less obvious. Mirissa is no longer a secret hideaway though; its popularity increases each year, prompting concerns about over-development. For the moment it remains one of the most idyllic places to relax along this stretch of coast.

The west end of the beach is popular with surfers, whilst further east, in the two beaches beyond the Giragala Village, is a reef where there is some good swimming. Giragala (or 'Parrot') Rock is a popular place to watch the sunset. Near here is a defile, known as Bandaramulla, where there is a Buddhist *vihara*.

Inland, you can explore the river, and there are some pleasant walks (or cycle trips) up into the jungle. In recent years Mirissa has become a centre for whale watching, and between December and April blue whales can be viewed offshore. Nearly every guesthouse and hotel now offers tours, as do three-wheeler drivers; quality varies.

ARRIVING IN MIRISSA
Getting there There are regular buses from Tangalla and the journey takes about 20-30 minutes. You can also take a three-wheeler.

Moving on From Mirissa, regular buses stop at both **Unawatuna** (see page 170, get off on the main road and walk a short distance) and **Galle** (see page 173). It is also possible to get a train to Galle from Weligama or Matara. Travelling between Unawatuna and Galle will take about half and hour.

Weligama is a busy centre for the surrounding fishing villages. Though the town itself is fairly unappealing, it has a picturesque location backed by the attractive Polwatte Ganga. There's a magnificent sheltered and sandy bay safe for diving and snorkelling beyond the usual season, and some good surf to the eastern end of the beach. The western end is the home of themany fishermen operating out of Weligama and there are catamarans everywhere. At the approach to the town there is a 4-m-high **statue of Kushta Raja**, sometimes known as the 'Leper King'. Various legends surround the statue believed by some to be of Bodhisattva Samantabhadra. Look out for the *mal lali* fret-work decorated houses along the road from the centre towards the statue. The area is also known for its handmade lace. Devil Dances are held in nearby villages.

Weligama is most famous however for its tiny **Taprobane Island**, walkable (at low tide) in the lovely bay. Once owned by the Frenchman, Count de Mauny, who built a magnificent house there, it was bought by American author Paul Bowles after his death. After a period of neglect, it was returned in the late 1990s to its former glory, and is now a luxury tourist retreat (see Where to stay).

The road running west from Weligama runs close to the sea offering wonderful views and linking a series of small attractive beaches. The area, with its white sandy beaches, attractive coves and first-class well-priced accommodation, is no longer known to just a few, though there still aren't the crowds that are found at Unawatuna. The coast between Weligama and Talpe was best known for its remarkable fishermen who perched for hours on poles out in the bay. Nowadays, this is a dying tradition. The most likely place to spot 'stilt' fishermen working is from Ahangama to Dalawella early in the morning or sometimes, if they're hungry, in the evening. At other times they tend to arrive only when visitors with cameras appear, and they expect a small tip for a photograph.

MIDIGAMA

The coast from Midigama to Ahangama is regarded as the best surfing area on the south coast, and consequently it is popular with long-term surfers. However, unless you are into surfing it is probably best avoided. It is full of very cheap guesthouses, catering for surfers on long stays.

KATALUVA

Purvarama Mahaviharaya, originally 18th century with late 19th-century additions, is 3 km along a minor road turning off at Kataluva (Km 132 mark); ask directions locally. The ambulatory has excellent examples of temple paintings illustrating different styles of Kandyan art. Young monks will happily point out interesting sections of the *Jataka* stories depicted on the wall friezes. Note the musicians and dancers on the south side and the European figures illustrating an interesting piece of social history. The priest is very welcoming and keen to speak with foreigners.

KOGGALA

Koggala has an attractive, tranquil lake with rocky islets to the north, and a Free Trade Zone with some light industry. The lake, actually a lagoon, is lined with mangrove and rich with birdlife. Boat trips run to the **Ananda Spice Garden** ① *T228 3805 for more details*, a temple and cinnamon island.

Just by the fortress gate, a road leads left over the railway line to the **Martin Wickramasinghe Folk Museum** ① *daily 0900-1700, Rs 200 (with explanatory leaflet), children Rs 100*. The museum houses the respected Sri Lankan writer's personal collection. His family home displays photographs and memorabilia, and some history about the area. Even if you are not a fan of Wickramasinghe, the museum is still worth visit as it contains some fascinating exhibits from traditional Sri Lankan life. Religious items and agricultural and fishing tools are well displayed behind glass cabinets, with some traditional games (from before cricket obsessed the nation). There's a colourful selection of *kolam* masks and puppets from the Ambalangoda area, and 101 different utensils for treating coconuts. The house and museum are set in an attractive garden with labelled trees, so you can swot up on your Sri Lankan flora.

TALPE AND DALAWELLA

Picturesque **Talpe** is just west of Koggala. An increasing number of upmarket hotels are beginning to open here and the accommodation is better value than in Unawatuna itself. The fine beaches continue to **Dalawella** which, despite being on the main road, has a lovely section of beach and a 'natural swimming pool' towards the eastern end.

Unawatuna's picturesque beach along a sheltered bay was once considered one of the best in the world. Although rather narrow, it is more suitable for year-round swimming than say, Hikkaduwa, as the bay is enclosed by a double reef, which lessens the impact of the waves. For divers, it is a good base to explore some of the wrecks in Galle Bay, and there is some safe snorkelling a short distance from shore (though you may be disappointed by the lack of live coral). Many find Unawatuna more appealing than its popular neighbour, Galle. However, this popularity has taken its toll. Beach restaurants have encroached to the point where the actual usable beach is very narrow, and the increasing number of visitors means that the beach is sometimes crowded, the western end of the bay particularly being popular with local day-trippers at weekends and public holidays. Some parts of the beach can also be very noisy, with music blaring until the early hours.

During the week, however, if you are seeking somewhere with a beach safe for swimming, a wide range of clean accommodation and a variety of good beachside restaurants, then Unawatuna is a good choice.

PLACES IN UNAWATUNA

Unawatuna's main attraction is unquestionably its beach but it isn't the only place worth visiting. There are some lovely walks in the area.

Rumassala kanda (hillock), the rocky outcrop along the coast, has a large collection of unusual medicinal herbs. In the *Ramayana* epic, Hanuman, the monkey god was sent on an errand to collect a special herb to save Rama's wounded brother Lakshmana. Having failed to identify the plant, he returned with a herb-covered section of the great mountain range, dropping a part of what he was carrying here. Another part is said to have fallen in Ritigala (see page 60). This area of forest is now protected by the state to save the rare plants from being removed indiscriminately. It offers excellent views across Galle Harbour towards the fort. On a clear day look inland to catch sight of Adam's Peak. The sea bordering Rumassala has the **Bona Vista reef** which has some of the best preserved coral in Sri Lanka. Recovery from the 1998 bleaching has been faster than elsewhere on the coast.

Jungle Beach, on the other side of the promontory, is pleasantly uncrowded and has some good snorkelling. Boat trips from some of the guesthouses run here and many three-wheelers will offer to take you. Alternatively, you can walk (around 45 minutes) from Unawatuna Beach. You might get lost but guides tend to appear as if by magic.

SOUTH COAST LISTINGS

WHERE TO STAY

Tangalla

$$$$ Amanwella, Godellawela,
T224 1333, www.amaresorts.com.
Luxury resort nestling in a crescent-shaped
bay. 30 suites, most hidden among the
trees, all with private plunge pools and
terrace. Beachfront infinity pool, restaurant,
contemporary design and furnishings.
The public beach is good for snorkelling.

$$ Mangrove Garden, Marakolliya,
T077-906018, www.beachcabana.lk.
6 chalets, reached by rope ferry but a bridge
is being built across the lagoon. Beach bar
and restaurant, rock-sheltered natural pool
for swimming, and a desert island feel.

$$-$ Green Garden Cabanas,
Goyambokka, T077-624 7628,
lankatangalla@yahoo.com. 3 wooden
cabanas and 1 of stone that would look at
home in the Alps, as well as a new family
cabana. A couple more are planned for next
year and all are dotted around the large
garden. Excellent food and a welcoming
and friendly family. Recommended.

$ Mangrove Beach Cabanas, Marakolliya.
Cabanas and mud houses in a beautiful
spot on a secluded beach, just down from
Mangrove Garden; check out the bathrooms.
Restaurant offers a good selection of food,
and staff are friendly and helpful.

Rekawa Beach

$$$$-$$$ Buckingham Place, T348
9447, www.buckinghamplace.lk. British-
owned luxury hotel right next to the Turtle
Conservation Project (see box, page 165).
11 spacious rooms and suites with colourful
splashes and modern decor, all overlooking
the lagoon and most with tubs and rain
showers. Excellent food, beautiful gardens,
pool, and almost deserted stretch of sand.
Boat trips on the lagoon and bikes available
for guests. Quiet and relaxing.

Matara

$$-$ Rest House, main fort area south
of bus station, Matara, T222 2299,
resthousemh@sltnet.lk. Offers modern,
clean rooms (cheaper ones have fans)
with thick mattresses, all finished to a high
standard. Restaurant has good Sri Lankan
breakfasts and views of the sea.

$ Sunny Lanka Guest House, Polhena Rd,
Polhena, T222 3504. Clean rooms in friendly
guesthouse, trips organized.

$ TK Green Garden, 116/1 Polhena Beach
Rd, Polhena, T222 2603. 11 good, clean a/c
and fan rooms, some with shared veranda,
though expensive restaurant, well-run,
quiet, pleasant garden.

Mirissa

$ Rose Blossom Guest House, look
for the sign opposite **Giragala Village**,
Bandaramulla, T077-713 3096, roseblossom.
mirissa@gmail.com. 3 rooms with hot
water, set in a large garden with a
restaurant serving good food. The couple
who run it are friendly and helpful.

Welligama

$$$$ Taprobane Island, T091-438 0275,
www.taprobaneisland.com. Probably
the most exclusive place to stay in Sri
Lanka. Rent the whole house, which has
5 bedrooms and resident staff, including
a private chef.

$$ The Green Rooms, T077-111 9896,
www.thegreenroomssrilanka.com. A surf
lodge at the eastern end of the beach
with very attractive wooden cabanas. The
whole place can be rented, or individual
rooms are available. Many visitors stay for
weeks and there's a family atmosphere. If
you want to learn to surf there are special
packages available. Also cookery lessons.
Recommended.

Koggala

$$$$ The Fortress, Matara Rd, Koggala, T438 9400, www.thefortress.lk. Large luxury beachfront hotel hidden behind high, imposing walls. Rooms, suites and apartments have huge beds and are tastefully decorated. All the facilities you'd expect, including diving trips and Ayurvedic treatments. Large swimming pool.

Unawatuna

$$ Black Beauty, Ganahena, signposted off the main road, T438 4978, www.black-beauty-sri-lanka.com. Look for the Ying Yang wooden door, which opens onto this very friendly, secluded guesthouse. Laid-back atmosphere, and good value (price includes breakfast), with sparkling clean rooms with a/c and hot water. Pool, play area. Can be booked up weeks and sometimes months in advance so call ahead. A good family choice.

$$ Nooit Gedacht, T222 3449, www.sri ayurveda.com. Beautiful colonial mansion (built 1735), steeped in history. Simple rooms with period furniture in the main house, or brighter and more modern ones in the new bungalows. Also full, authentic Ayurveda centre (€500 per week). Very peaceful and atmospheric.

RESTAURANTS

Tangalla

$$ Cactus Lounge, Pallikaduwa. Has a good setting on sheltered beach, fresh seafood, plus soups and snacks.
$$ Turtles' Landing, T071-684 0283. Offers similar fare to **Cactus Lounge**, see above.

Matara

$$ Rest House, see Where to stay. Restaurant serving good Sri Lankan rice and curry lunches, good views of the ocean.

Mirissa

$ Dewmini Roti Shop, 5 mins from the beach. Open 0700-2030. Serves excellent *kottu rotti*, the tourist favourites such as banana and honey rotti, and fried rice dishes. Tables set up behind with umbrellas for shade. Friendly family running it.

Unawatuna

$$ Blowhole, tucked away, past **Submarine Diving School**, turn right by the temple. In a great setting by the river (watch the wildlife), good place to stop on the way up to Jungle Beach or for a quiet breakfast. Simple but delicious food.
$ Hot Rock. Almost dropping into the sea (literally), this is a popular hangout serving seafood and Western dishes. Bright and colourful walls, friendly staff.

WHAT TO DO

Mirissa

Mirissa is awash with operators offering whale-watching trips, and quality and price vary greatly. Speak to other travellers to glean whose tours are currently the best.

Unawatuna
Cookery

Sonja's Health Food Restaurant, next to South Ceylon, Unawatuna Beach Rd, T224 5815, T077-961 5310. Karuna runs very popular cookery classes (1100-1500), which include a trip to Galle to visit the market for ingredients. Pupils are then taught how to make curries, sambol, etc. In the evening you eat what you've cooked and can bring a guest for free. Good value.

Diving

The diving season runs Nov-Apr. There are 5 or 6 wrecks nearby, some at a depth below 15 m. The best accessible wreck is the *Rangoon* in Galle Bay, though this is at a depth of 32 m. There are also some reefs and a rock dive on offer.

GALLE

Galle (pronounced in Sinhala as 'Gaal-le') is the most important town in the south and its fort area, with its mighty ramparts, encloses some wonderful examples of colonial architecture. A laid-back and enchanting place to wander, it was declared a UNESCO World Heritage Site in 1988. Rather removed from the busy modern town, the fort retains a villagey atmosphere, full of local gossip, and some find themselves staying far longer than they expected. Most, however, find that they have exhausted Galle's sites in a day or so.

ARRIVING IN GALLE

Getting there Some people choose to base themselves in Unawatuna and come to Galle for a day trip. If travelling from Mirissa to Galle catch one of the regular buses that runs along the coast from Matara. Alternatively, there are some slow train services that stop at Mirissa on their way to Galle, or take a three-wheeler to Matara and catch the train from there.

Moving on With your own transport, consider taking the A2 from Galle up to **Mount Lavinia** (see page 185), perhaps with a side trip en route to Brief Garden. If travelling by public transport, take a bus or train to Aluthgama and then arrange a three-wheeler to Brief Garden (consider overnighting in Bentota or around).

There is also the option of taking the train from Galle to Colombo and then a bus, train or three-wheeler to Mount Lavinia. Slow trains from Galle may also stop at Mount Lavinia. The Southern Expressway has cut the driving time from Galle to Colombo to under two hours and there are now buses travelling this route as well for those who are in a hurry to get back to the city and want to bypass the southwest coast.

Getting around The train and bus stations are both in the new town, 10-15 minutes' walk north of the fort walls and cricket stadium. Galle Fort is so small and compact that most of the guesthouses are very easy to find. To get to the upmarket hotels outside Galle, you will need to hire a taxi or three-wheeler.

Tourist information There is a branch of the **Ceylon Tourist Board** ① *Victoria Park, daily 0900-1600*, opposite the railway station.

BACKGROUND

Galle's origins as a port go back well before the arrival of the Portuguese. Ibn Batuta, the great Moroccan traveller, visited it in 1344. The historian of Ceylon, Sir Emerson Tennant, claimed that Galle was the ancient city of Tarshish, which had traded not only with Persians and Egyptians but with King Solomon. The origin of the name is disputed, some associating it with the Latin *gallus* (cock), so-called because the Portugese heard the crowing of cocks here at dusk, others with the Sinhala *gala* (cattle shed) or *gal* (rock).

Lorenzo de Almeida drifted into Galle by accident in 1505. It was a further 82 years before the Portuguese captured it from the Sinhala kings, and they controlled the port until the Dutch laid siege in 1640. The old Portuguese fort, on a promontory, was strengthened by the Dutch who remained there until the British captured Galle in 1796. Dutch East India Company, VOC (*Vereenigde Oost Indische Campagnie*) ruled the waves during the 17th and 18th centuries with over 150 ships trading from around 30 settlements in Asia.

A P&O liner called at Galle in 1842 marking the start of a regular service to Europe. In 1859, Captain Bailey, an agent for the shipping company, took a fancy to the spot where a small disused Dutch fort had stood in a commanding position, 3 km across the harbour. The villa he built, set in a tropical garden (now the **Closenberg Hotel**), was named 'Marina' after his wife. P&O's Rising Sun emblem can still be spotted on some of the old furniture.

Galle's gradual decline in importance dates back to 1875, when reconstruction of breakwaters and the enlarged harbour made Colombo the island's major port.

→PLACES IN GALLE

OLD TOWN AND FORT

The **fort**, enclosing about 200 houses, completely dominates the old town. You can easily spend a whole day in this area. Part of its charm is being able to wander around the streets; nothing is very far away. The Dutch left their mark here, building brick-lined sewers which the tides automatically flushed twice a day. The fort's main streets run over these old sewers and you can still see the manhole covers every 20 m or so.

There are two entry points. The more impressive **gate** is under the clocktower. The ramparts just here are massive, partly because they are the oldest and have been reinforced over the years on many occasions. There are three quite distinct bastions (Star in the west, Moon and Sun in the east). The clocktower (1883) itself is quite modern and sometimes has a huge national flag flying from it. In Queen Street is the second and much older gate.

The **ramparts**, surrounded on three sides by the sea, are marked by a series of bastions covering the promontory. The two nearest to the harbour are Sun and Zwart, followed by Aurora and Point Utrecht bastions before the **lighthouse**, then Triton, Neptune, Clippenburg, Aeolus, Star and Moon. Those on the west side are more accessible and stand much as they were built, although there is evidence of a signals post built in the Second World War on top of Neptune. The Sri Lankan army still has a base in the fort and so have a use for the Aeolus bastion. Under the ramparts between Aeolus and Star bastions is the tomb of a Muslim saint neatly painted in green and white, said to cover an old fresh water spring. The open space between Rampart Street and the ramparts is used as a recreational area and there is often an unofficial game of cricket in progress in the evenings and at weekends. Also on the Green is a small shrine; the main one, Sri Sudharmalaya temple, is across the street.

A **walking tour** around the ramparts is a must. You can try to do it on a clear evening and aim to reach the clocktower at sunset, starting at about 1630 and wandering slowly from **Amangalla** clockwise. An interesting route is to walk south from the hotels, all along Church Street, then east to the 20-m-high lighthouse which was built by the British in 1939, nearly on top of the old magazine with its inscription "AJ Galle den 1st Zeber 1782". You can get good views from the top, though you will need to get permission from the lighthouse keeper (ask in the gem store next door). You then return up Hospital Street past the Police Barracks (built in 1927 but failing to blend in with the older parts of the fort). The government offices on Hospital Street were once the Dutch 'factory' (warehouse). You then arrive at the square with the district court near the Zwart Bastion. Turn west along Queen Street which joins Church Street at the post office. The quiet fort streets are lined with substantial buildings, most with large rooms on the ground floor and an arched veranda to provide shade. The arched windows of the upper floors are covered by huge old louvered wooden shutters; the lower ones have glass nowadays. Unfortunately, quite a few of these fine houses are in need of restoration. The **Dutch Reformed Church** (1754), next to the **Amangalla** hotel, is certainly worth visiting. It was built as a result of a vow taken by the Dutch governor of Galle, Casparaus de Jong, and has a number of interesting memorials. Inside, the floor is covered by about 20 gravestones (some heavily embossed, others engraved), which originated in older graveyards which were closed in 1710 and 1804. The British moved them into this church in 1853. The organ loft has a lovely semicircular balustrade surrounding the organ while the pulpit, repaired in 1996, has an enormous canopy. Opposite the church is the old bell tower erected in 1701, while the bell, open to the elements, is hung in a belfry with a large dome on top of it. Next door is the Maritime

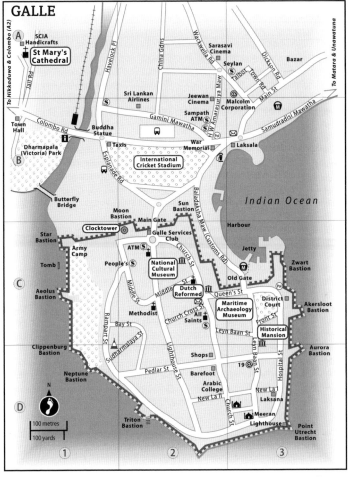

GALLE

Archaeology Museum (see below). The old **post office**, restored by the Galle Heritage Trust in 1992, is a long low building with a shallow red tiled roof supported by 13 columns. It is still functioning although it is very run down inside. Further down Church Street is the All Saints Church though it is not always open. This was built in 1868 (consecrated in 1871) after much pressure from the English population who had previously worshipped at the Dutch Reform Church. Its bell has an interesting history as it came from the Liberty ship *Ocean Liberty*. When the vicar asked the Clan Shipping Company whether they could help with the cost of a bell, the chief officer who had acquired the bell from the *Liberty* when it was scrapped (and named his daughter Liberty), presented it to the church in its centenary year, 1968. There is a particularly good view of the church with its red tin roof surmounted by a cockerel and four strange little turrets, from Cross Church Street. The old **Dutch Government House**, opposite the church, is now a hotel. Note the massive door in four sections at the Queen's Street entrance, was built for entry on horseback. At the end of Church Street lies the old **Arab Quarter** with a distinct Moorish atmosphere. Here you will find the Meeran Jumma Masjid in a tall white building which resembles a church with two square towers topped by shallow domes, but with the crescent clearly visible. Slender, tubular minarets are also topped by crescent moons. The mosque was rebuilt at the beginning of the 20th century where the original stood from the 1750s. The Muslim Cultural Association and Arabic College which was established in 1892, are here. It is still very active and you will see many Muslims in the distinctive skullcaps hurrying to prayer at the appointed hours.

The **Historical Mansion Museum** ⓘ *31-39 Leyn Bann St (well signed), T223 4114, 0900-1800 (closed on Fri 1230-1400 for prayers), free*, is a restored old house. There are a number of rooms around a small courtyard containing this potentially worthwhile collection of colonial artefacts. There are several interesting and rare items which are simply 'stored' here. The real aim of the museum becomes apparent when visitors are led to the gems for sale in the adjoining shop.

The **Maritime Archaeology Museum** ⓘ *Church St, opposite the post office, daily 0900-1700, Rs 550, children Rs 250*, is a new and enormous museum in an old Dutch warehouse, replacing the National Maritime Museum. Visitors enter on one level, follow the exhibits and leave by the exit on the lower floor. An interesting film is shown first that explains the various wrecks lying offshore, some artefacts of which are displayed in the museum. Look out for the beardman jug found at the *Avondster* wreck site in Galle harbour. Exhibits also explore how Sri Lankan dress and language (amongst other things) was influenced by visitors who came by sea to trade, and there are some interesting objects that were washed up after the tsunami. The museum currently feels a bit empty and it is disappointing that not all the objects were found, some are merely example of what would have been aboard the ships. However, there is much of interest to see.

The **National Cultural Museum** ⓘ *Church St (next to Amangalla), T223 2051, Tue-Sat 0900-1700, Rs 300, children Rs 150, cameras Rs 250, video cameras Rs 2000*, is in an old colonial stone warehouse. Exhibits include a model of Galle and the fort's Dutch and Portuguese inheritance.

NEW TOWN
This area was much worse hit by the 2004 tsunami, as everything inside the fort was offered a degree of protection by the walls. Cricket fans will want to visit the rebuilt

Galle International Cricket Stadium, where there is often a match going on. You can clamber up on the ramparts of the fort to find the spot from which Jonathan Agnew, the BBC's cricket correspondent, was forced to broadcast after the famous incident in February 2001 when he wasn't allowed into the ground.

The new town is quite pleasant to wander through and its bustle contrasts with the more measured pace of the fort. It is an easy walk out of the old gate and along by the sea with its rows of fishing boats neatly drawn up on the beach. On the Colombo Road to the west of Victoria Park, are several gem shops. If you take the road opposite them you can walk up to **St Mary's Cathedral** which was built in 1874 and has a very good view over the town. There is little of interest inside, though.

GALLE LISTINGS

WHERE TO STAY

$$$$ Amangalla, 10 Church St, T223 3388, www.amanresorts.com. 17 rooms and 8 suites, which retain the feel and elegance of Galle's most famous colonial hotel. Very attractive swimming pool, spa and good restaurant. Those who aren't staying can take a drink on the veranda or high tea in the lobby, and soak up some of the old-world atmosphere.

$$$$ Lighthouse Hotel (Jetwing), Dadella, 4 km north of Galle, T222 3744, www.jetwinghotels.com. Member of the Small Hotels of the World Association. 60 superbly furnished a/c rooms and 3 suites, panoramic views from sea-facing terrace, 2 restaurants including excellent **Cinnamon Room** for fine dining and 2 pools, one of which is saltwater.

$$$$-$$$ Galle Fort Hotel, 28 Church St, T223 2870, www.galleforthotel.com. Restored colonial mansion with large rooms and suites, all beautifully and thoughtfully decked out. Excellent food, bar and small pool. Attentive and helpful staff.

$$$ The Fort Printers, 39 Pedlar St, T224 7977, www.thefortprinters.com. Colonial mansion converted to a small hotel with 5 tastefully decorated suites. Small courtyard with pool, where meals and drinks are served.

$ Rampart View, 37 Rampart St, T222 6767, www.gallefortrampartview.com. 6 sizeable, clean a/c and fan rooms with attached bath in renovated colonial house. Wonderful views from the roof. Friendly, kind management. Free Wi-Fi.

RESTAURANTS

$$$ Galle Fort Hotel, 28 Church St, T223 2870, www.galleforthotel.com. Excellent European and Asian dishes served in relaxing surroundings overlooking the pool. Light lunches are available and there's a set menu in the evenings with a good choice of desserts. Not the best choice if you're in a rush.

$$-$ Serendipity Arts Café, Leyn Baan St. Open 0730-2130. Laid-back spot with friendly staff, serving sandwiches, burgers, Sri Lankan dishes and cake. There are books and magazines to flip through (some published over the road) and excellent walking tours of the fort leave from here (see What to do).

WHAT TO DO

Sri Serendipity, T077-683 8659, www. sriserendipity.com. Guided walking tours of Galle Fort. Also offers tours of Colombo. Tours leave from the **Serendipity Arts Café**.

GALLE TO COLOMBO

North of Galle lie the golden beaches that serve Sri Lanka's package tourism industry. To some, the southwest coast's wealth of quality accommodation, beach restaurants and bars makes for a perfect indulgent holiday; to others it has been spoilt by over-development. Yet away from the resorts traditional life continues. Many people still depend on fishing with fishermen bringing in catch at numerous points along the coast. The coconut palms that line the shore also provide a livelihood for many. The road and railway line hug the ocean as they go north towards Colombo's urban sprawl and the final stop on this route, Mount Lavinia – an enjoyable journey.

→HIKKADUWA

Hikkaduwa is Sri Lanka's beach party capital, so if you are looking for peace and a beach to yourself, then you might wish to avoid it. A victim of its own success, the island's original surfers' hangout is now its most popular resort with mass tourism bringing pollution and overcrowding, as well a reputation for unsavoury activities and beach boys. The beach here is gradually disappearing with the sea noticeably encroaching inland year by year. This said, the resort still has some appeal. This coastal stretch has a vast number of high quality hotels and guesthouses of all price ranges. The food, especially seafood, is often excellent and with so much competition, reasonably priced. And the opportunities for watersports – swimming, snorkelling, scuba diving (as long as you don't expect living coral) and especially surfing – is probably unrivalled on the island.

ARRIVING IN HIKKADUWA

Getting there The bus station is in the centre of Hikkaduwa town. All accommodation lies to the south. The train station is about 200 m north of the bus station. There are very frequent buses from Galle to Hikkaduwa and the journey takes about 30-45 minutes. It's also possible to take the train.

Moving on There are regular buses running from Hikkaduwa to destinations on the southwest coast and **Colombo** (see page 97), as well as train services that stop at Ambalangoda and Bentota. Slow trains stop at **Mount Lavinia** (see page 185). If travelling by public transport, you may decide to travel to Colombo and then take a train, bus or three-wheeler out to Mount Lavinia.

Getting around There are four parts to what is known collectively as 'Hikkaduwa'. At the northern end is **Hikkaduwa** proper, the original settlement. The beach tends to be somewhat narrower here and less appealing. Further south is **Wewala**, where the beach is a wider and more attractive. Along with **Narigama** this is the main 'centre' with numerous beach bars and restaurants, and the cheapest accommodation. At the southern end is **Thirangama**, which is less frantic, but has good surfing waves and a wider beach. It is possible to walk uninterrupted along much of the beach. Three-wheelers can be stopped along the Galle Road (bus drivers are less obliging), but you will need to negotiate the price. Cycles and motorbikes can be hired.

PLACES IN HIKKADUWA

Hikkaduwa's '**coral sanctuary**' is a shallow protected reef, close to the Coral Gardens Hotel. Once teeming with life, it was badly affected by 'bleaching' in early 1998, when sea temperatures rose causing the coral to reject the algae on which coral life fed. Recovery has been slow. The reef, and fish population, has also been degraded by tourism. Unregulated growth in the use of glass-bottomed boats to ferry visitors across the reef, dynamite fishing and the dumping of garbage from beachside hotels have all contributed to the denigration of the habitat, prompting the Department of Wildlife to upgrade the area to National Park status in 2002. However, it is still possible to see reef fish, which are fed by fishermen to provide an attraction for visitors. Glass-bottomed boats can be hired along the beach, though since the reef is shallow and close to shore, it is easy and less damaging to swim and snorkel to it. Despite the reduced diversity and population of coral and fish, Hikkaduwa is a good base for **scuba diving** and local operators run trips to up to 20 sites along the coast. Most rewarding close to Hikkaduwa are the rock formations, especially the deep Kirala Gala (21 m to 38 m), 10 minutes offshore, where there is also a wide range of pristine coral with groupers, barracuda and batfish. A number of wrecks, some in fairly shallow water, can also be visited, such as the *Earl of Shaftesbury*, though the wreck-diving is better in the bays further south at Galle or Weligama. Visibility varies from 8 m to 25 m, depending on the time of day (morning is better), and is at its best around the full moon period.

Hikkaduwa is Sri Lanka's **surf centre** from December to April, and has hosted numerous international competitions. It is particularly good for beginners as the waves are comparatively gentle, most breaking on the reefs rather than the beach. The focus is around the main break, known as the 'A-Frame' because of its distinctive apex, in Wewala, though this can be crowded in peak months. **Narigama** and **Thiragama** further south are usually quieter, though you will also need more experience.

HIKKADUWA AREA

To Baddegama (11km)
To Colombo, Telwatte Vihara & Ambalangoda
Gonapinuwala
A
HIKKADUWA
B12
WEWALA
NARIGAMA
THIRANGAMA
PUTUWATHA A2
Indian Ocean
Polgasduwa
B
N
DODANDUWA
Lagoon
To Galle
1 km
1 mile
(1)   (2)

AROUND HIKKADUWA

Alut Vihara (Totagama Rajamahavihara) at Telwatta, 2 km north of Hikkaduwa, dates from the early 19th century. It is the only temple to Anangaya on the island, where lovers make offerings to him. The carvings between the fine *makara* (dragon) arches leading to the sanctuary hide a cupid with his bow and flower-tipped arrows. The murals too are particularly impressive. Rarely visited by travellers, it is worth a trip and also makes a very pleasant bicycle ride. Also in Telwatta is the very simple but moving **Tsunami Photo Museum** ⓘ *0900-1800, donation*, which was originally set up with the help of Dutch woman Jacky van Oostveen. It charts the destruction and subsequent rebuilding in the region, and serves as a reminder not only of those who died but also those who survived. Well worth the time to visit.

Seenigama Temple, 6 km north, is on an island just offshore. The Devil's Temple here has enormous importance for local fishermen, who believe he will protect both their lives and wealth. You will need the services of a fisherman to get to the island. At another more easily accessible roadside temple, a few kilometres north on Galle Road, Sri Lankan travellers pay their respects, bringing most traffic to a temporary halt.

At Dodanduwa, **Kumarakanda Rajamahavihara**, 4 km south of Hikkaduwa just before Km 103 post, has some murals and statues, though it is on the tourist trail so expect a dancing monkey and 'school pen' collectors. The temple is reached by a long steep and narrow flight of stone steps. Donations are expected. The beach opposite has a very small private **Turtle Research Centre** ① *Rs 200*, which works to protect this endangered species. You can see eggs and different stages of development and a few posters under a shelter.

More relaxing as a break from the busy schedule at the beach is the picturesque **Ratgama Lake** which has abundant bird life and a large population of water monitors. There are three islands in the lagoon, one of which is **Polgasduwa**, where there is forest hermitage founded by a German monk. Touts offer trips from the beach. Once you are there you can explore the lagoon by paddleboat.

Baddegama, 11 km inland along the B153, is within easy reach of Hikkaduwa by bicycle or motorbike. The road is picturesque, cutting its way through coconut and banana groves, followed by several small plantations – rubber, tea and spices. About half way the road passes the **Nigro Dharama Mahavihara** (stupa) in Gonapinuwala. On a hill above the river in the grounds of Christ Church Girls College is the first Anglican church in Sri Lanka, built in 1818 and consecrated by Bishop Heber of Calcutta in 1825. Note the ironwood pillars.

→AMBALANGODA

The busy town of Ambalangoda is an important commercial and fish trading centre. With some local colour, and a fine sweep of sandy beach to its north, some visitors opt to stay here over its more touristy resort neighbours along the coast. The town is chiefly famous as the home of **devil dancing** and **mask making**, which many families have carried out for generations. It may be possible to watch a performance of *kolama* (folk theatre); ask at the museum or School of Dancing (see below). Ambalangoda is also famous as a major centre for cinnamon cultivation and production. Ask your hotel or guesthouse about visiting a plantation and factory. The colourful fish market is worth visiting early in the morning.

PLACES IN AMBALANGODA

There are actually two **Ariyapala Mask museums** ① *426 Patabendimulla, 0830-1730*, run by the two sons of the late mask-carver, who set up in competition. The museums are opposite one another: the smaller one houses the museum proper, while the other 'mask museum' is primarily a workshop and showroom. Some of the exhibits tracing the tradition of mask dancing are interesting and informative. The masks can be very elaborate. The *naga raksha* mask from the **Raksha Kolama** (Devil Dance), for example, has a fearsome face with bulging eyes that roll around, a bloodthirsty tongue hanging from a mouth lined with fang-like teeth, all topped by a set of cobra hoods (see box, page 182). You can watch the odd craftsmen at work carving traditional masks from the light *kaduru* wood. The carvings on sale in the

ON THE ROAD
Dance of the sorcerers

The **Devil Dance** evolved from the rural people's need to appease malevolent forces in nature and seek blessing from good spirits when there was an evil spirit to be exorcised, such as a sickness to be cured. It takes the form of a ritual dance, full of high drama, with a sorcerer 'priest' and an altar. As evening approaches, the circular arena in the open air is lit by torches, and masked dancers appear to the beating of drums and chanting. During the exorcism ritual, which lasts all night, the 'priest' casts the evil spirit out of the sick. There are 18 demons associated with afflictions for which different fearsome *sanni* masks are worn. There is an element of awe and grotesqueness about the whole performance and these dances have a serious purpose and are, therefore, not on offer as 'performances'.

The **Kolam Dance** has its origins in folk theatre. The story tells of a queen, who, while expecting a child, had a deep craving to see a masked dance. This was satisfied by the Carpenter of the Gods, Visvakarma, who invented the dances.

The *kolam* dances tell stories and again make full use of a wonderful variety of masks (often giant in size) representing imaginary characters from folk tales, Buddhist *jatakas*, gods and devils, as well as well-known members of the royal court and more mundane figures from day-to-day life. Animals (lions, bears) too, feature as playful characters. This form of folk dance resembles the more serious Devil Dance in some ways – it is again performed during the night and in a similar circular, torch-lit, open-air 'stage' (originally *kolam* was performed for several nights during New Year festivities). In spite of a serious or moral undertone, a sprinkling of cartoon characters is introduced to provide comic relief. The clever play on words can only be really appreciated by a Sinhalese speaker.

---

showroom are not of the best quality and are quite expensive. It is better to take your time to visit some of the smaller workshops around town on foot and compare prices and quality.

Traditional dancing shows take place about once a month at Bandu Wijesooriya School of Dancing ⓘ *417 Patabendimulla, T225 8948, www.banduwijesooriyadanceacademy.org*. A typical show will include a *kolam* dance, followed by several ritual dances, a village folk dance, and end up with some short Indian dances. Courses are also possible at the school, which is closed on Sunday, where they teach dance, drumming and mask-carving.

AROUND AMBALANGODA

At **Karandeniya**, 208 steps lead up to the **Galabuddha Temple**, which has a 33-m-long lying Buddha, which a sign proudly proclaims to be the biggest in South Asia. The murals are worthy of note. The temple is 11 km inland from Ambalangoda, along the Elpitiya Road.

At **Meetiyagoda**, 16 km inland, there is a moonstone quarry. The semi-precious stone, which often has a bluish milky tinge, is polished and set in silver or gold jewellery. The road sign claims that it's the 'only natural moonstone quarry in the world'.

→ AMBALANGODA TO INDURUWA

BALAPITIYA

A few kilometres north of Ambalangoda near the small town of Balapitiya, a bridge fords the Madu Ganga. The estuary is a major **wetlands** area, famous for its 64 islands. Tours are offered which usually include a visit to the 150-year-old **Koth Duwa temple**, and an island where you can watch cinnamon being cut and prepared, though bear in mind that the finished oil, bark and powder for sale is overpriced. You will also see some wildlife as the estuary is home to more than 300 varieties of plant, including 95 families of mangrove, marshes and scrub supporting 17 species of birds, and a wide variety of amphibians and reptiles; water monitors are common. River safari operators leave from either side of the bridge.

KOSGODA

Kosgoda's 4-km stretch of beach has the highest density of turtle nesting in the country. In August 2003, the **Turtle Conservation Project (TCP)** launched a programme with the financial assistance of the UNDP to protect 1 km of the beach with the assistance of former nest poachers, retrained as 'nest-protectors' and tour guides. The **Kosgoda Sea Turtle Conservation Project** ① *Galle Rd, T226 4567, www.kosgodaseaturtle.org, 0900-1700, Rs 200,* is open nearly every day and welcomes visitors and volunteers. Learn more about turtles and visit the hatchery. Contact them in advance if you want to take part in an evening turtle watch.

INDURUWA

Induruwa, with its pleasant stretch of beach, is being developed and some new hotels and guesthouses are opening up. Attractions in the area include several turtle hatcheries.

Visitors are welcome at the **turtle hatchery** ① *Galle Rd, Bentota South, T227 5850, Rs 200; donations appreciated.* Formerly part of the Victor Hasselblad Project, the hatchery has been running for about 20 years, buying eggs from local fishermen at a higher price than they would normally get if sold for food. The eggs are buried as soon as possible in batches of 50. After hatching, the baby turtles are placed in holding tanks for two to three days before being released into the sea in the evening under supervision. Depending on the time of year (best November to April), you can see the hatchlings of up to five species – green, olive ridley, hawksbill, leatherback and loggerhead – at any one time. An example of each species is also held in separate tanks for research purposes.

Note that concerns have been raised in recent years about the way hatcheries operate, so do some research before deciding if you want to visit them.

→ BENTOTA, ALUTHGAMA AND BERUWELA

BENTOTA

Bentota Bridge marks the border between the Western and Southern Provinces. The 40-ha **National Resort Complex** is built entirely for foreign tourists with shops, a bank and a post office. A full range of sports is available and the area is also gaining a reputation for providing first-class Ayurvedic healing centres, with many more under construction. South of Bentota, along Galle Road towards Induruwa, the area feels less of a tourist ghetto, and the natural beauty of the coastline returns. Here are some of the most sumptuous places to stay in the entire island. Unofficial 'guides' offer nearby river and lagoon trips and visits to temples, coir factories and woodcarvers. They are very overpriced.

ALUTHGAMA

Aluthgama, the principal town here, has a busy fish market and is famous for its oysters. The sand spit which separates the river from the sea where most of the hotels are built provides excellent waters for windsurfing and sailing. Many of the hotels referred to as being in Bentota are to the north of the Bentota Bridge and so are actually in Aluthgama.

BRIEF GARDEN

① T227 0462, guided tours daily 0800-1700, Rs 1000. From Aluthgama, take the road inland to Matugama, and then Dhargatown (8 km). From here, a 2-km rough track (right at the 1st fork and left at the 2nd) takes you to the gardens.

The splendid Brief Garden at Kalawila was created between 1929 and 1989 by the late Bevis Bawa, the landscape architect, writer, sculptor, bon vivant and brother to Geoffrey (see box, page 109) – the name refers to a court brief! It is an enchanting garden in an undulating landscape of paddies and scattered villages on a hillside. The 2-ha garden with cool, shady paths and many mature specimen trees, was really created as a series of wonderfully composed views, designed in different moods. There are many references to European- and Japanese-style gardens, with shade-loving anthurium and alocasia plants common throughout. Bawa's house though is the highlight, with its eclectic private collection of paintings, sculptures, photographs (note Edward VIII and Lord Olivier, both of whom stayed here) and furniture (many colonial antiques), providing an added incentive to visit. Some of the paintings were composed by Australian artist Donald Friend, who came for a week and stayed for six years. Bawa himself appears in a number of forms, both in the house and garden, at one point representing Bacchus, holding a birdbath shaped as a giant clam-shell. In his outside bathroom, he appears again as a water-spouting gargoyle with wild hair and blue marble eyes.

BERUWELA

The name Beruwela is derived from the Sinhalese word *Baeruala* ('the place where the sail is lowered'). It marks the spot where the first Arab Muslim settlers are believed to have landed in around the eighth century. **Kitchimalai Mosque**, on a headland 3 km north along the beach from the main hotel area, is worth seeing. It is a major pilgrimage centre at the end of **Ramadan** since there is also a shrine of a 10th-century Muslim saint; guides guides may tell you that it is the oldest mosque in Sri Lanka but this is unlikely to be true. Looking east from the mosque, **Beruwela harbour** is an interesting place to watch the fishermen unload their catch. The harbour has over 600 boats, many of which are quite sizeable since the fishermen spend up to two months at sea. The fish market is busy in the early morning – you may well see fresh shark or tuna change hands even before the sun is up. You can also hire a boat to the lighthouse raised on a small island offshore which offers an excellent view of the coastline from the top.

→ KALUTARA

Kalutara is a busy district capital renowned for its basket-making. Leaves of the wild date are dyed red, orange, green and black, and woven into hats, mats and baskets. To guard the spice trade the Portuguese built a fort on the site of a Buddhist temple here. The Dutch took it over and a British agent converted it into his residence. The site, by the bridge across the Kalu Ganga, now again has a modern Buddhist shrine, the **Gangatilaka Vihara**, with a sacred Bo tree outside. It is worth stopping to visit the hollow *dagoba* (actually a *dagoba* within a *dagoba*), as others on the island contain relics and are not accessible. Most remarkable are the extraordinary acoustics, which can be quite disorienting. There are 75 paintings inside, illustrating events from the Buddha's life.

Kalutara has a huge stretch of fine sand with **Wadduwa**, to the north, home to the area's top resorts. Kalutara itself divides into **Mahawaskaduwa** (Kalutara North) where the beach is more scenic, right down to **Katukurunda** (Kalutara South).

At **Palatota**, a little inland, is **Richmond Castle** ① *0830-1630, Rs 100, turn left immediately after the* vihara *along the Kalutara–Palatota road; after 2 km, a track leads left to the house*, a fine country house in a 17-ha fruit garden estate, it is now used as an education centre for underprivileged local children. Built in 1896, it originally belonged to landowner-turned-philanthropist NDA Silva Wijayasinghe, the local Padikara Mudah (village leader), and was used during the British period as a circuit bungalow for officials. Note the audience hall, with intricately carved pillars and beams (two shiploads of teak were brought from Burma for its construction) and a spiral staircase leading to a gallery. Another room shows some fascinating photographs from the time.

The large number of coconut palms along the coast road marks this as the centre of the arrack industry. The island's best quality mangosteen (introduced from Malaya in the early 19th century) and rubber are economically important. Graphite is also mined. Wild hog deer, introduced by the Dutch from the Ganga Delta, are reputedly still found nearby.

→ NORTH TO COLOMBO

Moratuwa, 23 km south of Colombo, has a large Catholic population, and some fine churches. The town is also noted for its furniture making and its college, and you will see by the side of the road furniture workshops carving wood into a wide variety of intricate designs. There is plenty of accommodation in Moratuwa, mainly by **Bolgoda Lake**, popular for local weddings and as a weekend escape from Colombo. Here you can fish for barramundi, or take boat trips out to the lake's islands.

Panadura, sits just to the south of a wide estuary, has many fine colonial mansions. From here, the A8 road leads east to Ratnapura and beyond, hugging the southern edge of the highlands. The town is known for producing some of the highest quality **batik** in Sri Lanka. It is well worth the small diversion to the workshop and showroom of **Bandula Fernando** ① *289/5 Noel Mendis Rd, just off the A2, T034-223 3369*. One of the foremost batik designers in Sri Lanka, Bandula Fernando combines traditional andmodern styles to produce some exceptionally vibrant and original batik designs. He is also credited with evolving mosaic art in batik, acknowledged as a uniquely individual style of batik. The designs on offer are quite different from those seen elsewhere on the island and are sold at fair prices considering the detail and excellence.

→ MOUNT LAVINIA

Just 8 km south of Colombo, Mount Lavinia is a pleasant place to stay for those put off by the noise and congestion of the capital. Once a fishing village, these days the drive along the busy Galle Road scarcely marks it apart from the rest of the city. The historic connection with British governors in the 19th century brings many seeking to sample something of that era in the famous **Mount Lavinia Hotel** here.

Some believe the town takes its name from a corruption of the Sinhalese 'Lihinia Kanda' (Gull Rock). The **Mount Lavinia Hotel** may contest the origins of the name. Literature suggests that British Governor Sir Thomas Maitland established the original building on the headland here in 1806 for himself and his secret lover Lovina, an exotic and beautiful dancer of mixed Portuguese and Sinhalese race – hence the name. It is said that for seven years she trysted secretly with him by creeping through a tunnel connecting her garden to Maitland's wine cellar! Later, the original Mount Lavinia Hotel was Governor Edward Barnes' weekend retreat. He had the bungalow significantly extended in the 1820s ('Governor's Wing'), but was forced to sell it as the government in England approved neither of the expenditure nor his luxurious lifestyle.

Mount Lavinia is famous for its 'golden mile' of beach, from which the high-rise buildings of central Colombo are easily visible. The attractive colonial villas and lovely scent of frangipani and bougainvillea, however, mask a slightly seedier side. Theft is more common than elsewhere and if visiting the beach do not take anything valuable with you; beware of walking around at night after the restaurants have closed.

The beach itself is cleanest south of **Mount Lavinia Hotel**, where it is 'private' for the use of the hotel residents only, although non-residents can pay for access as well as use of the pool. North of the hotel, it gets rather narrow and has a noticeable amount of litter especially at weekends and holidays. There are a number of bars/restaurants here, mostly run by the hotels immediately behind them.

Hotels close to the beach are also close to the railway line, with trains passing at regular intervals from early morning to late at night, invariably using their horns to alert pedestrians on the track. Take care when crossing the railway en route to the beach.

GALLE TO COLOMBO LISTINGS

WHERE TO STAY

Hikkaduwa

$$$$-$$ Suite Lanka, T227 7136, www.suitelanka. com. 6 beautifully furnished standard rooms, deluxe rooms and suites. Private verandas, pool, 2 bars (1 on beach), very quiet and intimate, good fresh seafood.

$$$-$$ Coral Sands, 326 Galle Rd, T227 7513, www.coralsandshotel.com. 75 clean and airy a/c rooms with balcony, not all sea facing and some newer than others, restaurant, bar, pools, diving school, friendly, reasonable value.

$ Neela's Guest House, 634 Galle Rd, Narigama, T438 3166, neelas_sl@ hotmail.com. Friendly and popular guesthouse offering fan rooms, or a/c rooms with sea views.

$ Surf Villa, Milla Rd, T077-760 4620. Down a side road but not far from the beach, this gem is hidden amongst a lush tropical garden. Rooms have fan or a/c and the bathrooms are enormous with bathtub and showers. Very clean and friendly, popular with surfers.

Bentota

$$$$ Saman Villas, Aturuwella, on a rocky headland 5 km south, T227 5435, www.samanvilla.com. 27 magnificent suites with sea views set on a spectacular rocky headland. All have attractive furnishings, and 'astonishing' open-air baths with rain shower. Superb pool high above sea which seems to merge with the ocean, panoramic views and access to long beaches either side. Good spa. Expensive but worth every rupee.

$$$$ The Villa (Paradise Rd), 138/18-22 Galle Rd (1.5 km south of Bentota), T227 5311, www.paradiseroadhotels.com. A former residence of Geoffrey Bawa, exquisite rooms in a large villa dated 1880, each individually designed, decorated and

furnished with antique furniture. Superb bathrooms (open-air bath), beautiful shaded garden, understated pool. Sublime.

$ Susantha, Resort Rd, Pitaramba, next to Bentota railway station (5 mins from beach, across from the rail track), T227 5324, www.hotelsusanthas.com. 18 spotless good-sized rooms with bath in pleasant chalets, prices vary according to facilities. Bar, good restaurant and Ayurvedic centre. Suites also available (**$$**).

Beruwela

$$$$-$$$ Eden Resort & Spa, Kaluwamodara, T227 6075, www.eden resortandspa.com. 158 rooms, suites and penthouses, grand entrance, large pool, spa, full entertainment and sports facilities. Friendly staff.

Barberyn Reef, Moragalla, T227 6036, www.barberynresorts.comcom. Opened in 1982, the 1st Ayurvedic centre in Sri Lanka. A range of rooms, some with a/c and some split-level with a living area. Extensive Ayurvedic health centre, safe swimming enclosed by a reef.

Mount Lavinia

$$$ Mount Lavinia, 100 Hotel Rd, T271 1711, www.mountlaviniahotel.com. Renovated and extended former governors' weekend retreat located on a small but prominent headland retaining a rich colonial atmosphere. 275 rooms and suites, many with sea views and retaining old world ambience, a 'must-stay'. Huge public areas and labyrinthine corridors, all facilities, range of restaurants, terrace bar (good for sunset drinks), nightclub, shopping arcade, sports including tennis, gym, elephant rides (Sun 1000-1400), impressive terrace pool, peaceful private beach (cleaner than public beach to the north).

$ Blue Seas Guest House, 9/6 De Saram Rd, T271 6298. Good clean rooms with a/c or fan (including breakfast), some with balconies, in family-run guesthouse. Quiet location, very friendly and helpful.

RESTAURANTS

Hikkaduwa
$$-$ Cool Spot, 327 Galle Rd, opposite Chaaya Tranz. Tasty curry and seafood, platters can be good value. Upstairs seating area is nicer, it feels further from the Galle Rd traffic.

Wewala
$ The Coffee Shop, Galle Rd. Simple but effective, homemade cake and tea or coffee. Good book exchange.

Narigama and Thirangama
$ Brother's Spot, Galle Rd. 5 little tables just off the road, serving Chinese, Italian and seafood dishes for lunch and dinner. A popular breakfast spot, the pancakes are superb and the bananas fresh from the owner's garden over the road.

Bentota
$$$ Diya Sisila, T077-740 2138. Not by the sea, but a popular place for excellent seafood with tables in a pleasant garden. The owner will pick guests up if requested. BYO, and be sure to book in advance.

$$ Susantha's, see Where to stay. Serves simple Sri Lankan and continental dishes.

Mount Lavinia
$$$ Governor's Restaurant, Mount Lavinia, see Where to stay. Atmospheric colonial surroundings.
$$$ La Rambla, 69 Hotel Rd, T272 5403. Tastefully decorated restaurant serving good-quality seafood and Mediterranean cuisine, desserts are a bit disappointing.
$$$-$$ La Voile Blanche, 43/10 Beach Rd, T456 1111. Unsurprisingly specializes in seafood, but has extensive menu with Asian and Western choices. Beachfront, with chilled atmosphere. Good cocktail list and range of spirits.
$$$-$$ Loon Tao, 43/12 College Av, T272 2723, www.loontao.com. Chinese restaurant serving predominantly seafood, but meat and tofu dishes also available. Extensive menu, upmarket beach hut feel.
$$ The Angler, 71 Hotel Rd. Family-run, also 4 **$** rooms and apartment to let. Good Sri Lankan, Chinese and Western dishes.

WHAT TO DO

Hikkaduwa
The diving season along the southwest coast is Nov-Apr, and Hikkaduwa has the most dive schools on the island, though the not the best local sites. There are several other dive schools in addition to those listed here. Check that they are SSI or PADI qualified before agreeing to a dive or course. Snorkelling equipment can be hired from shops along the main street. Glass-bottomed boats can be hired from a number of places just north of the Chaaya Tranz. Some travellers find there are too many boats chasing too few viewing spots, turtles are disturbed unnecessarily and that the glass is not as clear as you might hope.

PRACTICALITIES

INS AND OUTS

→ BEST TIME TO VISIT SRI LANKA

The island lies just north of the equator and temperatures remain almost constant throughout the year. However, rainfall varies widely. Sri Lanka is affected by two main monsoon seasons, sweeping over the country at different times of year. The **southwest monsoon** (June-October) brings heavy rain to the south; the best time to visit this area is from late October to early March, after the monsoon has finished. The **northeast monsoon** (October-January) can be a good time to visit despite the rain as the countryside becomes lush with tropical vegetation. The north and east are dry but hot from June to October. The Central Highlands are much cooler throughout the year, but are very wet both during the southwest monsoon and the northeast monsoon.

→ GETTING TO SRI LANKA

AIR

All international flights arrive at Katunayake, 30 km north of Colombo, although a new airport has been built near Hambantota and will soon be accepting international flights. International airlines flying to Sri Lanka include: Aeroflot, British Airways, Cathay Pacific, El Al, Emirates, Gulf Air, Indian Airlines, Korean Airlines, Kuwait Airways, Lufthansa, Malaysia Airlines, Oman Air, Pakistan International Airways, Qatar Airways, Royal Jordanian, Saudi Arabian, Singapore Airlines and Thai International. Sri Lankan Airlines ① *www.srilankan.lk*, the national carrier, flies to over 20 countries, and has offices all over the world. A source of great national pride, it compares favourably with the best of the Southeast Asia airlines for comfort and service. At the time of writing, Sri Lankan Airlines was still the only airline offering direct flights from London to the island.

November to March is high season with Christmas, New Year and Easter the most expensive times to visit. Shop around, book early and if using a 'bucket shop' confirm with the airline that your name appears on their list. It is possible to get a significant discount from a reputable travel agent especially outside European holiday times, most notably from London. The airlines invariably quote a higher price as they are not able to discount tickets but off-load surplus tickets on agents who choose to pass on part of their commission to passengers. It is possible to get Christmas bargains, but the lowest prices are often during May-June when it's monsoon season in the south.

A number of charter companies offer package tours, operating mainly from Western Europe (Germany, Italy, etc). These can work out cheaper than scheduled flight fares, but may have limitations. They are not available to Sri Lankan nationals and usually must include accommodation. You can also arrange a stop-over in Sri Lanka on a 'Round the World' and other long-distance tickets.

From the UK and Ireland Sri Lankan Airlines flies eight to nine times a week direct from London to Colombo and British Airways flies three times a week via India. Jet Airways offers some good deals, transiting through India. It is usually cheaper to fly via the Middle East; Gulf Air, Emirates, Oman Air and Qatar Airways tend to offer similar fares.

There are various discount flight booking agencies which offer significantly better deals than the airlines themselves.

From the USA and Canada From the east coast, it is best to fly from New York via London or pick up a direct flight from the UK but this will usually involve a stopover in London. From the west coast, it is best to fly via Hong Kong, Singapore or Bangkok using one of those countries' national carriers.

From Australasia via the Far East There are no direct flights to Colombo from Australia or New Zealand, but **Cathay Pacific**, **Malaysian Airlines**, **Singapore Airlines** and **Thai International** are the main linking airlines and offer the best deals. **Sri Lankan Airlines** also flies to the major Southeast Asian regional capitals.

From South Asia **Sri Lankan Airlines** flies to a growing number of Indian destinations, including Bangalore, Chennai, Delhi, Kochi, Mumbai, Thiruvananthapuram and Tiruchirappalli, as well as Male in the Maldives. **Jet Airways** flies to Colombo from Chennai and Delhi.

AIRPORT INFORMATION

Disembarkation Cards are handed out to passengers during the inward flight. Complete parts 1 and 2 and hand them in at the immigration counter on arrival along with your passport. Keep your baggage identification tag safe as this must be handed in when leaving the Arrivals hall.

Bandaranaike International Airport, at present Sri Lanka's only international airport (although a new one will be opening in the south of the island), is at Katunayake, 30 km north of Colombo. It has modern facilities including duty free shops (with a large selection of electrical goods). Major banks are represented by branches in the Arrivals hall, offering a good rate of exchange, and there is an ATM which accepts most cards. The tourist information counter has limited information although it is worth picking up copies of *Travel Lanka* and the *Sri Lanka Tourist Board Accommodation Guide*.

There is a pre-paid taxi stand and several hotel and tour company booths just after the Arrivals hall. Outside, porters will offer to transport your luggage; alternatively, the trolleys are free. There are several hotels and guesthouses within a few kilometres of the airport, and a wider choice of accommodation at Negombo, 6 km away (see page 35).

A few flights each night arrive in Sri Lanka in the small hours. If you are going to arrive late, it is best to book a hotel or guesthouse in Negombo for the first night (and arrange in advance to be picked up from the airport) and move to Colombo or another beach resort the following day. Avoid accommodation touts. The airport bank exchange counters and taxis operate 24 hours, though public transport does not.

On departure, give yourself enough time to pass through security. Travellers are not allowed into the terminal building before their luggage has been x-rayed and their documents have been scrutinized.

SEA

Cruise ships occasionally stop at Colombo and you may be able to get a berth on a cargo or container ship from ports in the Gulf region or Southeast Asia but it is impossible to book trips in advance. Sailors in their own vessels may be able to berth in Galle, although immigration formalities should be carried out in Colombo. Check with your nearest Sri Lankan representative in advance.

→ TRANSPORT IN SRI LANKA

Public transport in Sri Lanka is very cheap and, in the case of buses, island-wide. Due to overcrowding on buses, train is a (marginally) more comfortable alternative, although the network is limited and there are often delays. The majority of travellers hire a car – whether self-drive or with a chauffeur – for at least part of their stay, especially if only here for a short time. Note that some areas of the north remain out of bounds.

AIR

SriLankan Air Taxi (operated by Sri Lankan Airlines) and Cinnamon Air have a code share agreement and fly from Colombo's Bandaranaike International Airport to Koggala, Dickwella, Kandy, Trincomalee and Batticaloa. FitsAir ① www.fitsair.com, formerly ExpoAir, has regular scheduled flights from Colombo's domestic airport at Ratmalana to Jaffna. Visitors with money to burn can charter planes or helicopters to take them to their destination.

ROAD

The main roads in Sri Lanka are generally well maintained but traffic often moves very slowly, especially in Colombo and its surrounds. There has been some investment in recent years and there are now 'carpet' roads from Colombo to Kandy, Puttalam and Galle.

Bus Government-run CTB buses are the cheapest, slowest and most uncomfortable of the options as they are always very crowded. Private buses follow the same routes, offer a higher degree of comfort (if you can get a seat) and cost a little more.

Private intercity buses are often air-conditioned minibuses (sometimes coaches on popular routes). They cost about double the fare of ordinary buses but they are quicker and you are guaranteed a seat since they operate on a 'leave when full' basis. They can be quite cramped, especially if you have a lot of luggage (if it takes up a whole seat you will probably have to pay for it) but on the whole they are the best option for travelling quickly between the main towns. They are generally non-stop but will let you off on request en route (ask the conductor in advance) although you will still have to pay the full fare to the end destination. If you do want to get off en route it is best to sit near the door since the aisle is used by passengers on fold-away seats. The fare is usually displayed on the front or side window.

In general it is best to board buses at the main bus stand in order to get a seat. Once out on the road it is normally standing room only.

Car hire Many people choose to travel by car for at least part of their trip. This gives you greater flexibility if you want to tour, giving you the chance to see some places that are almost inaccessible any other way. Sharing a vehicle can make this possible for even those travelling on a small budget. On the downside however it cuts out some of the interaction with local people which can be one of the most rewarding aspects of public transport, and may give you a lesser sense of 'achievement'.

There are several **self-drive** car hire firms based in Colombo including some linked to international firms. You have to be 25-65 years old and have an International Driving Permit (contact your local Automobile Association) in order to get a Sri Lankan driving permit through their AA. To get this 'recognition permit', which is issued up to the expiry date of your International Driving Permit, is a simple process and costs Rs 2800. Just call at the **Automobile Association of Sri Lanka** ① *3rd floor, 40 Sir MM Markar Mawatha, Galle Face, Colombo 3, T242 1528, Mon-Fri 0830-1630*. Some hire firms (eg **Avis**) will arrange this. If you do not have an International Driving Permit but do have your national licence, you must apply for a temporary Sri Lankan Driving Licence from the **Register of Motor Vehicles** ① *Department of Motor Traffic, 341 Elvitigala Mawatha, Colombo 5, T269 4331*. Temporary Driving Licences are issued on payment valid for a month up to a maximum of three months.

The rule of 'might is right' applies in Sri Lanka, and the standard of driving can be appalling. Many foreign visitors find the road conditions difficult, unfamiliar and sometimes dangerous. If you drive yourself it is essential to take great care and you should attempt to anticipate the mistakes that Sri Lankan road users might make. Most Sri Lankan drivers appear to take unbelievable risks, notably overtaking at inopportune times, such as when approaching a blind bend. Pedestrians often walk along, or in the middle of, a narrow road in the absence of pavements and cattle and dogs roam at will. Never overtake a vehicle in front of you which indicates to the right. It usually means that it is unsafe for you to overtake and rarely means that they are about to turn right. Flashing headlights mean 'get out of the way, I'm not stopping'. In these circumstances it is best to give the oncoming vehicle space, since they usually approach at great speed. Roundabouts are generally a free-for-all, so take your chance cautiously. Horns are used as a matter of course, but most importantly when overtaking, to warn the driver being overtaken.

It may actually be safer (and more relaxing) to hire a **car with a driver**. These are available through travel agents and tour operators, or you can book with a freelance driver direct (the latter usually works out considerably cheaper). A driver may be helpful in being able to communicate with local people and also make a journey more interesting by telling you more about the places and local customs. Before setting off, however, you should agree some ground rules, as there are a number of potential pitfalls. First, check that the driver is content for you to pick the route and accommodation, as some can be inflexible. It is best not to depend on the driver for suggestions of hotels, restaurants and gift shops since you may not get an unbiased opinion. Most large hotels have free driver accommodation and will provide a meal for them, but guesthouses and hotels off the beaten track often do not – in these instances you should agree in advance who will pay for drivers' accommodation. It is also worth checking that the driver will stop for photographs; that his allowance will cover parking fees at sites; and, if you plan a long trip, that he is prepared to spend the time away from home. Hire charges vary according to make and mileage and can be very high for luxury models.

Self-drive The following rates quoted by Malkey ① *www.malkey.lk*, were valid in 2013. Suzuki Alto: €250 per day, plus €0.14 per excess kilometre. Toyota Camry: €284 per week, plus €0.48 per kilometre. A refundable deposit of Rs 25,000 is required, which covers insurance for accidental damage and loss (with a police report) up to this value, and taxes of 12% are added. It is prohibited to drive in wildlife sanctuaries. Petrol costs, which are extra, are rising fast.

Car with driver Suzuki Alto €77 per week (up to 100 km), plus €0.24 per excess kilometre. Mercedes Benz: €110 per day, plus €1.10 per excess kilometre. Fuel is included but taxes of 12% are added. Chauffeur's subsistence is an extra Rs 1500 per day (Rs 2000 in the north and east). Alternatively, some companies charge a flat rate. Much cheaper rates are possible with freelance drivers.

Quickshaw's ① www.quickshaws.com, offers car and driver rates from £36 per car per day for two people. The price includes an air-conditioned car with English-speaking chauffeur/guide; a daily minimum of 100 km per day, averaged out over a number of days (£0.36 per extra kilometre); and insurance.

Red Dot Tours ① www.reddottours.com/sri-lanka-holidays-getting-around-car-and-driver.htm, has a useful calculator for car and driver trips, which allows you to work out an estimated the cost for specific trips.

Cycling Cycling is very worthwhile in Sri Lanka as it gives you the opportunity to see authentic village life well off the beaten track. Foreign cyclists are usually greeted with cheers, waves and smiles. It is worth taking your own bike (contact your airline well in advance) or mountain bikes can be hired from **Adventure Sports Lanka** ① www.actionlanka.com, in Colombo and other adventure tour companies, though they may not be up to international standards. Bicycles can be transported on trains, though you will need to arrive two hours ahead at Colombo Fort station. While cycling is fun on country byways, hazardous driving means that you should avoid the major highways (especially the Colombo–Galle road) as far as possible. Cycling after dark can be dangerous because of the lack of street lighting and poor road surfaces. Take bungee cords (to strap down a backpack), spare parts and good lights from home, and take care not to leave your bike parked anywhere unattended. Repair shops are widespread and charges are nominal. Always carry plenty of water.

Local bikes tend to be heavy and often without gears but on the flat they offer a good way of exploring short distances outside towns. Many people choose to hire one to explore ancient city areas such as Polonnaruwa and Anuradhapura.

Hitchhiking This is rare in Sri Lanka, partly because public transport is so cheap.

Motorcycling Motorcycles are popular locally and are convenient for visiting different beaches and also for longer distance sightseeing. Repairs are usually easy to arrange and quite cheap. Motorcycle hire is possible in some beach resorts (eg Hikkaduwa, Mirissa) or in towns nearby. You will generally need to leave a deposit or your passport. Check all bikes thoroughly for safety. If you have an accident you will usually be expected to pay for the damage. Potholes and speed-breakers add to the problems of a fast rider.

Taxi Taxis have yellow tops with red numbers on white plates, and are available in most towns. Negotiate the price for long journeys beforehand. **Radio cabs** (eg Ace, Quick,

GNTC) are more expensive and have a higher minimum charge, but are fixed price, very reliable, convenient and some accept credit cards. They are air-conditioned, have digital meters and are available 24 hours at the airport, Colombo and Kandy. The car usually arrives within 10-15 minutes of phoning (give your exact location).

In tourist resorts, taxis are often Toyota **vans** which can carry up to 10 people. Ask at your hotel/guesthouse for an estimate of the fare to a particular destination. There is usually a 'going-rate', but you will probably have to bargain to reach this. Agree on the fare before getting in.

Three-wheeler These three-wheeled motorized tricycles, the Indian auto-rickshaws made by Bajaj, move quickly through traffic but compare poorly against taxis for price. Sri Lanka's three-wheeler drivers are always keen to procure business, and you will be beeped constantly by any without a passenger. An alarming 40% lack licences, and the driving is frequently of the kamikaze variety but they are often the only option available. More and more three-wheelers have metres, but you may have to ask the driver to turn it on before you set off, and he may try and take you to sights en route to boost his fare. If travelling in an unmetred three-wheeler, ensure you agree a price before setting off and bargain hard. You can offer about 60% of the asking price though it is unlikely that you will get to pay the same rate as locals.

TRAIN

Although the network is limited there are train services to a number of major destinations. Journeys are comparatively short, and very cheap by Western standards. Train journeys are leisurely (bar the intercity service between Colombo and Kandy) and an ideal way to see the countryside and meet the people without experiencing the downside of a congested bus journey through dusty crowded roads. You should be aware of touts on major train routes (especially Colombo to Kandy and Galle).

There are three principal 'lines':

1 Northern Line This runs from Colombo up to Anuradhapura and continues north to Vavuniya, though no longer to Jaffna or Mannar (although work is currently underway to repair the line). A line branches east at Maho (67 km south of Anuradhapura) towards Habarana, then splitting at Gal Oya junction, the northern section terminating at Trincomalee, the southern section continuing via Polonnaruwa to Batticaloa.

2 Main Line East from Colombo Fort to Kandy (with a branch line to Matale) with the ascent starting at Rambukkana. From Peradeniya the Main Line continues to Badulla through the hills, including stops at Nanu Oya (for Nuwara Eliya), Hatton (for Adam's Peak), Ohiya (for the Horton Plains) and Ella. This line is very scenic and a recommended way of travelling to the hill country, though book well in advance (up to 10 days).

3 Colombo–Matara Line Originating at Maradana/Fort, this line heads south following the coast to Galle and as far as Matara, connecting all the popular coastal resorts. Running initially through the commuter belt south of the city, it can be crowded in rush hour. There is also work underway to extend this line.

There are also the following lines: on the **Puttalam Line**, there are slow trains north from Fort to Puttalam via Katunayake (for the airport), Negombo and Chilaw. The **Kelani Valley Line** goes from Maradana to Avissawella.

Third class has hard seats; second has some thin cushioning; first class is fairly comfortable. Many slow trains may have second- and third-class coaches only, with first-class only available on some express trains. The time of the next train in each direction is usually chalked onto a blackboard. A seat on a luxury private train from Colombo to Kandy in 2013 costs Rs 1450; a standard first class/observation car costs Rs 500; second class Rs280; 3rd class Rs 180.

Intercity trains There are air-conditioned intercity trains running to Kandy and Vavuniya (via Anuradhapura), which should be booked in advance. Some Kandy trains also have a first-class observation car, which must be booked well in advance as it is very popular and runs only once a day. There are also new, 'luxury' cars operating on these routes that are targeted at tourists. They offer a food service, air conditioning and a few have an observation platform. On other services, the ones that run more frequently, you will have to settle for looking out the window from your first-class comfort. You will need to specify your return date at the time of booking the outward journey as tickets are not open-ended.

There are also some special through trains such as a weekly service from Matara all the way to Anuradhapura, and another from Matara to Kandy, both via Colombo. Extra services are put on during festivals and holidays, eg from January for four months to Hatton (for the Adam's Peak pilgrimage season); April holiday season to the hills; in May and June for full moon days to Buddhist sites such as Kandy, Anuradhapura, Mihintale; and July/August for **Kandy Perahera**.

MAPS

The Survey Department's *Road Map of Sri Lanka* (scale 1:500,000), available at Survey Department branches in large towns, as well as some shops, including Odel in Colombo, is useful and up-to-date. It has some street maps for larger towns. For more detail the department's four large sheet maps covering the island (scale 1:250,000) are the best available. These may not be available to buy for security reasons but you can ask to consult these at the Survey Department's Map Sales Branch in Colombo. *Arjuna's Atlas of Sri Lanka*, Arjuna, 1997 (see www.lankadotcom.com) is a comprehensive demographic survey of Sri Lanka. Sri Lanka Tourist Board branches both in Sri Lanka and abroad gives out a 1:800,000 Sri Lanka itinerary map plus several city and site guides with sketch maps free, but these are not particularly clear.

There are a number of user-friendly fold-out sheet maps produced abroad. These are mainly 1:500,000 scale and show tourist sights. Some have town street maps and some tourist information. Insight and Berndtson & Berndtson maps are both nicely laminated; Periplus's has some tourist information and clear street maps of Colombo, Kandy, Anuradhapura, Galle, Negombo, Nuwara Eliya and Polonnaruwa; Nelles Verlag also has some city insets; the Reise *Know How* map is probably the most detailed.

PRICE CODES

WHERE TO STAY

$$$$ over US$175   **$$$**   US$100-175
$$ US$40-99   **$**   under US$40

Prices refer to the cost of a double room with breakfast, not including service charge or other meals unless otherwise stated.

SERVICE CHARGE

Note that a service charge of 10% is applied to some accommodation. Up to 16% government tax, which is added to food and drink as well, can also apply. The more upmarket the establishment, the more likely these will be added to the total. Enquire beforehand about additional taxes, otherwise it can give you a nasty shock when you come to pay.

RESTAURANTS

$$$ over US$15   **$$**   US$6-15   **$**   under US$6

Prices refer to the cost of a two-course meal for one person including a soft drink, beer or glass of wine.

→ WHERE TO STAY IN SRI LANKA

Sri Lanka has a surprisingly uneven range of accommodation. At the top end, there are international five-star hotels in Colombo (a high minimum rate has been imposed on hotels in Colombo by the government, going some way to explaining the prices) and a handful of very exclusive 'boutique' hotels in some other areas. Below this level, you can stay safely and relatively cheaply in most major tourist areas, where there is a choice of quality hotels offering a full range of facilities (though their food can be bland and uninspired). At the lower end of the scale, there is an increasing range of family-run guesthouses in tourist areas offering bed and breakfast (and sometimes other meals). In smaller centres even the best hotels are far more variable and it may be necessary to accept much more modest accommodation. In the high season (December to March for much of the island) bookings can be extremely heavy. It is therefore best to reserve rooms well in advance if you are making your own arrangements, and to arrive reasonably early in the day.

Prices are highly inflated in Kandy during the **Esala Perahera** festival and in Nuwara Eliya during the April holiday season. 'Long weekends' (weekends when a public holiday or **poya** day falls on a Thursday, Friday, Monday or Tuesday) also attract a substantial increase in room rates in Nuwara Eliya. Many hotels charge the highest room rate over Christmas and New Year (between mid-December to mid-January). Large reductions are made by hotels in all categories out-of-season in most resorts. Always ask if any is available. During the monsoon rooms may feel damp and have a musty smell.

International class hotels Mainly in Colombo, Kandy and the main tourist destinations, these have a full range of facilities with prices and standards comparable to the West. These are often genuinely luxurious.

ON THE ROAD

Ayurvedic healing

Ayurveda (the science of life/health) is the ancient Hindu system of medicine – a naturalistic system depending on diagnosis of the body's 'humours' (wind, mucus, gall and sometimes blood) to achieve a balance. In the early form, gods and demons were associated with cures and ailments; treatment was carried out by using herbs, minerals, formic acid (from ant hills) and water, and hence was limited in scope. Ayurveda classified substances and chemicals compounds in the theory of *panchabhutas* (five 'elements'). It also noted the action of food and drugs on the human body. Ayurvedic massage using aromatic and medicinal oils to tone up the nervous system has been practised for centuries.

This ancient system, which developed in India over centuries before the Buddha's birth, was written down as a *samhita* by Charaka. It probably flourished in Sri Lanka up to the 19th century when it was overshadowed by the Western system of allopathic medicine.

In addition to the use of herbs as cures, many are used daily in the Sri Lankan kitchen (chilli, coriander, cumin, fennel, garlic, ginger), some of which will be familiar in the West, and have for centuries been used as beauty preparations.

Boutique hotels and villas One of the fastest growing sectors of the market, these can be quite special offering a high degree of luxury, superb and very personal service, and a sense of privacy and exclusiveness lacking in resort-style hotels. Often they are innovatively designed with environmental sensitivity. Some sumptuous villas can also be rented by the day or week – see www.villasinsrilanka.com.

Colonial-era hotels The colonial period has left a legacy of atmospheric colonial-era hotels, notably in Colombo, Kandy and Nuwara Eliya. Some were purpose built, others converted from former governors' residences, etc. A number have been carefully modernized without losing their period charm. Some very good deals are available.

Resort hotels Catering mainly to tourists on package holidays, most larger tourist hotels on beaches and near important sites come into this category. Some are luxurious with a good range of facilities, others, notably in some west coast resorts, are rather tired and dated. Food served here tends to be of the 'all-you-can-eat' buffet variety. It pays to make bookings through tour operators, which offer large discounts on most resort-style hotels.

Guesthouses Guesthouses are the staple of budget travellers, and are in plentiful supply in tourist haunts such as the west and south coasts, as well as in Kandy, Nuwara Eliya, Anuradhapura and a few other towns. Some are effectively small hotels, usually at the upper end of the price bracket; others are simpler and more basic affairs. At their best, usually when family owned, they can be friendly, homely, and rich sources of local information. Those offering quality home cooking are well worth searching out. In addition, some private homes in Colombo, Kandy and some beach areas offer rooms, which can be very good value.

Ayurvedic resorts   Mainly on the west coast, very popular with tourists from mainland Europe, these offer a degree of luxury combined with ready or tailor-made programmes of Ayurveda treatment. The authenticity of the treatments on offer tends to vary. **Ayurveda Pavilions** in Negombo, and **Siddhalepa Ayurveda Health Resort** in Kalutara, are two of the most highly regarded resorts, while more basic accommodation is offered with treatment at the Ayurvedic hospitals in Mount Lavinia.

Government rest houses   These are sometimes in converted colonial houses, often in superb locations and although occasionally run down and overpriced with poor service, in some cases they are the best (or only) option in town. **Ceylon Hotels Corporation (CHC)** ① *Central Reservations: 2 Galle Rd, Colombo 3, T558 5858, www.ceylonhotels.lk*, is responsible for management of several of the old government rest houses across the island. It's best to book through Central Reservations as occasionally an individual rest house may not honour a direct booking. Prices charged by some on arrival may vary from what is quoted on the phone or the CHC's 'official' typed list showing the tariff which only a few managers acknowledge exists. Rice and curry lunches at rest houses are often good, though more expensive than similar fare elsewhere.

National park accommodation   National park bungalows are expensive, with accommodation costs, national park fees, service charges and linen charges. If the bungalow is within the park boundaries then you will have to pay park entrance fees for two days for an overnight stay. Camping is also possible in many national parks. Accommodation must be booked at the **Department of Wildlife Conservation** ① *www.dwc.gov.lk*, in Colombo but at the time of writing, excessive demand, the complex lottery system and the difficulty in getting to the office was making this difficult to arrange. The bungalows and campsites also have to be booked up to a month in advance. Another option if you want to stay in the park is to arrange a camping safari with **Leopard Safaris** (see pages 42, 155 and 162).

Plantation bungalows   Some attractive rubber and tea plantation bungalows in the hill country can be rented out by small or large groups and provide an interesting alternative place to stay. A caretaker/cook is often provided. There is no centralized booking agency, but see Tea Trails bungalows (page 143), speak to the tourist board or contact Red Dot Tours, www.reddottours.com.

Circuit bungalows   Designed mainly for government workers, these may be the only option in areas well off the beaten track. They should be booked through the government offices in Colombo. Contact details are given under individual entries.

Railway Retiring Rooms   Railway Retiring Rooms may be hired for up to 24 hours. However, there are only a few stations with rooms and they are generally rather poor value. Some are open to people without rail tickets and can be useful in an emergency. Stations with rooms include: Anuradhapura, Galle, Kandy, Mihintale, Polgahawela, Maho and Trincomalee.

Although it shares some similarities with Indian cooking, Sri Lankan cuisine is distinct from its neighbour. While at its heart lies the island's enviable variety and bountiful supply of native vegetables, fruits and spices, Sri Lanka's history of trade and colonization has contributed to the remarkable range of dishes available today. Even before the arrival of the Europeans, Indians, Arabs, Malays and Moors had all left their mark. The Portuguese brought chilli from South America, perhaps the most significant change to food across the East, while the Dutch and even the British have also bequeathed a number of popular dishes. Sampling authentic Sri Lankan fare is a highlight of any trip.

CUISINE → *See Food glossary, page 218.*

Rice and curry is Sri Lanka's main 'dish', but the term 'curry' conceals an enormous variety of subtle flavours. Coriander, mustard seeds, cumin, fenugreek, peppercorns, cinnamon, cloves and cardamoms are just some of the spices that, roasted and blended, give a Sri Lankan curry its richness, while most cooks also add Maldive fish, or dried sprats. *Rampe* (screw-pine leaf) and tamarind pulp are also distinctive ingredients. The whole is then usually cooked in coconut milk.

Sri Lankan food is renowned for being fiery, and **chilli** is the most noticeable ingredient in some curries. While most tourist restaurants, aware of the sensitivity of some Western palates, normally tone down its use, real home cooking will usually involve liberal quantities. If a dish is still too hot, a spoonful of rice or curd, or a sip of beer or milk (not water) will usually tone down its effects.

A typical Sri Lankan meal would comprise a large portion of rice, with a 'main curry' – for Buddhists usually fish, although chicken, beef and mutton are also often available – and several pulse and vegetable and (sometimes) salad dishes. *Dhal* is invariably one of these, and vegetable curries may be made from jackfruit, okra, breadfruit, beans, bananas, banana flowers or pumpkin, amongst others. Deliciously salty poppadums are also usually served, and the offering is completed by numerous side dishes: spicy pickles, sweet and sour chutneys and 'sambols', made of ground coconut (*pol sambol*) or onion mixed with Maldive fish, red chilli and lime juice (*seeni sambol*). *Mallung,* a milder dish prepared with grated coconut, shredded leaves, red onions and lime, is an alternative to try. *Kiri hodhi* is a mild 'white' curry prepared with coconut milk.

Rice-based alternatives to rice and curry include the Dutch-inspired *lamprais*, rice boiled in meat stock with curry, accompanied by dry meat and vegetable curries, fried meat and fish or meat balls (*frikkadels*), then parcelled in banana leaf and baked; and the ubiquitous *buriyani*, a Moorish dish of rice cooked in stock with pieces of chopped spiced meat and garnished with sliced egg.

The **rice** generally served is usually plain white boiled rice but it is worth searching out the healthier red rice. There are some tasty alternatives. '**String hoppers**', a steamed nest of thin rice flour noodles, are often eaten with thin curries at breakfast but are available at any time. '**Hoppers**' (*appam*), a breakfast speciality, are small cupped pancakes made from fermented rice flour, coconut milk and yeast. Crispy on the edges (like French crêpes), thick at the centre, they are often prepared with an egg broken into the middle of the pan ('egg hoppers'). *Pittu* is a crumbly mixture of flour and grated coconut steamed in a bamboo mould, usually served with coconut milk and sambol.

As befits a tropical island, Sri Lanka's **fish** and **seafood** is excellent. The succulent white seerfish, tuna and mullet, usually grilled and served with chips and salad, are widely available along the coast, while crab, lobster and prawns (often jumbo prawns) are magnificent and reasonably priced. Cuttlefish is very versatile and prepared a number of ways. Meat varies in quality; though it is cheap and usually better than you get in India.

Unsurprisingly, **Indian** food is also popular, particularly from the south. Cheap filling traditional 'plate' meals (*thali*) are available in Colombo, the north and east, as are *dosai*, crispy pancakes made from rice and lentil-flour batter, often served with a spiced potato filling.

Sri Lanka has a spectacular variety of superb tropical **fruit**, and this is reflected in the variety of juices on offer. Available throughout the year are pineapple, papaya (excellent with lime) and banana, of which there are dozens of varieties (red bananas are said to be the best). The extraordinarily rich jack (*jak*) fruit is also available all year. Seasonal fruit include the lusciously sweet mango (for which Jaffna is especially famous), the purplish mangosteen (July to September), wood-apple, avocado, the spiky foul-smelling durian and hairy red rambutan from July to October. In addition to ordinary green coconuts, Sri Lanka has its own variety – the golden king coconut (*thambili*); the milk is particularly sweet and nutritious.

BREAKFAST

The tendency amongst most smaller hotels and guesthouses is to serve a 'Western breakfast' comprising fruit and white bread with some jam. It is well worth ordering a Sri Lankan alternative in advance – ie the night before. This could comprise hoppers, string hoppers, *kiribath* (see Desserts, below) or, best of all, the delicious **rotty** (*rotti/roti*), a flat circular unleavened bread cooked on a griddle. In larger hotels breakfast will usually be a buffet of Western and Sri Lankan dishes.

LUNCH

Lunch is the main meal of the day for many Sri Lankans. Rice and curry is the standard, often served in larger hotels as a buffet or in many local and tourist restaurants. A cheaper and quicker alternative is to pick up a **'lunch packet'**, available from local restaurants and street vendors. This takeaway option usually comprises a portion of rice, a meat, fish or vegetable curry, plus *dhal*, all wrapped up in a paper parcel. This is a cheap and filling meal. A lighter alternative still is a plate of **short eats**, a selection of meat and vegetable rolls, 'cutlets' (deep-fried in bread crumbs), *rotis* and *wadais*, a Tamil speciality of deep-fried savoury lentil doughnut rings, sometimes served in yoghurt (*thair vadai*). You will normally be given a full plate and charged for however many you eat. Bear in mind though that plates are left on the table, people finger them choosing which ones to eat, and then when they've finished the leftovers go back to be served again. Try and intercept a fresh batch just out of the fryer.

DINNER

In larger hotels, dinner is usually the main meal of the day, often with enormous all-you-can-eat buffets. Sri Lankans tend to eat late but light, and be aware that outside Colombo and the major tourist centres, the offering in guesthouses and restaurants may be limited unless you order in advance. It may not be possible to get rice and curry but Chinese food, such as fried rice, and devilled dishes are nearly always available.

DESSERTS

Sri Lankans tend to have a sweet tooth. Rice forms the basis of many Sri Lankan sweet dishes, palm treacle (*kitul*) being used as the main traditional sweetener. This is also served on curd as a delicious dessert (*kiri peni*) and boiled and set into *jaggery*. *Kavun* is an oil cake, made with rice flour and treacle and deep-fried until golden brown. Malay influence is evident in the popular *watalappam*, a steamed pudding made with coconut milk, eggs and jaggery, rather reminiscent of crème caramel. *Kiribath*, rice boiled in milk, is something of a national dish, often served at weddings and birthdays. It can be eaten with jaggery or as a breakfast dish with *seeni sambol*. Sri Lankan ice cream varies in quality; the best is made by soft drinks company **Elephant House**. Jaffna is also famous for its 'cream houses'.

EATING OUT

Eating out in Sri Lanka is remarkably cheap. Most restaurants serve a choice of Indian, Chinese and continental dishes. Sadly, it is not easy to get good Sri Lankan food in most resort hotels which tend to concentrate on Western dishes. The upmarket hotels in Colombo, however, serve first-class buffets at lunch and dinnertime, and there are an increasing number of excellent Sri Lankan restaurants in the city. Upcountry, home cooking in family-owned guesthouses is often unbeatable. It is essential to order well in advance as Sri Lankan curries take a long time to prepare. This is one of the reasons for the universal popularity of Chinese and 'devilled' dishes available throughout the island, which can be knocked together in a few minutes. **Vegetarian** food is much less common in Sri Lanka than in India, and in places can be difficult to get. Check out www.lankarestaurants.com, for interesting and helpful reviews of restaurants, including food and ambience.

DRINKS

As they are year-round fruits, fresh papaya, pineapple and lime **juice** are always excellent. Sour-sop and wood-apple juice are two more unusual alternatives worth trying. One of the most popular and widespread drinks is King Coconut (the golden *thambili*). Always pure, straight from the nut, it is very refreshing. Mineral **water** is available everywhere, though is relatively expensive. There is a huge variety of bottled **soft drinks**, including international brands. Local favourites include ginger beer, cream soda, lemonade and Necto. These are perfectly safe but always check the seal. **Elephant House** is the main soft drinks manufacturer, and all their products are palatable. One potent soft drink is **Peyawa**, a ginger beer made with pepper and coriander for added kick.

The island's **coffee** harvest failed in 1869, and it would seem that Sri Lankans have never quite forgiven it, such are the crimes committed in the name of the drink. Colombo's upmarket hotels do however serve decent coffee, and there are a couple of new Western-style coffee bars opening up. As befits one of the world's great producers, **tea** is of course a much better option, although the highest quality varieties are generally exported.

Drinking **alcohol** in Sri Lanka is a no-nonsense male preserve. Bars, except in Colombo and tourist areas, tend to be spit-and-sawdust affairs. **Beer** is strong (5%+), popular and served in large 660 ml bottles. **Lion**, **Carlsberg** and **Three Coins** are the three main brands, each producing a Pilsner-style lager slightly thin to Western tastes but quite palatable. **Three Coins** make some good specialist beers: their 8% **Sando** stout is smooth and chocolatey, and **Riva** is a more than passable wheat beer. The locally brewed **arrack**, distilled from palm toddy, is the most popular spirit and a cheaper option than beer. Superior brands include **Old Arrack, Double distilled**, the matured VSOA and **seven-year-old** arrack. The frothy, cloudy cider-like **toddy** is the other national drink, produced from the fermented sap of coconut, kitul (palm treacle) or palmyra palms. It is available from very basic toddy 'taverns', usually makeshift shacks that spring up in toddy-producing areas. Alcohol is not sold on *poya* days (see box, page 204). Orders for alcoholic drinks in hotels are usually taken on the previous day. Note that hotels and restaurants will serve foreign tourists expensive, imported spirits and beers unless told otherwise.

→ FESTIVALS IN SRI LANKA

Since the significant days of all four of its religions are respected, Sri Lanka has an remarkable number of festivals, and probably more public holidays (29) than anywhere else in the world – a matter of increasing consternation to the island's business leaders. In mid-April, the **Sinhala** and **Tamil New Year** celebrations are colourful and feature traditional games. In May and June the **Wesak** and **Poson Poya** (full moon) days are marked with religious pageants. **Esala Perahera** (around July-August full moon) is the most striking of all, particularly in Kandy though major festivals are also held in Colombo, Kataragama and other major temples. Drummers, dancers, decorated elephants, torch-bearers and whip-crackers all add colour and drama to the 10 days of celebrations. All full moon (*poya*) days are holidays, as are Saturday and Sunday. There are also several secular holidays. Most religious festivals (Buddhist, Muslim and Hindu) are determined by the lunar calendar and therefore change from year to year. Check at the tourist office (www.srilankatourism.org) for exact dates.

HOLIDAYS AND FESTIVALS

Jan Duruthu Poya Sri Lankan Buddhists believe that the Buddha visited the island. There is a large annual festival at the Kelaniya Temple near Colombo.

Tamil Thai Pongal On 14th, observed by Hindus, celebrating the first grains of the rice harvest.

Jan/Feb Navam Poya In late-Jan/early Feb, this is celebrated at Colombo's grandest *perahera* at Gangaramaya Temple, with caparisoned elephants, dancing, drummers and processions.

Feb National (Independence) Day Celebrated on the 4th and involves processions, dances, parades.

Feb/Mar Maha Sivarathri Marks the night when Siva danced his celestial dance of destruction (*Tandava*), celebrated with feasting and fairs at Siva temples, preceded by a night of devotional readings and hymn singing.

Mar/Apr Easter Good Friday with Passion plays in Negombo and other coastal areas, in particular on Duwa Island.

Mar Medin Poya Day.

Apr Bak Poya Day.

Sinhala and Tamil New Year Day
The 13-14th is marked with celebrations (originally harvest thanksgiving), by closure of many shops/restaurants. Many Colombo residents decamp to the highlands, see box, page 122.

May May Day 1 May.

Wesak Poya Day The day following is the most important *poya* in the calendar, celebrating the key events in the Buddha's life: his birth, Enlightenment and death. Clay oil-lamps are lit across the island and there are also folk theatre performances. Wayside stalls offer food and drink free to passers-by. These are special celebrations at Kandy, Anuradhapura and Kelaniya (Colombo).

FESTIVALS
Full moon festivities

Full Moon *poya* days of each month are holidays. Buddhists visit temples with offerings of flowers, to worship and remind themselves of the precepts. Certain temples hold special celebrations in connection with a particular full moon, eg Esala at Kandy. Accommodation may be difficult to find and public transport is crowded during these festivals. No alcohol is sold (you can however order your drinks at your hotel the day before) and all places of entertainment are closed.

National Heroes' Day On the 22nd of the month but not a public holiday.

Jun Poson Poya Day Marks Mahinda's arrival in Sri Lanka as the 1st Buddhist missionary; Mihintale and Anuradhapura hold special celebrations.

Bank Holiday On the 30th.

Jul/Aug Esala Poya The most important Sri Lankan festival. It takes place in Jul/ early Aug with grand processions of elephants, dancers, etc, honouring the Sacred Tooth of the Buddha in Kandy lasting 10 days, and elsewhere including Dewi Nuwara (Dondra) and Bellanwila Raja Maha Vihare, South Colombo. Culmination of the **Pada Yatra** pilgrimage to Kataragama, where purification rituals including firewalking are held.

Munneswaram (Chilaw) Vel Festival and in Colombo from Sea St Hindu temple, procession to Bambalapitiya and Welawatta.

Nikini Poya Day Celebrations at Bellanwila, Colombo.

Sep Binara Poya Day A Perahera is held in Badulla.

Oct/Nov Wap Poya Day.

Deepavali Festival of Lights, celebrated by Hindus with fireworks, commemorating Rama's return after his 14 years exile in the forest when citizens lit his way with earthen oil lamps.

Nov Il Poya Day.

Dec Unduwap Poya Day Marks the arrival of Emperor Asoka's daughter, Sanghamitta,

with a sapling of the Bodhi Tree from India. Special celebrations at Anuradhapura, Bentota and Colombo.

Christmas Day Bank holiday on 25th.

Special Bank Holiday 31st.

Muslim holy days

These are fixed according to the lunar calendar. According to the Gregorian calendar, they tend to fall 11 days earlier each year, dependent on the sighting of the new moon.

Ramadan Start of the month of fasting when all Muslims (except young children, the very elderly, the sick, pregnant women and travellers) must abstain from food and drink from sunrise to sunset.

Id ul Fitr The 3-day festival marks the end of Ramadan.

Id-ul-Zuha/Bakr-Id Muslims commemorate Ibrahim's sacrifice of his son according to God's commandment; the main time of pilgrimage to Mecca (the Hajj). It is marked by the sacrifice of a goat, feasting and alms giving.

Muharram When the killing of the Prophet's grandson, Hussain, is commemorated by Shi'a Muslims. Decorated *tazias* (replicas of the martyr's tomb) are carried in procession by devout wailing followers who beat their chests to express their grief. Shi'as fast for the 10 days.

ESSENTIALS A-Z

Accident and emergency Emergencies T119/118. **Police** T243 3333; **Tourist Police** T243 3342; **Fire and ambulance** T242 2222; **Hospital** (Colombo) T269 1111.

Children

Children of all ages are widely welcomed and greeted with warmth which is often extended to those accompanying them. Sri Lanka's beaches and wildlife are especially likely to appeal, and of course a visit to Pinnawela Elephant Orphanage (see page 115). Keep children away from stray animals which may carry parasites or rabies; monkeys can be aggressive.

Care should be taken when travelling to remote areas where health services are primitive since children can become ill more rapidly than adults. Extra care must be taken to protect children from the strong sun by using high factor sun cream, hats, umbrellas, etc, and by avoiding being out in the hottest part of the day. Cool showers or baths help if children get too hot. Dehydration may be counteracted with plenty of drinking water – bottled, boiled (furiously for 5 mins) or purified with tablets. Preparations such as 'Dioralyte' may be given if the child suffers from diarrhoea. Moisturizer, zinc and castor oil (for sore bottoms due to change of diet) are worth taking. Mosquito nets or electric insect repellents at night may be provided in hotel rooms which are not a/c. To help young children to take anti-malarial tablets, one suggestion is to crush them between spoons and mix with a teaspoon of dessert chocolate (for cake-making) bought in a tube. Wet wipes and disposable nappies are not readily available in many areas.

In the big hotels there is no difficulty with obtaining safe baby foods. For older children, tourist restaurants will usually have a non-spicy alternative to Sri Lankan curries. Grilled or fried fish or chicken is a good standby, often served with boiled vegetables, as are eggs. Fruit is magnificent but should be peeled first. Toast and jam are usually served for breakfast, or hoppers (with bananas). Fizzy drinks are widely available, although king coconut is a healthier and cheaper alternative. Bottled water is available everywhere.

Many hotels and guesthouses have triple rooms, at little or no extra cost to the price of a double, or you can ask for an extra bed. The biggest hotels provide babysitting facilities.

Buses are often overcrowded and are probably worth avoiding with children. Train travel is generally better (under 12s travel half-price, under 3s free) but hiring a car hire is by far the most comfortable and flexible option; see page 192.

Customs and duty free

On arrival visitors to Sri Lanka are officially required to declare all currency, valuable equipment, jewellery and gems even though this is rarely checked. All personal effects should be taken back on departure. Visitors are not allowed to bring in goods in commercial quantities, or prohibited/restricted goods such as dangerous drugs, weapons, explosive devices or gold. Drug trafficking or possession carries the death penalty, although this is very rarely carried out on foreigners. In addition to completing Part II of the Immigration Landing Card, a tourist may be asked by the Customs Officer to complete a Baggage Declaration Form.

Duty free

You are allowed 1.5 litres of spirits, 2 bottles of wine, 200 cigarettes, 50 cigars or 250 g rolling tobacco, a small quantity of perfume and 250 ml of eau de toilette. You can also import a small quantity of travel souvenirs not exceeding US$250 in value. For more information visit Sri Lanka Customs, www.customs.gov.lk.

Export restrictions

Up to 10 kg of tea is allowed to be exported duty free. Note that the 'Ceylon Tea' counter at the airport outer lobby accepts rupees. The following are not permitted to be exported from Sri Lanka: all currencies in excess of that declared on arrival; any gems, jewellery or valuable items not declared on arrival or not purchased in Sri Lanka out of declared funds; gold (crude, bullion or coins); Sri Lankan currency in excess of Rs 250; firearms, explosives or dangerous weapons; antiques, statues, treasures, old books, etc (antiques are considered to be any article over 50 years old); animals, birds, reptiles or their parts (dead or alive); tea, rubber or coconut plants; dangerous drugs.

Import of all the items listed above and in addition, Indian and Pakistani currency, obscene and seditious literature or pictures is prohibited.

If transiting through another country after leaving Sri Lanka, check beforehand that any duty free alcohol you purchase will be accepted, if you not you may find yourself in India or the Middle East pouring it down a sink in front of customs officials.

Disabled travellers

The country isn't geared up specially for making provisions for the physically handicapped or wheelchair-bound traveller. Access to buildings, toilets, pavements and kerbs and public transport can prove frustrating but it is easy to find people to give a hand with lifting and carrying. Provided there is an able-bodied companion to scout around and arrange help, and so long as you are prepared to spend on at least mid-price hotels or guesthouses, private car hire and taxis, Sri Lanka should prove to be rewarding.

Some travel companies now specialize in exciting holidays, tailor-made for individuals depending on their level of disability. **Global Access – Disabled Travel Network Site**, www.globalaccessnews.com, is dedicated to providing information for 'disabled adventurers' and includes a number of reviews and tips from members of the public. You might want to read *Nothing Ventured* edited by Alison Walsh (Harper Collins), which gives personal accounts of world-wide journeys by disabled travellers, plus advice and listings.

Organizations in Sri Lanka include **Sri Lanka Federation of the Visually Handicapped (SLFVH)**, 74 Church St, Col 2, Colombo, T011-243 7758, www.slfvh.org.

Drugs

Penalties for possession of, use of, or trafficking in illegal drugs in Sri Lanka are strict, and convicted offenders may expect jail sentences and heavy fines.

Electricity

230-240 volts, 50 cycles AC. There may be pronounced variations in the voltage, and power cuts are common. 3-pin (round) sockets are the norm. Universal adaptors are widely available.

Embassies and consulates

For embassies and consulates of Sri Lanka, see www.embassiesabroad.com.

Health

Local populations in Sri Lanka are exposed to a range of health risks not encountered in the Western world. Many of the diseases are major problems for the local poor and destitute and, although the risk to travellers is more remote, they cannot be ignored. Obviously 5-star travel is going to carry less risk than backpacking on a budget.

Healthcare in the region is varied, with the best being facilities being available in Colombo where there are some excellent private clinics/hospitals. As with all medical care, first impressions count. It's worth contacting your embassy or consulate on arrival and asking where the recommended (ie those used by diplomats) clinics are. You can also ask about locally recommended medical do's and don'ts. If you do get ill, and you have the opportunity, you should also ask your medical insurer whether they are satisfied that the medical centre/hospital you have been referred to is of a suitable standard.

Before you go

Ideally, you should see your GP or travel clinic at least 6 weeks before your departure for general advice on travel risks, malaria and vaccinations. Make sure you have travel insurance, get a dental check (especially if you are going to be away for more than a month), know your blood group and if you suffer a long-term condition such as diabetes or epilepsy make sure someone knows or that you have a Medic Alert bracelet/necklace with this information on it. Remember that it is risky to buy medicinal tablets abroad because the doses may differ there is the risk of being given fake drugs.

A-Z of health risks

If you are unlucky (or careless) enough to receive a venomous **bite or sting** by a snake, spider, scorpion or sea creature, try to identify the creature, without putting yourself in further danger (do not try to catch a live snake). Snake bites in particular are very frightening, but in fact rarely poisonous – even venomous snakes bite without injecting venom. Victims should be taken to a hospital or a doctor without delay. Commercial snake bite and scorpion kits are available, but are usually only useful for the specific types of snake or scorpion. Most serum has to be given intravenously so it is not much good equipping yourself with it unless you are used to making injections into veins. It is best to rely on

local practice in these cases, because the particular creatures will be known about locally and appropriate treatment can be given. To prevent bites, do not walk in snake territory in bare feet or sandals – wear proper shoes or boots and walk heavily to warn the snake you are coming. For scorpions and spiders, keep beds away from the walls and look inside your shoes and under the toilet seat every morning. Certain tropical sea fish when trodden upon inject venom into bathers' feet. This can be very painful. Wear plastic shoes if such creatures are reported. The pain can be relieved by immersing the foot in hot water (as hot as you can bear) for as long as the pain persists. Citric acid juices in fruits such as lemon are reported as being useful.

Chikungunya is a relatively rare mosquito-borne disease that has had outbreaks in Sri Lanka, particularly during the monsoon when flooded areas encourage the carrier mosquitoes to breed. The disease manifests within 12 days of infection and symptoms resemble a severe fever, with headaches, joint pain, arthritis and exhaustion lasting from several days to several weeks; in vulnerable sections of the population it can be fatal. Neither vaccine nor treatment are available, so rest is the best cure.

Unfortunately there is no vaccine against **dengue fever** and the mosquitoes that carry it bite during the day. You will be ill for 2-3 days, then get better for a few days and then feel ill again. It should all be over in 7-10 days. Heed all the anti-mosquito measures that you can.

The standard advice for **diarrhoea** prevention is to be careful with water and ice for drinking. If you have any doubts about where the water came from then boil it or filter it and treat it. There are many filter/treatment devices now available on the market. Food can also transmit disease. Be wary of salads (what were they washed in, who handled them), re-heated foods or food that has been left out in the sun having been cooked earlier in the day. There is a simple adage that says wash it, peel it, boil it or forget it. Also be wary of unpasteurized dairy products, these can transmit a range of diseases from brucellosis (fevers and constipation), to listeria (meningitis) and tuberculosis of the gut (constipation, fevers and weight loss).

The key treatment with all diarrhoea is rehydration. Try to keep hydrated by taking the right mixture of salt and water. This is available as Oral Rehydration Salts (ORS) in ready-made sachets or can be made up by adding a teaspoon of sugar and a half teaspoon of salt to a litre of clean water. You can also use flat carbonated drinks. Drink at least 1 large cup of this drink for each loose stool. Alternatively, Immodium (or Pepto-Bismol, used a lot by Americans) is useful if you have a long coach/train journey or on a trek, although is not a cure. Antibiotics like Ciproxin (Ciprofloxacin) – obtained by private prescription in the UK – can be a useful antibiotic for some forms of travellers' diarrhoea. If it persists beyond 2 weeks, with blood or pain, seek medical attention. One good preventative is taking probiotics like Vibact or Bifilac which are available over the counter.

If you go **diving** make sure that you are fit to do so. The **British Sub-Aqua Club (BSAC)**, Telford's Quay, South Pier Rd, Ellesmere Port, Cheshire CH65 4FL, UK, T01513-506200, www.bsac.com, can put you in touch with doctors who do medical examinations. Protect your feet from cuts, beach dog parasites (larva migrans) and sea urchins. The latter are almost impossible to remove but can be dissolved with lime or vinegar. Keep an eye out for secondary infection. Check that the dive company know what they are doing, have appropriate certification from BSAC or **PADI**, Unit 7, St Philips Central, Albert Rd, St Philips, Bristol, BS2 OTD, T0117-300 7234, www.padi.com, and that the equipment is well maintained.

Hepatitis means inflammation of the liver. The most obvious symptom is a yellowing of your skin or the whites of your eyes. However, prior to this all that you may notice is itching and tiredness. Early on, depending on the type of hepatitis, a vaccine or immunoglobulin may reduce the duration of the illness. There are vaccines for hepatitis A and B; the latter spread through blood and unprotected sexual intercourse, both of these can be avoided. Unfortunately there is no vaccine for hepatitis C or the increasing alphabetical list of other hepatitis viruses.

If infected with **leishmaniasis**, you may notice a raised lump, which leads to a purplish discolouration on white skin and a possible ulcer. The parasite is transmitted by the bite of a sandfly. Sandflies do not fly very far and the greatest risk is at ground levels, so if you can avoid sleeping on the jungle floor do so, under a permethrin-treated net and use insect repellent. Seek advice for any persistent skin lesion or nasal symptom. Several weeks of treatment is required under specialist supervision.

Various forms of **leptospirosis** occur throughout the country, transmitted by a bacterium which is excreted in rodent urine. Fresh water and moist soil harbour the organisms, which enter the body through cuts and scratches. If you suffer from any form of prolonged fever consult a doctor.

A **malaria** risk exists throughout the year in Sri Lanka, predominantly in the area north of Vavuniya and the northeastern coastal districts. There is a low to no risk in the rest of the country. In the UK we still believe that Chloroquine and Paludrine are sufficient for Sri Lanka.

For **mosquito repellents**, remember that DEET (Di-ethyltoluamide) is the gold standard. Apply the repellent 4-6 hrs but more often if you are sweating heavily. If a non-DEET product is used check who tested it. Validated products (tested at the London School of Hygiene and Tropical

Medicine) include Mosiguard, Non-DEET Jungle formula and non-DEET Autan. If you want to use citronella remember that it must be applied very frequently (hourly) to be effective. If you are a target for insect bites or develop lumps quite soon after being bitten, carry an Aspivenin kit.

Prickly heat is a common intensely itchy rash, avoided by frequent washing and by wearing loose clothing. It is cured by allowing skin to dry off through use of powder – and spending a few nights in an a/c hotel.

Rabies is endemic in most districts in Sri Lanka, so avoid dogs that are behaving strangely. If you are bitten or licked over an open wound by a domestic or wild animal, do not leave things to chance: scrub the wound with soap and water and/or disinfectant, try to at least determine the animal's ownership, where possible, and seek medical assistance at once. The course of treatment depends on whether you have already been satisfactorily vaccinated against rabies. If you have (and this is worthwhile if you are spending lengths of time in developing countries) then some further doses of vaccine are all that is required. If you are not already vaccinated then anti-rabies serum (immunoglobulin) may be required in addition. It is important to finish the course of treatment. Note that Sri Lanka suffers from shortages of immunoglobulin, so if planning to spend time in rural areas it may be worth investing in the pre-travel vaccine.

The range of visible and invisible **sexually transmitted diseases** is mind-boggling. Unprotected sex can spread HIV, hepatitis B and C, gonorrhea (green discharge), chlamydia (nothing to see but may cause painful urination and later female infertility), painful recurrent herpes, syphilis and warts, just to name a few. You can cut down the risk by using condoms, a femidom or avoiding sex altogether.

Make sure you protect yourself from the **sun** with high-factor sun screen and don't forget to wear a hat.

Ticks usually attach themselves to the lower parts of the body often after walking in areas where cattle have grazed. They swell up as they start to suck blood. The important thing is to remove them gently, so that they do not leave their head parts in your skin, because this can cause a nasty allergic reaction later. Do not use petrol, Vaseline, lighted cigarettes, etc, to remove the tick, but, with a pair of tweezers remove the gently by gripping it at the attached (head) end and rock it out in very much the same way that a tooth is extracted.

Certain **tropical flies** which lay their eggs under the skin of sheep and cattle also occasionally do the same thing to humans with the unpleasant result that a maggot grows under the skin and pops up as a boil or pimple. The best way to remove these is to cover the boil with oil, Vaseline or nail varnish to stop the maggot breathing, then to squeeze it out gently the next day.

Vaccinations

If you need vaccinations, see your doctor well in advance of your travel. Most courses must be completed by a minimum of 4 weeks. Travel clinics may provide rapid courses of vaccination, but are likely to be more expensive. The following vaccinations are recommended: typhoid, polio, tetanus, infectious hepatitis and diptheria. For details of malaria prevention, see page opposite.

The following vaccinations may also be considered: rabies, possibly BCG (since TB is still common in the region) and in some cases meningitis and diphtheria (if you're staying in the country for a long time). Yellow fever is not required in Sri Lanka but you may be asked to show a certificate if you have travelled from Africa or South America. Japanese encephalitis may be required for rural travel at certain times of the year (mainly rainy seasons). An effective oral cholera vaccine (Dukoral) is now available as 2 doses providing 3 months' protection.

Useful websites
Blood Care Foundation (UK), www.bloodcare.org.uk
British Travel Health Association (UK), www.btha.org
Fit for Travel, www.fitfortravel.scot.nhs.uk
Foreign and Commonwealth Office (FCO) (UK), www.fco.gov.uk
The Health Protection Agency, www.hpa.org.uk
Medic Alert (UK), www.medicalalert.co.uk
Travel Screening Services (UK), www.travelscreening.co.uk
World Health Organisation, www.who.int

Human rights
In the last few years Sri Lanka and its human rights have been in the news for all the wrong reasons. There have been reports of restrictions on freedom of expression and freedom of the press, and disappearances of journalists. Sri Lanka has also so far refused to undertake an independent investigation into what happened at the end of the civil war – it is widely held that war crimes were committed by both sides during the final weeks of the conflict.

Insurance
Although Sri Lanka does not suffer from being a crime-ridden society, accidents and delays can still occur. Full travel insurance is advised but at the very least get medical insurance and coverage for personal effects. There are a wide variety of policies to choose from, so it's best to shop around. Your local travel agent can also advise on the best and most reliable deals available. Always read the small print carefully. Check that the policy covers the activities you intend or may end up doing. Also check exactly what your medical cover includes, eg ambulance, helicopter rescue

or emergency flights back home. Also check the payment protocol. You may have to pay first before the insurance company reimburses you. **STA Travel**, www.statravel.co.uk, offers a range of good-value policies.

Internet
Internet access is now widespread across Sri Lanka but prices can vary considerably. Hotels and guesthouses are beginning to offer Wi-Fi, and in the main tourist areas cafés are also getting in on the act. Most major towns will usually have communication centres where terminals are available. Connections are usually much slower and less reliable and charges rise. Sometimes post offices offer the cheapest internet connection in town, so it is worth dropping in to ask. Skype is increasingly available.

Language
Sinhala and Tamil are the official languages, but English is widely spoken and understood in the main tourist areas though not by many in rural parts. Some German is spoken by a growing number of Sri Lankans in the southwestern beach resorts.

Media
Newspapers and magazines
It is well worth reading the newspapers, which give a good insight into Sri Lankan attitudes. The *Daily News* and *The Island* are national daily newspapers published in English; there are several Sunday papers including the *Sunday Observer* and *Sunday Times*. Each has a website with archive section which is worth investigating. In Colombo and some other hotels a wide range of international daily and periodical newspapers and magazines is available. The *Lanka Guardian* is a respected fortnightly offering news and comment. *Lanka Monthly Digest* is aimed primarily at the business world but has some interesting articles.

Travel Lanka is a free monthly tourist guide available at larger tourist offices and in major hotels. It has some useful information and listings for Colombo and the main tourist areas, though much is out of date. If the copy on display in the tourist office is months out of date ask for the more recent edition, it's usually tucked away in a cupboard. For a more contemporary view, pick up a copy of *Leisure Times*. Also monthly, it has the latest restaurant, bar and nightclub openings, and a rundown of the month's events in Colombo. Free copies are available at the airport, big hotels, shopping complexes, and some bars and clubs.

Radio and television

Sri Lanka's national radio and television network, broadcasts in Sinhalese and English. **SLBC** operates between 0540 and 2300 on 95.6 FM in Colombo and 100.2 FM and 89.3 FM in Kandy. **BBC World Service** (1512khz/19m and 9720khz/31m from 2000 to 2130 GMT) has a large audience in both English and regional languages. Liberalization has opened the door to several private channels and an ever-growing number of private radio stations. **Yes FM** (89.5 FM), **TNL** (101.7 FM) and **Sun FM** (99.9 or 95.3 FM) broadcast Western music in English 24 hrs a day.

The 2 state TV channels are **Rupavahini** which broadcasts 24 hrs a day, and **ITN**. Many Sri Lankans now watch satellite TV with a choice of channels, which offer good coverage of world news and also foreign feature films and 'soaps'.

Money → *£1 = Rs 204, US\$1= Rs 132, €1= Rs 174 (Aug 2013)*

The Sri Lankan rupee (LKR) is made up of 100 cents. Notes in denominations of Rs 1000, 500, 200, 100, 50, 20, 10 and coins in general use are Rs 10, 5, 2 and 1. Visitors bringing in excess of US\$10,000 into Sri Lanka should declare the amount on arrival. All Sri Lankan rupees should be re-converted upon leaving Sri Lanka. It is also illegal to bring Indian or Pakistani rupees into Sri Lanka, although this is rarely, if ever, enforced. See Customs, page 205. It is now possible to bring Sri Lankan rupees into the country but at the time of writing the limit was set at Rs 5000 and it was only available at some foreign exchange desks in the UK and had to be ordered in advance.

It is best to carry credit cards in a money belt worn under clothing. Only carry enough cash for your daily needs, keeping the rest in your money belt or in a hotel safe. Keep plenty of small change and lower denomination notes as it can be difficult to change large notes, this is especially helpful if taking 3-wheelers or bargaining for goods.

Banks

Banks are generally open Mon-Fri 0900-1500, although some banks in Colombo have extended opening hours. Private banks (eg **Commercial Bank**, **Hatton National Bank**, **Sampath Bank**) are generally more efficient and offer a faster service than government-owned banks like **Bank of Ceylon** and **People's Bank**.

ATMs are common in Sri Lanka. A small fee will be charged on your bill at home and will vary depending of your bank. The majority of Sri Lankan banks now accept Visa, MasterCard and Cirrus, but check the sign for assurance. Queues at ATMs can be very long on public holidays.

Changing money

There is an ATM and several 24-hr exchange counters at the airport which give good rates of exchange. Larger hotels often have a money exchange counter (sometimes open 24 hrs), but offer substantially lower rates than banks. In the larger cities and resorts you will often find private dealers who will exchange cash notes or travellers' cheques. Rates are comparable to banks and are entirely above board. There is no black market money-changing in Sri Lanka, although it may be useful to carry some small denomination foreign currency notes (eg £10, US$10) for emergencies.

Keep the **encashment receipts** you are given when exchanging money, as you may need at least 1 to re-exchange any rupees upon leaving Sri Lanka. Unspent rupees may be reconverted at a commercial bank when you leave. Changing money through unauthorized dealers is illegal.

Ensure you change your rupees before checking in at the airport, there are no exchange facilities in the departure lounge.

Cost of travelling

The Sri Lankan cost of living remains well below that in the industrialized world, although is rising quite sharply. Food and public transport, especially rail and bus, remain cheap, and accommodation, though not as cheap as in India, costs less than in the West. The expensive hotels and restaurants are also less expensive than their counterparts in Europe, Japan or the US.

Budget travellers (sharing a room) could expect to spend about Rs 2500 each per day to cover the cost of accommodation, food and travel. Those planning to stay in fairly comfortable hotels and use taxis or hired cars for travelling to sights should expect to spend at least Rs 9000 a day. Single rooms are rarely charged less than about 80% of the double room price.

Many travellers are irritated by the Sri Lankan policy of '**dual pricing**' for foreigners – one price for locals, another for tourists. Sites that see a lot of tourists, particularly in Kandy and the Cultural Triangle, carry entrance charges comparable to those in the West, while national park fees have increased exponentially in recent years and carry a catalogue of hidden extra taxes. Hotels have one price for Sri Lankans and expats and another for foreign tourists. In common with many other Asian countries, some shops and 3-wheeler drivers will try to overcharge foreigners – experience is the only way to combat this.

Credit cards

Major credit cards are increasingly accepted in the main centres of Sri Lanka both for shopping and for purchasing Sri Lankan rupees, but do not let the card out of your sight. Ensure that transactions are carried out in front of you and check the amounts before confirming payment. Larger hotels also accept payment by credit card. Cash can also be drawn from ATMs using credit cards but charges will be applied. Notify your bank in advance that you will be using your credit card and/or debit card whilst in Sri Lanka to avoid the card being stopped. It is also recommended that you check your statements on returning home.

Service charge

A service charge of 10% is applied to some accommodation, and a further 15% government tax, which is added to food and drink as well, can also apply. The more upmarket the establishment the more chance these will be added to the total. Enquire beforehand about additional taxes, otherwise it can give you a nasty shock when you come to pay.

Opening hours

Banks Mon-Fri 0900-1500 (some 1300), some open Sat morning
Government offices Mon-Fri 0930-1700, some open Sat 0930-1300 (often alternate Sat only).
Post offices Mon-Fri 1000-1700, and Sat mornings.
Shops Mon-Fri 1000-1900 and Sat mornings with most closed on Sun. Sun street bazaars in some areas.
Poya days (full moon) are holidays and government offices, etc, will be closed. In tourist areas more is open that elsewhere.

Post

Try to use a franking service in a post office when sending mail, or hand in your mail at a counter. Many towns often have private agencies which offer most postal services.

For valuable items, it is best to use a **courier**, eg **DHL Parcel Service** in Colombo. It takes 2-3 working days to the UK or USA; 3-4 working days to mainland Europe.

Poste restante at the GPO in larger towns will keep your mail (letters and packages) for up to 3 months.

Safety
Restricted and protected areas

Some places in the north and east of the island remain no-go or have limited access due to high security and/or land mines. Check www.fco.gov.uk for the latest information. Travel off road should not be undertaken.

Other areas with restricted access include certain archaeological sites, national parks and reserves which require permits before visiting. Refer to the relevant sections of the travelling text for details.

Confidence tricksters

Confidence tricksters and touts who aim to part you from your money are found in most major towns and tourist sites. It is best to ignore them and carry on your own business while politely, but firmly, declining their offers of help.

Accommodation touts are common at rail and bus stations often boarding trains some distance before the destination. After engaging you in casual conversation to find out your plan one will often find you a taxi or a 3-wheeler and try to persuade you that the hotel of your choice is closed, full or not good value. They will suggest an alternative where they will, no doubt, earn a commission (which you will end up having to pay). It is better to go to your preferred choice alone. Phone in advance to check if a place is full and make a reservation if necessary. If it is full then the hotelier/guesthouse owner will usually advise you of a suitable alternative. Occasionally, touts operate in groups to confuse you or one

may pose as the owner of the guesthouse you have in mind and tell you that it is sadly full but able to 'help' you by taking you to a friend's place.

Another trick is to befriend you on a train (especially on the Colombo to Galle or Kandy routes), find out your ultimate destination and 'helpfully' use their mobile to phone for a 3-wheeler in advance, telling you that none will be available at the station. Once at the other end, the 3-wheeler driver may take you on an indirect route and charge up to 10 times the correct fee. In fact, 3-wheeler drivers are nearly always waiting at major stations. It's worth checking the distance to your destination.

Another breed of tout is on the increase especially in Colombo around Galle Road and Fort, and in towns attracting tourists (Kandy, Galle). Someone smartly dressed may approach on the street, saying they recognize you and work at your hotel. Caught off-guard, you feel obliged to accept them as your guide for exploring the sights (and shops), and so are ripe for exploitation. Some may offer to take you to a local watering hole, where at the end of your drinking session the bill will be heavily inflated. Be polite, but firm, when refusing their offer of help.

A gem shop may try to persuade you to buy gems as a sample for a client in your home country – usually your home town (having found out which this is in casual conversation). A typical initial approach is to request that you help with translating something for the trader. The deal is that you buy the gems (maybe to the value of US$500 or US$1000) and then sell them to the client for double the price, and keep the difference. Of course, there is no client at home and you are likely to have been sold poor-quality gems or fakes. Only buy gems for yourself and be sure of what you are buying. This is a common trick in Galle and Ratnapura where various methods are employed. It is worth getting any purchase checked by the State Gem Corporation in Colombo. It is also essential to take care that credit cards are not 'run off' more than once when making a purchase.

Travel arrangements, especially for sightseeing, should only be made through reputable companies; bogus agents operate in popular seaside resorts.

Personal security

In general the threats to personal security for travellers in Sri Lanka are small. In most areas it is possible to travel without any risk of personal violence, though violent attacks, still very low by Western standards, are on the increase. Care should be taken in certain lesser visited areas of popular beach resorts such as Hikkaduwa, Negombo and Mirissa, and don't walk along the beach at night after the restaurants and bars have closed.

Basic common sense needs to be used with respect to looking after valuables. Theft is not uncommon especially when travelling by train or crowded bus. It is essential to take good care of personal possessions both when you are carrying them, and when you have to leave them anywhere. You cannot regard hotel rooms as automatically safe. It is wise to use hotel safes for valuable items, though even they cannot guarantee security. It is best to keep passports with you at all times. Money belts worn under clothing are one of the safest options, although you should keep some cash easily accessible in a purse.

Police

Even after taking all reasonable precautions people do have valuables stolen. This can cause great inconvenience. You can minimize this by keeping a record of vital documents, including your passport number in a separate place from the documents themselves, with relatives or friends at home, or even email them to yourself before setting off. If you have items stolen, they should be reported to the police as soon as possible. Larger hotels will be able to help in contacting and dealing with the police.

Many tourist resorts now have an English-speaking tourist police branch. The paper work involved in reporting losses can be time consuming and irritating, and your own documentation (eg passport and visas) will normally be demanded. Tourists should not assume that if procedures move slowly they are automatically being expected to offer a bribe. If you face really serious problems, for example in connection with a driving accident, you should contact your consular office as quickly as possible.

Student travellers

Full-time students qualify for an **ISIC** (International Student Identity Card) which is issued by student travel and specialist agencies at home (eg **STA Travel**). A card allows some few travel benefits (eg reduced prices) and acts as proof of student status. Only a few sites in Sri Lanka will offer concessions, however.

Telephone

Dialling Sri Lanka from abroad: T+94. National operator: T1200. International operator: T101 to change to T1201. Directory enquiries: T1234 International directory enquiries T1236.

Calls within Sri Lanka STD codes are listed for each town in the text. Dial the local number within the town but use the STD area code first (eg Kandy 081) when dialling from outside the town. Mobile prefixes are 071, 072, 077 and 078.

IDD (International Direct Dialling) is now straightforward in Sri Lanka with many private call offices throughout the country. Calls made from hotels usually cost a lot more (sometimes 3 times as much). They can be made cheaply from post offices though you may need to book. There are also IDD card-operated pay phones, phone cards can be bought from post offices, kiosks near the pay phones and some shops. Pay phones can of course be used for local calls as well.

The cheapest way to phone abroad is to use **Skype**, and this is becoming increasingly available in Sri Lanka at internet cafés and some guesthouses.

Mobile phones

Mobile phones or 'hand phones' are very popular in Sri Lanka and networks extend across much of the island. Most foreign networks are able to roam within Sri Lanka; enquire at home before leaving. If staying in Sri Lanka for several weeks, consider getting a pay-and-go SIM card. You will need to provide a copy of your passport for their records, but topping up is straightforward once everything is set up. When topping up in shops the process is completed by the shopkeeper and you are not handed a voucher, wait until the confirmation text comes through before leaving the premises. The main mobile phone providers are **Etisalat**, **Mobitel** and **Dialog**. Dialog currently has the best island coverage.

Time

GMT + 5½ hrs. Perception of time is sometimes rather vague in Sri Lanka (as in the rest of South Asia). Unpunctuality is common so you will need to be patient.

Tipping

A 10% service charge is added to room rates and meals in virtually all but the cheapest hotels and restaurants. Therefore it is not necessary to give a further tip in most instances. In many smaller guesthouses staff are not always paid a realistic wage and have to rely on a share of the service charge for their basic income.

Tour companies sometimes make recommendations for 'suitable tips' for coach drivers and guides. Some of the figures may seem modest by European standards but are very inflated if compared with normal earnings.

Taxi drivers do not expect to be tipped but a small extra amount over the fare is welcomed.

Tourist information

The **Sri Lanka Tourist Board**, 3rd floor, Devonshire Sq, London EC2M 4WD, T0845-8806 3333, www.srilanka.travel, has some information for planning your trip. The website has details of sights, accommodation and transport. There are Sri Lanka Tourist Board offices in Colombo and a few major tourist centres, such as Kandy. They are listed in the relevant sections throughout the book.

Useful websites

www.divesrilanka.com Information on dive sites, and when and where to dive.
www.infolanka.com Has an extensive list of travel links, some useful articles, recipes and downloadable Sri Lankan music files.
www.lakdasun.org A site for Sri Lankans rather than foreign tourists, but useful tips

about accommodation and transport can be found on the forum.

www.reddottours.com Tailor-made tours and accommodation listings. Based in the UK. Also has a useful calculator for car and driver trips, to work out the estimated cost of a journey.

www.srilanka.travel The official website of the Sri Lanka Tourist Board, with useful general tourist information.

www.tamilnet.com Has a fairly balanced Tamil perspective of what's happening in Sri Lanka.

Visas and permits

A visa must be obtained before travelling to Sri Lanka via the online visa service (www.eta.gov.lk), unless you are a citizen of Singapore or the Maldives and can travel without one. Visas are initially for 30 days (single- or double-entry) but can be extended. They range in cost from US$15-30 depending of your country of origin. Transit passengers must also apply for their visas in advance.

A 60-day **extension** is available to nationals of all countries upon paying a fee, which varies according to the charge to Sri Lankans of entering your country. This can be arranged before leaving for Sri Lanka, or apply in person during office hours, to the **Department of Immigration and Emigration**, 41 Ananda Rajakaruna Mawatha, Col 10, Colombo, T94-11-532 9000, www.immigration.gov.lk. Bring passport, flight information and passport photo. It is not necessary to wait until shortly before the expiry of your original visa. Extensions will be granted at any time within the original 30-day period.

Women travellers

Travelling solo as a woman in Sri Lanka is relatively easy compared with many other countries but you will probably encounter a lot of unwanted attention and have unsavoury remarks directed at you. In recent years, a number of women travellers have expressed concern about travelling alone and there have been some incidents of assault. Travelling with a male companion does not guarantee a quiet life, although those travelling solo may want to invent an imaginary husband and consider wearing a fake wedding ring, or joining forces with other travellers met along the way.

Modest dress for women is always advisable: loose-fitting, non-see through clothes. Cover the shoulders, and wear skirts, dresses or shorts that are at least knee-length. Don't walk through towns in bikinis and take the time to cover up. Make a note of how the local women are dressing and act accordingly, you'll soon notice a difference between say Colombo and Trincomalee town.

It is always best to be accompanied when travelling by 3-wheeler or taxi at night. Do not get into a taxi or 3-wheeler if there are men accompanying the driver and consider asking your hotel/guesthouse or restaurant to arrange a 3-wheeler for you. Travelling on buses can be uncomfortable because of the number of people packed into a small space, and wandering hands occur. If someone is pressing themselves against you a little too enthusiastically, jam your bag in between or just get off at the nearest stop and take another bus. If travelling alone, try and sit next to another woman, on the East coast this is expected of you and they will pat the seat to invite you to join them. Do the same on trains, or sit with a family. Try not to find yourself alone in a railway carriage and be particularly wary on sleeper services.

Remember that what may be considered to be normal, innocent friendliness in a Western context may be misinterpreted by some Sri Lankan men. It's not recommended for women to frequent the local bars, instead drink in hotel bars or restaurants.

Avoid visiting remote areas of archaeological sites such as Polonnaruwa late in the day (ie after the tour groups have left) and care should be taken in certain lesser visited areas of popular beach resorts such as Hikkaduwa, Negombo and Mirissa.

As at home, do not walk around alone at night, or on deserted stretches of beach, and use your common sense. Solo women travellers will have the added bonus of meeting and speaking to Sri Lankan women. Most trips will pass without incident but it is always better to be safe than sorry. If a situation makes you feel uncomfortable, extricate yourself, if a guesthouse gives you the creeps find another one.

Working in Sri Lanka

All foreigners intending to work need **work permits**. No one is allowed to stay longer than 6 months in a calendar year, or to change their visa status. The employing organization should make formal arrangements. Apply to the Sri Lankan representative in your country of origin.

FOOD GLOSSARY

Basic vocabulary	Sinhalese	Tamil
bread	*pān*	*rotti/pān*
butter		*butter/vennai*
(too much) chilli	*miris wadi*	*kāram*
drink	*bīma*	*kudi*
egg	*biththara*	*muttai*
fish	*malu*	*min*
fruit	*palathuru*	*palam*
food	*kama*	*unavu*
jaggery	*hakuru*	*sini/vellam*
juice	*isma*	*sāru*
meat	*mus*	*iraichchi*
oil	*thel*	*ennai*
pepper	*gammiris*	*milagu*
pulses (beans, lentils)	*parippu*	*thāniyam*
rice	*buth*	*arisi*
salt	*lunu*	*uppu*
savoury		*suvai*
spices	*kulubadu*	*milagu*
sweetmeats	*rasakevili*	*inippu pondangal*
treacle	*pani*	*pāni*
vegetables	*elawalu*	*kai kari vagaigal*
water	*wathura*	*thanneer*

Fruit		
avocado	*alkigetapera*	
banana	*keselkan*	*valaippalam*
cashew	*cadju*	*muruthivi*
coconut	*pol*	*thengali*
green coconut	*kurumba*	*pachcha niramulla thengai*
jackfruit	*(jak) kos ambul*	
mango	*amba*	*mangai*
orange	*dodam*	
papaya	*papol*	*pappa palam*
pineapple	*annasi*	*annasi*

Vegetables		
aubergine	*vambatu*	*kathirikai*
beans (green)	*bonchi*	*avarai*
cabbage	*gowa*	*muttaikosu*
gourd (green)	*pathola*	*pudalankai*
mushrooms		*kalān*
okra	*bandakka*	*vendikkai*
onion	*luunu*	*venkayam*
pea		*pattani*
pepper	*miris*	*kāram*
prawns	*isso*	*irāl*
potato	*ala*	*uruka kilangu*
spinach	*niwithi*	*pasali*
tomato	*thakkali*	*thakkali*

Meat, fish and seafood

chicken	kukulmas	koli
crab	kakuluvo	nandu
pork	ōroomas	pantri
potato	ala	uruka kilangu
spinach	niwithi	pasali
tomato	thakkali	thakkali

Ordering a meal in a restaurant: Sinhalese

Please show the menu	menu eka penwanna
sugar/milk/ice	sini/kiri/ice
A bottle of mineral water please	drink botalayak genna
do not open it	arinna epa

Order a meal in a restaurant: Tamil

Please show the menu	thayavu seithu thinpandangal patti tharavum
sugar/milk/ice	sini/pāl/ice
A bottle of mineral water please	oru pothal soda panam tharavum

Sri Lankan specialities

amblulthial sour fish curry

kaha buth kaha rice (yellow, cooked in coconut milk with spices and saffron/turmeric colouring) kiri rice is similar but white and unspiced, served with treacle, chilli or pickle

biththara rotti rotti mixed with eggs

buriyani rice cooked in meat stock and pieces of spiced meat sometimes garnished with boiled egg slices

hoppers (āppa) cupped pancakes made of fermented rice flour, coconut milk, yeast, eaten with savoury (or sweet) curry

lamprais rice cooked in stock parcelled in a banana leaf with dry meat and vegetable curries, fried meat and fish balls and baked gently

mallung boiled, shredded vegetables cooked with spice and coconut

pittu rice-flour and grated coconut steamed in bamboo moulds, eaten with coconut milk and curry

polos pahi pieces of young jackfruit (tree lamb) replaces meat in this dry curry

rotty or rotti flat, circular, unleavened bread cooked on a griddle

sambol hot and spicy accompaniment usually made with onions, grated coconut, pepper (and sometimes dried fish)

sathai spicy meat pieces baked on skewers (sometimes sweet and sour)

'short eats' a selection of meat and vegetable snacks (in pastry or crumbled and fried) charged as eaten.

string hoppers (indiappa) flat circles of steamed rice flour noodles eaten usually at breakfast with thin curry

thosai or *dosai* large crisp pancake made with rice and lentil-flour batter

vadai deep-fried savoury lentil dough-nut rings

Sweets (rasakavilis)

curd rich, creamy, buffalo-milk yoghurt served with treacle or jaggery

gulab jamun dark, fried spongy balls of milk curd and flour soaked in syrup

halwal aluva fudge-like, made with milk, nuts and fruit

kadju kordial fudge squares made with cashew nuts and jaggery

kaludodol dark, mil-based, semi solid sweet mixed with jaggery, cashew and spices (a moorish delicacy)

rasgulla syrup-filled white spongy balls of milk-curd and flour

thalaguli balls formed after pounding roasted sesame seeds with jaggery

wattalappam set 'custard' of coconut, milk, eggs and cashew, flavoured with spices and jaggery

INDEX

CREDITS

Footprint credits
Editor: Nicola Gibbs
Production and layout: Emma Bryers
Maps: Kevin Feeney
Cover: Pepi Bluck

Publisher: Patrick Dawson
Managing Editor: Felicity Laughton
Advertising: Elizabeth Taylor
Sales and marketing: Kirsty Holmes

Photography credits
Front cover: Dhammika Heenpella/
Images of Sri Lanka/Getty Images
Back cover: Honza Hruby/Shutterstock.com;
takepicsforfun/Shutterstock.com;
antloft/Shutterstock.com
Inside front flap: Galyna Andrushko/
Shutterstock.com; Klemen Misic/
Shutterstock.com.
Colour pages: title page: 9photos/Shutterstock.com.
p2: slava296/Shutterstock.com; Natalia Davidovich/
Shutterstock.com. p3: Klemen Misic/Shutterstock.com;
paytai/Shutterstock.com. p4: k86/Shutterstock.com.
p5: Kenneth Dedeu/Shutterstock.com.
p6: Anton Gvozdikov/Shutterstock.com; Sergieiev/
Shutterstock.com. p7: Nazzu/Shutterstock.com.
p8: Filip Fuxa/Shutterstock.com. p9: Kenneth Dedeu/
Shutterstock.com; Kaetana/Shutterstock.com;
SurangaWeeratunga/Shutterstock.com.
p10: Anton Gvozdikov/Shutterstock.com;
SurangaWeeratunga/Shutterstock.com.
p11: DMSU/Shutterstock.com. p12: John Copland/
Shutterstock.com. p13: Calvste/Shutterstock.com.
p14: SurangaWeeratunga/Shutterstock.com.
p16: suronin/Shutterstock.com; PETER HATCH/
Shutterstock.com; Jan Wlodarczyk/Alamy.
p18: Nazar Niyazov/Dreamstime.com; Valery Shanin/
Shutterstock.com; David Noton Photography Alamy.
p19: EpicStockMedia/Shutterstock.com.
p20: Toxawww/Dreamstime.com. p21: itsmejust/
Shutterstock.com; Jorg Hackemann/Shutterstock.com.
p22: Jorg Hackemann/Shutterstock.com.
p24: Eric Gevaert/Shutterstock.com. p25: Filip Fuxa/
Shutterstock.com. p26: Elisa Locci/Shutterstock.com;
filmlandscape/Shutterstock.com. p27: EMJAY SMITH/
Shutterstock.com. p28: Peter Schickert/Alamy.
p29: fbxx/Shutterstock.com; Super Prin/Shutterstock.
com; Robert Harding Picture Library Ltd/Alamy.
p30: Sebastien Burel/Shutterstock.com.
p32: Iryna Rasko/Shutterstock.com.

Publishing information
Footprint DREAM TRIP Sri Lanka
1st edition
© Footprint Handbooks Ltd
September 2013

ISBN: 978 1 907263 75 0
CIP DATA: A catalogue record for this book
is available from the British Library

® Footprint Handbooks and the Footprint
mark are a registered trademark of
Footprint Handbooks Ltd

Published by Footprint
6 Riverside Court
Lower Bristol Road
Bath BA2 3DZ, UK
T +44 (0)1225 469141
F +44 (0)1225 469461
footprinttravelguides.com

Printed in Spain by GraphyCems

Every effort has been made to ensure that
the facts in this guidebook are accurate.
However, travellers should still obtain
advice from consulates, airlines etc about
travel and visa requirements before
travelling. The authors and publishers
cannot accept responsibility for any loss,
injury or inconvenience however caused.

Distributed in the USA by Globe Pequot
Press, Guilford, Connecticut